Theology and Canon Law

New Horizons for Legislation and Interpretation

Ladislas Örsy, S.J.

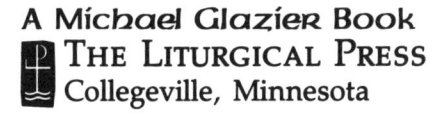

A Michael Glazier Book
THE LITURGICAL PRESS
Collegeville, Minnesota

Cover design by David Manahan, O.S.B.

A Michael Glazier Book published by The Liturgical Press

Copyright © 1992 by The Order of St. Benedict, Inc., Collegeville, Minnesota. All rights reserved. No part of this book may be reproduced in any form or by any means, electronic or mechanical, including photocopying, recording, taping, or any retrieval system, without the written permission of The Liturgical Press, Collegeville, Minnesota 56321. Printed in the United States of America.

1   2   3   4   5   6   7   8   9   10

Library of Congress Cataloging-in-Publication Data

Orsy, Ladislas M., 1921–
   Theology and Canon Law : new horizons for legislation and interpretation / Ladislas Orsy.
     p. cm.
   "A Michael Glazier book"
   Includes bibliographical references and indexes.
   ISBN 0-8146-5011-2
   1. Canon law. 2. Catholic Church—Doctrines. I. Title.
LAW
262.9—dc20   91-42699
                                                                    CIP

Contents

Abbreviations 4
Foreword 7
1 New Attitude of Mind: An Inquiring Spirit 9
2 New Attitude of Mind: Searching for New Horizons 18
3 Interpretation: The Law and Its Interpreters 35
4 Interpretation: Guiding Principles 53
5 Implementation through Reception 83
6 Values and Laws 89
7 Integrated Interpretation or
  The Role of Theology in Interpretation 102
8 Moral Theology and Canon Law:
  The Quest for a Sound Relationship 119
9 Models of Law and Their Impact on Interpretation 139
10 Theology and Canon Law: An Inquiry into Their Relationship 158
Acknowledgments 190
References 192
Bibliography 194
Analytical Index 207
Index of Persons 210

Abbreviations

AAS	Acta Apostolicae Sedis
ABBOTT	The Documents of Vatican II (in English translation)
CCL-GBI	The Code of Canon Law in English Translation, prepared by The Canon Law Society of Great Britain and Ireland
CCL-USA	Code of Canon Law: Latin-English Edition. Translation prepared under the auspices of the Canon Law Society of America
CLD	Canon Law Digest
DS	Enchiridion Symbolorum, 35th edition.
JUR	The Jurist
LTK	Lexikon für Theologie und Kirche
NCE	New Catholic Encyclopedia
SC	Studia Canonica
TS	Theological Studies

This messianic people is invested
with the dignity and freedom of those
who were born from God;
the Holy Spirit dwells in their hearts
as in his temple.
Their law is the new commandment to love
as Christ loved us (cf. John 13:34).
Their goal is the kingdom of God,
inaugurated by God himself on earth,
and to be extended further
until it is brought to perfection by him
at the end of time.

Cf. Lumen gentium, 9

Foreword

This book was born from a wonder that prompted the question: how can we find the right harmony between Christian beliefs and the laws governing the life of the community; or, between the divine mysteries and the norms of human creation?

Such harmony is an indispensable condition for the well being of the church. Too many laws can obscure the vision of the mysteries and can strangle the sensitivity of the people to an all-pervading divine presence; the lack of good laws can leave inner gifts and energies wasted in idle passivity or heedless activity.

To find an answer is all the more necessary because the divine assistance given to the church in practical matters is somewhat different from that granted in the resolution of doctrinal issues. In the proclaiming of the evangelical message, the church is ultimately protected by the gift of infallibility: God's people cannot become victim of falsehood. In the making of a law, or in issuing a precept, the church is not guaranteed the highest degree of prudence: the best judgments must be searched for with the help of grace and wisdom. This does not imply though that the pilgrim church can lose its way toward the fullness of the Kingdom, but it does admit that less than perfect decisions can slow its progress and diminish its capacity to be sign of salvation among the nations—as history proves abundantly. We need to know the ideal in order to handle the real.

The ideal, however, is not easy to find. To discover it, we must pay sustained attention to the ineffable mysteries and, at the same time, take into consideration our own human limitations; both belong to the church. To balance such opposites well and to bring them into harmony is a daunting task; perhaps no human person can do it perfectly. Yet, we can search for it. The means are accessible: we need to clarify concepts, formulate principles, evaluate concrete situations, and suggest balanced decisions.

Indeed, I offer this work more as a documentation of this on-going search than as an advocacy of its final conclusions. For this reason, the questions it raises might be of greater importance than the answers it reaches. Good questions are like the good seed: once sown, they can bring forth fruit a hundredfold.

If my approach is different from that of others who have written on the relationship of theology and canon law, it is because I see the issue within the framework of a cognitional theory that stresses both the unity and distinction between reaching out for unbounded knowledge and taking a decision for a specified action. In theology the church seeks a deeper understanding of God's mysteries: *fides quaerens intellectum*, a never ending task. In making a law, the church binds the faithful to a specific action, *fides quaerens actionem*, a decision that must lead to a clearly defined act. The two operations must be harmoniously linked, but the one cannot be the other.

I learned this epistemological approach mainly from Bernard Lonergan. As a philosopher, his aim was not so much to communicate a theory (as most others do) but to teach a method that can lead an alert, intelligent, reasonable, and responsible inquirer to make his or her own discoveries. Lonergan's method has the characteristics of great (hence rare) philosophical initiatives: it takes some time and much effort to penetrate through the complexities surrounding it, but once entered into and firmly possessed, it reveals its astounding simplicity.

Beyond that I am indebted to those who over many years helped me by raising pertinent questions: students and colleagues, speakers and writers, sympathizers and adversaries, in various schools and in many countries. To them, and to all who contributed to this project in other ways, great or small, I offer my thanks.

If this book does no more than keep alive the wonder that has inspired it, prompt some new questions, and lead to increased discussions, then, it will have already fulfilled, and in good measure, its intended scope.

1

New Attitude of Mind: An Inquiring Spirit

The question

The expression "new attitude of mind," *novus habitus mentis*, can create an impression that we are dealing with something mysterious and unattainable, with an ideal that can be a source of inspiration but not the object of rational definition. The position of this study is the opposite. It seeks to establish that the expression has a down to earth meaning, hence that it can be defined and attained. The ordinary canon lawyer can not only possess it, but has a duty to work for it, acquire it, and live by it.

The expression comes from Paul VI. He used it repeatedly. Here are a couple of examples: On December 14, 1973, in his allocution to the students of the "Course of Renewal in Canon Law" of the Gregorian University, he spoke of

> the germane force and significance of the revised canon law which, in accord with the new attitude of mind introduced by the said Vatican Council, contributes very much to the pastoral care and new needs of the people of God.[1]

On February 4, 1977, he stressed the same point in another allocution to the judges of the Roman Rota:

1. Cf. CLD 8: 100-101.
For more information concerning the pronouncements of Paul VI and John Paul II from 1963 to 1985 on canon law see the section "Canon 8" in each of the volumes from 6 through 11 of *Canon Law Digest.* They give an extensive list of references (to original texts and comments in periodicals) together with quotes from major addresses. *See* also Paulus VI, *Allocutiones de iure canonico,* ed. J. Beyer (Rome: Universitas Gregoriana, 1980).

10 New Attitude of Mind: An Inquiring Spirit

> Let these principles be kept before your eyes in the execution of the office entrusted to you to the extent that from them a new attitude of mind may be brought about.[2]

When we read these and similar texts from Paul VI, wise pope that he was, we find that he was strongly convinced that without this new attitude of mind present in those who are serving the people in the ministry of justice, the laws of the church cannot be correctly understood, still less can they fulfill their purpose of bringing peace and order into the life of the community. But we find also that the pope does not give any exhaustive description, let alone a technical definition of this new attitude of mind. He has intuited something, enough to point out the direction we have to take, but otherwise he has left to us the task of exploring the idea further, discovering its full meaning and determining its practical implications. It is our duty, therefore, to seek a more precise and critically correct answer to the question: What is this new attitude of mind?[3]

Discarding some misconceptions

Let us begin by discarding some misconceptions: once the ground is cleared we are in a better position to build.

This new attitude of mind cannot be adequately defined by saying that it consists in translating a few new doctrinal insights into practical propositions, such as collegiality, subsidiarity, and so forth. An attitude of mind is more than the application of any particular point of doctrine.

The new attitude of mind cannot be identified either with some virtues newly emphasized in interpreting and implementing the laws,

---

2. CLD 8: 111. This allocution is rich in insights; it can be read also as a charter as to what canon law should be in the church. Another passage deserves to be quoted:
> the law of the Church has a truly spiritual character and must be actually informed by the Spirit of Christ, the Holy Spirit. Led on by this kind of reasoning, the council demanded that the law of the Church be an instrument of its spiritual life (CLD 8:105).

3. This is the normal process of discovery. Someone has the intuitive perception of an object at a distance, which is enough to prompt a closer investigation. Then comes the search for helpful informational data, the formulating of various hypotheses, and finally the critically sound proofs that the object of the initial intuition is indeed real and existing. Of course, the investigation may conclude the opposite: the initial intuition is not born out by facts.

such as mercy, compassion, equity and the like. Such virtues have been well known to canonists of all ages; they would not be new.

Further, this new attitude cannot be some kind of gnostic knowledge reached through an internal enlightenment available only to a few. Quite the opposite: Paul VI spoke of it as a quality of any good canon lawyer involved in the daily business of the church and often in direct contact with people who are in difficulties and in need of help.

The new attitude introduced by the council

An attitude of mind cannot be anything else than a permanent disposition of the human spirit, the spirit that by its very nature is both contemplative and active. It is contemplative because it has the capacity to seek the truth, to recognize it, and to surrender to its imperative. It is active because it has the capacity to reach out for values, to make responsible decisions and to transform the world through constructive actions. It follows that a new attitude of mind must consist in an internal capacity to operate in new ways; that is, in an improved method of searching for the truth and in an increased determination to reach out for values not noticed before.[4]

Paul VI insisted that this new disposition was introduced by Vatican Council II. So our question should be: what was so very new in the operation of the council itself? If we can find the answer to this question we shall be in a good position to say how the legislator, the interpreter or the administrator of the laws should operate in these post-conciliar times.

To find this newness, we must turn to the council.

There are two radically different ways of looking at the council, and the distinction between the two is important for us. One way is to see the council as a past assembly whose task was to give us a collection of documents with a cohesive body of doctrine. In this conception the council is a concluded historical event: it has come and gone. All that can be of interest to us now are the ideas and norms contained in its documents. Our duty is to assimilate them or to obey them.

Another way of looking at the council is to see it as an event: the beginning of a new movement. The documents that it has given us are certainly important, but even more important are the dynamics that produced them. Our task is more than to learn about the doctrine and

---

4. The precise object of renewal is the living mind itself (that is, the tool by which we acquire knowledge and progress in it); the object of renewal here and now is not what is contained in the mind, be it ideas or propositions.

to obey the norms; we must also appropriate and use the method the council followed in its effort to renew the church. The council did more than teach or legislate: it started a movement that must continue. It taught us a new method of operation.

The new attitude of mind at the council

The question is now: in what did the new method of the council consist?

I shall seek the answer to this question in two steps: first, by recalling some achievements of the council; second, by showing how the council operated. First, the objective results; second, the method that produced them.

Discoveries at the council. The achievements of the council could be called, quite legitimately, new discoveries—not in the sense that illegitimate innovations were added to the deposit of the revelation but in the sense that the fathers reached new insights into those sacred realities that the church has possessed from its origins.[5]

We can be in possession of a truth and progress in its understanding. The council did indeed move from limited perceptions to deeper comprehensions. Such movements can easily be demonstrated by comparing some dominant trends and opinions before the council with those that actually prevailed at the council. Here are some examples.

• *From imperium to communio.* Ever since the Middle Ages there has been a tendency to perceive the structures of the church on the pattern of the classical Roman household where the *paterfamilias*, the head of the extended family, had *imperium*: that is, all power over persons and things was concentrated in his hands. The centralization that ensued after the Reformation and the definitions of Vatican Council I reinforced this trend. Vatican Council II moved away from it and stressed the fact that the church was *communio*, an organically constituted body where every single member is endowed with the power of the Spirit,

---

5. Not all ecumenical councils operated in this way—perhaps none. Virtually all previous councils responded to a crisis; they acted as judges between contending parties concerning the meaning of the evangelical message. Hence there were affirmations and condemnations. Vatican Council II arose out of the desire of Pope John XXIII to renew, *aggiornare*, the proclamation of our Christian doctrine in function of the needs of the modern world. This meant to take a good look at the world and all creatures in it, and then to see what the significance of the evangelical message was for them.

even if this power works in different ways in the various members: a hierarchical communion (cf. *Lumen gentium*).

• *From confessional conflict to ecumenical vision.* The centuries before Vatican Council II were marked by sharp and inimical conflicts among Christian churches and communities. None of them paid much attention to the unity that results from our common baptism and our common beliefs in many mysteries. The council moved away from such hostile attitudes and came to a better understanding of an existing bond of unity, notwithstanding our differences. This movement gave a new direction to the Catholic church in ecumenical matters and created a much more favorable climate for the work of reunion (cf. *Orientalium Ecclesiarum, Unitatis redintegratio*).

• *From defensive isolation to expansive presence.* The shock in the wake of the fragmentation of the Western church in the sixteenth century provoked a strong defensive attitude in the Catholic church, followed by a policy of isolation. The intent was a noble one: to preserve the integrity of faith and morals. But the policy was one-sided and the method of enforcing it unfortunate. More than once it led to bitter confrontations not only with other confessions but also with respectable secular movements advocating social reform or scientific progress. The council pulled down the battlements, and let the church meet the world. Also, it took a new look at this planet Earth, and saw that it was good. It spoke in a new way of earthly values and of human persons whose faith, hope, and love are known to God alone. Of course, in such a blessed universe, even if it is marked by sin and evil, Christians should not remain isolated. Their mission is to "build the earth" and proclaim God's mighty deeds to every creature (cf. *Gaudium et spes*).

• *From a static world view to a dynamic one.* Ever since the Middle Ages, faithful to the Aristotelian foundations of its systematic theology, the church has tended to see this creation as an immensely complex structure of immutable essences, subject only to accidental changes. Such a vision was not favorable to an evolutionary explanation of the universe, since it was not able to perceive the full meaning and importance of history. In this steady and static framework the church appeared as a place where time does not have its impact on institutions and propositions. The council was humble enough to proclaim that, while there is continuity from the original proclamation of the evangelical message to its contemporary preaching, there is also a developmental process that affects our understanding of it. Once God planted his gifts in a changing and evolving universe, he let them become parts of our human history (cf. *Dei verbum*).

Enough of the examples. Even if they are but a few, they show the movement that took place at the council. In each case the fathers left behind a narrow vision and arrived at another one based on broader foundations. In this lies the achievement of the council.

The mind of the council

In no way is it easy to speak of the mind of a large assembly such as the council. In truth, there were many individual minds, no two perfectly identical. Yet the many minds displayed a common attitude that became manifest during the first session at the time of the debate on "The Sources of Revelation." From then on, gradually but forcefully, most of the material contained in the previously prepared schemata was discarded. New committees were formed. A new method of work was introduced. Instead of merely reaffirming the known, the council began to raise questions and with the help of them moved more and more into exploring the field of the unknown. There was a new method: the spirit of defensive affirmation had given place to the spirit of expanding inquiry.

But inquiry in itself is not enough. After all, any fool can raise a question, but it takes a learned person to raise a good question, because good questions flow from enhanced knowledge. As the mind moves forward to a broader context, old and familiar things acquire a new meaning and reveal new problems.

At this point a simple "thought experiment" example could be more enlightening than a long explanation. I may know the house in which I live, every single part of it. I may think that my knowledge is so perfect that nothing can be added to it. But if one day I am lifted up into the air, well above the house, I may come to a new perception of its proportions and of its relationship to all other features on the ground. The house would be still the same old building, but my perception of it would have changed. I would be looking at the same object from a higher viewpoint, and that is enough to bring me some new knowledge and help me to raise new questions.

This "thought experiment" illustrates quite well the transformation that took place in the mind of the council fathers. In the realm of the spirit, they were able to ascend to new heights and from there take a fresh look at the world that was so familiar to them. They were able to perceive the unchanging mysteries of our faith from a viewpoint higher than the one to which they were accustomed, and, once that happened, the dynamics caused by enhanced knowledge took over. Questions flowed easily and abundantly.

Thus the inquiring mind of the council was well grounded; it proceeded from enhanced knowledge.

The new method

We are now in a position to state the requirement for the acquisition and operation of the new attitude of mind. With the help of increased knowledge, the mind can *move into a higher viewpoint, take a fresh look at familiar things, and have the basis to raise new questions.* The answers will be a felicitous synthesis of old and new, just as happened at Vatican II.

That this was indeed the case, let me demonstrate through the already familiar examples.

• *The movement from imperium to communio* was made possible by the immense progress before the council in historical research which brought into the forefront the ancient idea and practice of *communio*. From a higher viewpoint, *imperium* lost its attraction.

• *The change from confessional conflict to ecumenical understanding* was facilitated by a fresh look at all the Christian churches and communities. While earlier observers saw in them nothing but abomination, the council perceived among them the signs of God's grace in the presence of the Word and the sacraments they possessed. From that higher perspective, the mutual relationships between them and the Roman Catholic community appeared differently. Thus the heretics and schismatics became our brothers and sisters.

• Similarly, *the move from defensive isolation to an appreciation of secular values* and to a more direct service of the human family could happen only because the council fathers came to a better perception of the goodness of all things in this creation and of the dignity of every human person in it. From contemplating our whole planet and listening to the cry of the needy everywhere, they came to a much better understanding of the mission of the church.

• Also, *the council moved away from a philosophy that could think in static categories only.* Inspired by the discoveries of empirical sciences and informed by historical data, the fathers accepted a developmental view of the universe. This new stance helped them to reach a better understanding of how the word of God keeps developing in our midst without ever losing its original meaning.

Such examples could be multiplied but there is no need for more. The evidence is strong enough to show that whenever the fathers reached a new discovery, it was due to their enhanced knowledge and the spirit of inquiry that animated them. They looked at many familiar things from a higher viewpoint, they raised new questions and, as a result, they were able to come up with fresh answers. Theirs was not a mere intellectual achievement: the impulse of the Spirit, trust in him and courage were needed to move beyond the known and pierce the veil of the unknown.[6]

Conclusion

There is nothing mythical about the new habit of mind that canon lawyers should acquire. In the future, a good canon lawyer should do the same that the council did: move beyond the familiar into a higher viewpoint that only enhanced knowledge can give, then raise new questions and have the courage to accept fresh answers.

He may well take encouragement from the words of John Paul II in the *Apostolic Constitution* promulgating the new Code:

> The instrument, such as the Code is, fully accords with the nature of the Church, particularly as presented in the authentic teaching of the Second Vatican Council seen as a whole, and especially in its ecclesiological doctrine. In fact, in a certain sense, this new Code can be viewed as a great effort to translate the conciliar ecclesiological teaching into canonical terms. If it is impossible perfectly to transpose the image of the Church described by conciliar doctrine into canonical language, nevertheless the Code must always be related to that image as to its primary pat-

---

6. There would be many ways of expanding the above reflections further and illustrating them by examples. It would not be difficult to show how in the drafting of the new Code of Canon Law both attitudes of mind were active. At times the drafters were able to look at an issue from a higher viewpoint; then they produced significantly better norms animated by a new spirit: the introduction of the scriptural concept of covenant into the law of marriage would be a good example of this. At times they remained within the confines of the familiar; then the result was the substantial reaffirmation of the old rules, as happened in the matter of courts and procedures. Many more examples of the impact of the old and new attitude of mind could be gathered from the Code, e.g., concerning the role of the laity, the position of the hierarchy, the attitude of the law toward change, and so forth. At times these different attitudes of mind resulted in conflicting trends in the new legislation; e.g., a new exaltation of the dignity of the Christian faithful coupled with a certain distrust in the wisdom and prudence of the laity; a new declaration of episcopal collegiality with hardly any practical possibility of exercising it. For more examples of different trends in the new Code see Ladislas Örsy, *The Council and the Code: From Vision to Legislation,* Père Marquette Theology Lecture (Milwaukee, Wis.: Marquette University Press, 1985).

tern, whose outlines, given its nature, the Code must express as far as is possible.[7]

We could add that the method of understanding and interpreting the Code should be related also to the method of the council.

All this seems a deceptively simple program—as long as one has not tried it. Once tried, however, it reveals itself as more demanding than anything that canon lawyers have ever tried.

But those who have acquired this new attitude rooted in an inquiring mind can never again be mere lawyers. No matter if they are legislators, interpreters, or judges, if their business is to make, or impose, or explain laws, they will always be ready to move to a higher viewpoint, should the case so warrant it. That vantage point may be provided by theology, or philosophy, or history, or by any combination of the different branches of learning. From there they will be able to see the legal norms in a broader context, raise new questions, discover new answers, and then integrate the same norms into the life of the community in a happy combination of old and new so that each and all can experience, taste, and enjoy the freedom that was given to us, citizens of the Kingdom.

---

7. *See* Apostolic Constitution *Sacrae disciplinae leges, The Code of Canon Law in English Translation* (London: Collins, 1983) xiii–xiv.

2

New Attitude of Mind: Searching for New Horizons

A broader landscape

In the preceding chapter I suggested that the new disposition of the mind required from the canonists consisted in the developing of a spirit of inquiry. Indeed, the documents of the council were born from such a spirit, from a disposition of the mind which does not simply rest in the possession of some acquired knowledge, but continues to inquire in order to progress relentlessly toward the fullness of truth. Hence—I affirmed—a new habit of the mind means to take a new look at our laws from a higher viewpoint, and then to raise new questions.

This statement is more weighty than it appears; it means that there is no scientific understanding of canon law which does not ultimately ask for the *why?* of every single norm. But it is worth the while. If the church is always to be reformed, *ecclesia semper reformanda*, its laws cannot be an exception to this universal rule: they too must be subject to an on-going revision, *leges ecclesiae semper reformandae*. There is no better assurance for this on-going reform than that many lawyers should be in the habit of raising questions. When this happens, we shall have far more penetrating and incisive commentaries.[1]

---

1. I am anticipating here a point to which I shall return later in this chapter: the ascent of the mind from merely paraphrasing the law to inquiring into the ultimate reasons of the law is also the ascent of the mind into a higher horizon where it sees all objects differently; it is a move from the level of common sense to the level of abstraction. This is a distinct move (upwards, a vertical one) on the part of the subject, hence it is a development in the *subjective* component of the horizon. When the field of vision expands (to include other fields with other objects, hori-

This explanation I retain but I wish to integrate it into a broader landscape by carrying further the reflections on the meaning of *novus habitus mentis*. I wish to suggest and demonstrate that to acquire a new disposition of the mind means to enter into a new field of vision; that is, into a new horizon.[2]

The doctrine of horizon

A foundational doctrine. The doctrine of horizon as an articulated philosophical theory was not known either to the ancient Greek philosophers or to the medieval scholastic thinkers. It has been developed mainly in our century. Yet, as is the case with many basic philosophical discoveries, once understood (and lived by), it appears obvious and simple—certainly less complicated than Aristotle's teaching on the categories.[3]

---

zontally), there is a distinct development also, but in the *objective* component of the horizon.

In simpler terms: I can understand all things better within my field of vision if the operations of my mind reach greater refinement; I can see more objects if my field of vision expands. When I learn the abstract laws behind the moving stars, I understand their movement better. When I look at the sky with a telescope, I can see more stars. In both cases my knowledge expands.

The previous chapter in this book speaks mainly of the development in the subjective component of the horizon of the canon lawyer; this one focuses more on the expansion of the objective component. The two together help authentic progress.

This anticipation in explanation should also help the reader to become aware, right from the beginning, that the doctrine of horizon is of universal application; it applies to physics no less than to canon law. There is a community of all sciences!

2. I have invoked many times the doctrine of horizon in my writings, but this essay, brief as it is, is the first one dedicated exclusively to this topic. In no way, however, is it a full treatment of the issue; its main purpose is to draw the attention of the reader to an important advance in cognitional theory.

Since Paul VI asked for a *novus habitus mentis*, for this writer, at least, it was quite easy and natural to turn to the doctrine of horizon, which is precisely a well grounded and verifiable theory about the dispositions of the mind.

I have no doubt that, once applied to the field of canon law, that is, to the whole process of making, applying and interpreting the norms, it will yield abundant returns.

3. Ample explanations of the doctrine of horizon can be found throughout David Tracy's book *The Achievement of Bernard Lonergan* (New York: Herder & Herder, 1970). See also Lonergan's *Method in Theology* (New York: Herder & Herder, 1972);

The doctrine of horizon contributes greatly not only to our comprehension of the process of knowing, from its initial to its final stages, but also provides a significant clue for a better understanding of the conditions for communications. It is not enough to exchange ideas; it is necessary to pass from one horizon into another. Words can sound the same from one horizon to another, but their meaning can be significantly different—a deceptive situation. To establish communications, the horizons should be adjusted first, and the exchange of ideas should follow.[4]

This doctrine asserts that the mental operations and their results in human persons are essentially dependent on and limited by their field of vision. In other terms, the meaning of everything that happens subjectively and is expressed objectively in the mind of a person can be fully grasped only if the extent of the field of vision of that person is taken into account.

Neither Aristotle nor Aquinas adverted to this fact. For them, every concept was complete in itself; once the essence of a thing was grasped, the environment added little. Hence progress in knowledge was achieved by strict logical operations, by deductive or inductive arguments, but not by conversion to a broader horizon.[5] They did not see that when such a conversion happens, everything in the old horizon

---

he explicates the various types of conversion: intellectual, moral and religious, each of them an entry into a new horizon. For Gadamer, the interpretation of a text consists in the resolution of a conflict of horizons, from which a new meaning arises; see *Truth and Method* (New York: Seabury, 1975). Gadamer is certainly not far from the truth when a law has been made in one cultural context, and then is interpreted in another.

4. This rule is of capital importance for the success of ecumenical dialogues. We must acknowledge first that the centuries of separations created different horizons for the various denominations, which had an impact on the commonly held propositions. To reach the goal of reunion, a common horizon ought to be created which will have to be broader than any of the existing ones. Once the horizons are expanded and adjusted, some of the conceptual and propositional problems may simply vanish, and others are likely to become more tractable.

5. Because of this philosophy, spread far and wide in the schools and absorbed by many, until fairly recent times the church experienced great difficulties in accepting any other development in doctrine than the one which is the conclusion of a logical deduction from already known premises.

Today we can say with some assurance that a development in the understanding of the Christian doctrine takes place when the horizon of the believers expands, either by their ascending to a higher level of operations, or through the broadening of their field of vision, or both.

receives a new shade of meaning because everything is put into a new context.[6]

Testing the theory

Testing it by observing others. If this doctrine is rooted in experience, some of the observable facts must be within the reach of each one of us. Indeed, they are. Who has not met persons who have demonstrated high intelligence within a well defined (and circumscribed!) frame of reference but whom no human effort (or argument, for that matter) could move to consider facts and ideas outside of it?[7] We have seen such persons among philosophers: if they happened to be Platonist, no force could ever move them to let Aristotle's ideas penetrate their mind. We have seen them among theologians: if they have accepted the tightly knit system of predestination, no amount of reasoning could budge them to give some consideration to the role of free will. In more

---

6. Aquinas himself entered into new horizons when he began to see the Christian mysteries in an Aristotelian context. His explanation of the mysteries is full of new shades of meanings originating in the Aristotelian universe; e.g. he used the categories of substance and relation to protect the mystery of the Trinity from the accusation of contradiction; he defined the sacraments using the categories of matter and form, etc. It seems, however, that his inquiring mind never turned to the phenomenon that he experienced: the move into a broader horizon.

7. The capacity to function intelligently within a given horizon should never be confused with the capacity to move into another horizon.
From time to time we hear the exclamation: "But how can such and such a person who is so intelligent be so narrow minded?" A puzzling predicament, undoubtedly. But the theory of horizon accounts for such personalities. Someone may handle questions within a given frame of reference with the highest intelligence, but cannot bring himself or herself to accept questions from outside the well known field of vision. For that, a re-adjustment of the whole person would be needed, with an acceptance of the insecurity that it brings. Thus, someone may be exceptionally intelligent and competent, yet unable to undergo such a conversion. How many times have scientists of the highest accomplishment in one frame of reference shown themselves incapable of accepting a new insight and re-modelling their knowledge and operations accordingly?! Nearly every great discovery *within a new horizon* is followed by a display of polite or violent resistance by intelligent persons. Conversion to a new way of thinking does not necessarily come after some conceptually correct information. Needless to say, theology is not exempt from such events. After the second world war, many Catholic theologians were moving into new horizons (creating the so-called "new theology" movement) but encountered strong resistance from those who lived and thought in the traditional ones. A similar struggle developed after Vatican Council II.

practical matters, we have encountered them as dedicated physicians who declared themselves faithful believers in old and proven remedies, not realizing that they were losing out on the new and more effective medicines. Also, we have met, or have heard of, farmers who, content with their old ways of production, could not bring themselves to accept new methods of cultivation.[8]

What is common to all such groups? They are enclosed within their clearly defined field of vision and are not willing to look beyond it. Hence, their knowledge is not disturbed: everything they know makes good sense within their frame of reference. They have no incentive to leave the world in which they are at home. Of course, ultimately they are the losers: their mind remains devoid of new information, their spirit does not know the joy of discovery. The cry *Eureka!* is not for them.

All such groups display a common attitude: they dislike questions which point beyond their field of vision. When they hear them, they shake them off politely (or otherwise) as inopportune or irrelevant. The inborn human thirst for knowledge is no longer felt by them.[9]

It is not difficult to verify the theory of horizon in our own society.

Testing the theory by observing ourselves. After all, this doctrine is primarily a cognitive theory, hence there must be an even more appropriate testing ground for it in our own inner world. Every one who is an attentive, insightful and rational inquirer should be able to perform the test by self-observation.

---

8. Such a problem with farmers has been reported many times in the press: farmers to whom aid was granted in underdeveloped countries refused to switch to modern methods of cultivation. Then the issue for development was not in the productivity of the soil, but in the broadening of the mind of the farmers. The most urgent need for aid was not in farming but in education.

9. There are many other fields of observation where the theory of horizon can be tested and where it can be demonstrated how far the field of vision of human persons shapes their knowledge. Negatively, every oppressive regime goes to extraordinary lengths to restrict the horizon of its citizens, so that they cannot perceive anything that could start a thought process critical of the government. As a rule, such a regime begins by obliterating history: the citizens should look at the present only, without any rival. When no comparison is possible, the worst can be acclaimed as the best.

Liberation comes through the perception of a new horizon; the French revolution broke out because the field of vision of the people expanded to a political system where there was *liberté, égalité, fraternité,* even if the actual realization of that system has fallen short of the ideal.

Innumerable examples could be introduced from history, past and contemporary.

Almost certainly, we have all experienced an inner broadening. On a not too deep level this may have occurred as the effect of a journey abroad: after an encounter with other cultures many of our earlier concepts and judgments changed. It is not that they lost all significance; rather, they received new shades of meaning. What earlier appeared as absolutes had to be reassessed in function of our new frontiers of knowledge.

Similarly we all must have experienced a narrowing of our horizon. It may have occurred when we dedicated ourselves too much to one occupation, or focused exclusively on a restricted object of study, so that eventually our interest in other topics decreased, and our field of vision was reduced.

This self observation could be turned into a critical self examination. We can ask ourselves whether or not there were situations in which we refused an invitation to enter into a broader horizon. Such an invitation, if it existed, came probably in the guise of new questions to which no answer could be found within our own field of vision. Although the questions may have been prompted by facts puzzling enough, to accept them would have meant to exchange our security for uncertainty. We recoiled from entering into the unknown. When we refused to respond, we did not do so by demonstrating rationally that the questions were without base, but by politely turning away from them.

The experience of transition. The transition from one horizon into another is probably not beyond our experience either. The point of departure is always our home field where we operate in great security. There everything is twice known: we can understand all the questions, and we can find all the answers.

But beyond this horizon of the known there is another one, the contents of which we perceive clearly enough to see pertinent questions but not well enough to construe satisfactory answers; there is an element of the unknown in it. In such situations the whole of our humanity reacts. To progress into a new horizon is not a matter of deduction or induction or any other kind of logical operation. It is a matter of courage and determination to accept the uncertainty that the new environment brings. To face such a new field of vision which is partly known, partly unknown is an act of the whole human person: feelings, perceptions, understandings, moral sense of values, all play their part. We progress at our risk.

Further, we all are aware that somewhere out there, entirely beyond our field of vision, there is an immense world which is totally unknown to us. We do not even have those fragments of knowledge which would be necessary to raise questions about it; it is twice unknown, in the questions that it hides, and in the answers that it keeps beyond our reach. Not surprisingly, it provokes reluctance in our humanity to enter it—ever!

Changing horizons in the history of canon law

Authentic history includes changing horizons. An adequate and critically correct history of canon law can never be written without including the history of changing horizons. The reason for this is that both the law makers and the interpreters of the law did think and act within a given horizon; thus history cannot be complete without including the environment in which they operated and which influenced everything they thought and practiced.

Canon law underwent significant changes of horizon in the course of its history.

• *Non-critical and non-scientific approach: the horizon of Christian wisdom. From the beginning to Gratian.* The development of canon law during the first millennium and somewhat beyond it was the gradual crystallization of the practical wisdom of the community. It consisted of conciliar legislations, decisions in decretal letters, local and universal customs, often gathered in collections but not subject to much critical evaluation and not organized scientifically into a coherent system held together by abstract principles. In making the laws, the church was mostly inspired by pastoral considerations, or by pastoral expediency— in the holy sense of the term.

• *Critical and scientifically organized approach: the horizon of scientific abstraction. From Gratian to Trent.* Gratian led the entry into the new horizon of critical thinking and scientific organization. Through an adaptation of the method *sic-et-non,* he let canons confront canons, and thus reveal their harmony or dissonance. Whenever there was a conflict among them, he tried to resolve it with the help of critical reasoning, by assessing the relative importance and authority of each canon. This was the beginning of a critical and scientific operation in the true sense of the terms. In this Gratian and his successors were helped not only by the dialectics of the *sic-et-non* method developed in the schools, but by re-discovery in the West of the ancient Roman law, which in its classical period had reached a sophisticated degree of abstraction.

• *The loss of critical spirit: the horizon of literal exegesis. From Trent to Vatican II.* Since the sixteenth century the whole body of canon law has been placed ("re-located" would be a better term) into the horizon of the Council of Trent and of the counter-reformation movement: it has become not so much an instrument of expansion as an instrument of defence against both internal and external enemies. There occurred a narrowing of horizons. The *why?* of the laws was no longer investigated and critical inquiry into the values behind the laws virtually ceased. Many commentaries offered no more than a narrowly literal exegesis of the texts. Little attention was paid to the theological roots of canon law. Even the philosophical explanation of its foundations shifted from *reason* to the *will of the lawgiver;* law was no longer seen as *ordinatio rationis* but *ordinatio voluntatis.*

- *The impact of the "perfect society" theory: a secular horizon.* Meanwhile, there was another development, a change of horizon—but not in the right direction. New vistas were opened by the theory of the "perfect society" which both church and state were presumed to be. While this theory originated with the medieval scholastics, it had its full impact on canon law in the post-Tridentine period. The problem was not so much with the theory as with the fact that its secular model was uncritically applied to the church.[10] The church had to be a "perfect society" *in the same sense* as the state was, and elements of secular organization and jurisprudence were increasingly imported into the

---

10. As is well known, the scholastics defined a "perfect society" as a society having all the means at its disposal to reach its own end. They did not imply that such a society was perfect morally, or in fact used all the means available to pursue its goal faithfully. Hence, in their thinking, a society could be perfect in theory and imperfect through and through in practice. They knew how to distinguish the two.

Even if one accepts the validity of this theory, which is debatable, clearly the expression "perfect society" could be applied to the state and the church *analogically* only; they could not be perfect societies *in the same sense* since their goals are radically different.

The fatal flaw in reasoning and practice occurred when this analogy was lost from sight, and the idea of the perfect society *as it applied to the state* was used as a model for the church.

In other terms, the idea of perfect society became the vehicle for the transfer of secular modes of thought, institutions and proceedings to a religious community. A classical example of this process is the first Code of Canon Law: under several aspects it was conceived and composed following the model of civil codes.

For some time there has been much talk in theology about demythologization, and indeed some false myths have been swept away and the truth has become all the more visible for it. We should ask ourselves if our laws are not in need of some de-secularization in order to let the truth and beauty of the church become more visible for all, believers and unbelievers.

community of believers, whether on a superficial level, as in some titles and offices, or in more substantial matters, such as the increasing centralization in the government of the church.

• *The search for a theological horizon. Our age.* At Vatican Council II, through the ministry of the bishops, the whole church moved into new horizons on a scale and at a rate probably unprecedented in history.[11] The Catholic church's field of vision was pushed outward to include the whole church of Christ (of which the boundaries go beyond the Catholic church); even more, to embrace the welfare of the whole human family. All the categories and judgments which originated in the Middle Ages and in the post-Tridentine centuries had to be reassessed. Canon law had to be reconstructed accordingly. But in this process the issue was no longer the conversion of bishops to a new vision (as happened at the council), but the restructuring of living institutions. No wonder the work took a long time, and even with the new Code, it remains incomplete.

In the course of this history, two types of changes in the varying horizons can be observed. One concerns the *operations* of the canon lawyers: under the leadership of Gratian they moved to a higher level of abstraction and achieved a broader field of vision. The other refers to the *incorporation of new fields into their vision*: today we see canon law as embedded in theology. The first could be called the expansion of the subjective pole of the horizon (it takes place in the subject, the knower), the second the broadening of the objective pole of the horizon (it takes place in the object, the known).[12]

---

11. Pope John Paul II in his allocution on October 29, 1981, to the members of the Pontifical Commission for the Revision of the Code of Canon Law drew their attention to the new horizons opened up by the council:
> However, as it is well known, when the Second Vatican Ecumenical Council directed its attention to the mystery of the Church (in the constitution, *Lumen gentium*) and to its role or mission in the world of the present time (in the constitution, *Gaudium et spes*), it proffered a much fuller view of ecclesiology and opened up much vaster horizons in evaluating the relationship of the Church with the world itself.
>
> As a result, there is the necessity that the laws of the Church be so structured that they square with that same prospectus and that they harmonize with those horizons. Moreover, this relationship had already been clearly declared by the council itself when it observed that the mystery of the Church must be kept in view in the elaboration of canon law. (CLD 9: 37)

12. As I mentioned earlier in this chapter, in every horizon there is a subjective and an objective pole. The subjective pole is the manner (mode, level) of opera-

This gives us a starting point for determining how the horizon of the canon lawyer should expand today. In other terms, we have come closer to making practical suggestions as to how a new disposition of the mind can be built and maintained.

Transitions into new horizons

A precondition. The precondition for entering into a new horizon is a God given natural and internal drive in the person that compels him or her to seek ever more knowledge. Without such desire, there will be no movement of life—not in the mind, anyway. Obviously this does not mean that the spirit should not be disciplined, or that it should not be prevented from sweeping up all kind of useless information; it means only that it should be alive and properly channelled. The sign that the overall disposition of a person is right is the readiness of the person to raise well grounded questions. Thus the entry into a new horizon is open.

tions; it responds to the question, how the person "in charge" (the subject) is operating. The objective pole is the content of the field of vision; it responds to the question, what is actually included in the person's field of vision (the objects).

To the first: A horizon may be confined to operations on the level of common sense: when a person accumulates wisdom from experience, without perceiving the world of abstract principles and laws, he or she is operating within the horizon of common sense.

One day, however, the person may come to an insight that pulls together many cases under one ordering principle, and then may reassess and correct all previous judgments and decisions accordingly. For the person "in charge" this would be no less than a passage from the world of experimental operations into the world of critical judgments and decisions based on abstract principles; a passage into a new horizon. Such a passage will compel a re-evaluation of all that he or she has thought and done before, and will set a new mode of operation.

This is to enter into a new horizon by ascending to a higher level of operation. The person sees more and sees it better.

To the second: A horizon can be confined to a specific field of knowledge, such as the analysis of the text of an ancient conciliar decree. A person may have come to important conclusions from the text itself. But if that text is a response to an intellectual movement, he or she will never be able to come to a full understanding of what is contained there unless the field of vision includes also the ideas which inspired that movement in the first place. For an adequate historical account the person must move from the horizon of textual criticism (an indispensable starting point) into the horizon of current ideas—probably not even mentioned in the text. By expanding the field of vision, he or she sees more and better.

Ascending to higher types of operations. Canon lawyers can enter into new horizons by ascending into the higher viewpoint of values. This will have an impact on the manner of their operations, no matter what their activities are: the planning, implementing or interpreting of the laws.

In every case, this means to understand and explain the meaning of a law in function of the value that it intends to serve.

In theory, this may seem obvious; so much so that it hardly needs justification. Laws are norms of action. An action that is not in pursuit of a value is a misguided effort: it is not an *ordinatio rationis,* a rational disposition. It should be called *ordinatio sine ratione,* or *contra rationem*— an a-rational or irrational disposition.

In practice, however, the habit of the post-Tridentine centuries still tends to prevail: critical questions about values are scarce, and the need for such an inquiry is by no means universally accepted. Many commentaries stay with the text of the law, without offering any reflections on the values the law intends to uphold. Yet, no vigorous, healthy, and well balanced development of the law and of its interpretation is possible without our canon lawyers gradually entering into the new horizon of the value oriented evaluation of the norms.

On the part of those who plan the law this calls for a sustained critical effort; before any law is enacted its connection with the intended value must be well established. Such a healthy approach cannot be anything else than the result of a new disposition of the mind. The issue is not new knowledge, but rather a new way of operating.[13]

---

13. A similar development took place in biblical exegesis at the beginning of this century. The new approach put a virtual end to literal expository explanations and introduced modern hermeneutics, which eventually helped to produce a much better understanding of the Bible.

But the term "critical" ought to be understood rightly. It does not mean a spirit of idle or unsympathetic criticism, it means simply (as in every science) that every bit of information is confronted with the question of *why?* In canon law, this *why?* must reach out to the full extent of the norms. This means that the ministry of the interpreter does not consist in merely paraphrasing the law, or in construing imaginary cases through which the text is better understood, but in seeking to account for the *raison d'être* of every single norm: why is it there? This is bound to lead him or her into the heart of the matter: the explanation of the values that the law intends to uphold.

It will lead him or her to an inquiry concerning the legislator's own horizon. Remember, interpretation has been described as a conflict of horizons; it could be described also as a blending of horizons.

Entering into new fields of vision. The governing rule for the needed expansion of horizon is that it should take place according to the organic connections that canon law has with other fields of ecclesiastical arts and sciences. The following are only examples.

• *The redeeming church.* The first expansion of horizon should be in the direction of ecclesiology: the understanding of the nature of the church should govern the understanding of its laws. Since the church is, in an analogous sense, the continuation of the incarnation, we may say that it exists for the sake of redeeming human persons. To understand canon law as having a function in our redemption is to distinguish it sharply from civil law, and to collocate it in a spiritual order which is never purely juridical.

If the horizon of a canonical legislator, or of an interpreter, does not include this perspective, his or her handling of the law will be deficient, no matter how perfect it may appear from a purely technical point of view—perfect, that is, on the model of civil law. The inclusion of the redeeming character of the church into the horizon affects the meaning of every single concept in canon law.

• *The whole church of Christ.* To enter and remain in the ecumenical dimension is supremely important. Many a time in its history the Roman Catholic church has been accused of excessive legalism; today the same accusation is still heard at ecumenical gatherings, in a gentler tone maybe but no less firmly. If we are perceived as carrying an excessive baggage of legalism, burdened by heavy centralization, occupied with legal quibbles about the devotional life of the church, we are not (in the existential order) attractive to our separated brothers and sisters—no matter what the ecumenical dialogues on doctrine may conclude. Union between large religious communities will never come by propositional agreements alone; in some way each must enter into the horizons of the others. There was a doctrinal agreement between the East and the West at the Council of Florence, but the intended union did not materialize because the two churches never came together within the same field of vision.

• *The image of God.* This may sound like an unusual demand: the horizon of canon law should include a theologically well developed image of God. But, after all, our laws are meant to please God, and we determine how to please him according to the image we have of him.[14]

---

14. If this sounds far fetched, a reading of the four gospels may bring home the same truth. Jesus spent much of his time in correcting the image that the scribes and the experts in the law had of God. He told them that the God of Israel was

In canonical manuals we read little about such things, yet there is no doubt that in any given age, canon law reflected to a high degree the contemporary perception of the personality of God. The image of God shaped the law. Let me refer to two contrasting approaches.

In the first centuries this image was dominated by the still fresh memory of the risen Christ; hence there was little preoccupation with administrative details and there was a great deal of room for generosity and forgiveness.[15] Nothing else would have fitted well with the personality of the Risen One.

The post-Tridentine age has seen the growth of a legal system with myriads of details and penalties. Behind it, undoubtedly, there was a conception of God as a meticulous administrator and a punctilious judge.

To enter today into the dimension of the image of God as an inspiring source for making and interpreting the laws means to be in vital touch with the best of theological thinking on the most burning and proper question theology can ever raise: who is our God?[16]

- *The horizon of service.* In looking at the structures of the church, we see a need for the horizon of service, as distinct from the horizon of power. The new Code stresses the "sacred power" in the form of the *potestas regiminis,* but for such power to be well placed and to operate satisfactorily, in the practical life of the church it must be consistently balanced by the duty to serve.

---

not one who was concerned more with the washing of the hands than with the purity of the heart. He was not one who liked long lamentations; on the contrary, he was pleased with a few words coming from a contrite heart; and so forth.

We should not think that all those who, at various times in our past history, imposed on the community and administered seemingly cruel or senseless laws were necessarily evil or corrupt people. Many of them were convinced that they were doing a service to God; they thought God was the type of person who thought in the same way as they did.

15. This remains true in spite of excessive severity which certainly existed under some aspects, such as in the matter of penance. But we should recall that proportionally very few persons in a community were subject to such discipline, and only in the case of major and mostly public offenses. For ordinary Christians, the signs of mercy and forgiveness were abundant in various liturgical celebrations.

16. Vatican Council II has done much to correct our image of God, and our laws have changed accordingly. Examples: the council conveyed that God is a person who calls all to holiness, and the laws granted a greater role to the laity; he is one who extends his grace to non-Catholic Christians, and the laws on mixed marriages were revised.

• *The horizon of modern empirical sciences.* Let me put this very practically by way of an example. Canon 1095 of the new Code describes as unable to contract a valid marriage those who lack the use of reason or suffer from a serious defect in judgment, or who for psychological reasons cannot assume marital obligations. Should such defects be judged from the horizon of scientific psychology, or from the horizon of canonical rulings? If the first alternative is chosen, canon law *receives* the verdict based on medical evidence; otherwise it has very little to say except to insure that the vision of an authentic Christian anthropology is not violated. If the second alternative is chosen, canon law tries to decide a medical issue which is beyond its competence; the sign of such an approach is likely to be interminable analyses of legal precedents.

More examples could be given of horizons into which canon law can or, as the case may be, must expand.

Practical applications

The task after Vatican Council II. It has been said many times that the new Code must be interpreted in function of the doctrine of Vatican Council II, and not vice-versa. More specifically one could say that there is no correct and faithful interpretation of the new Code unless it takes place in the new horizons into which the council itself entered.

• *Education.* Quite rightly, there arises the question of what impact the need for a new habit of mind should have on the training of canonists. The documents *Sapientia Christiana* and the following *Ordinationes* are mainly concerned with the content of courses. But the most important aspect of education is the leading of the students into new horizons. One could play with the etymology of the word *e-ducere*: to educate means to lead the candidates *out* of their habitual world, and to lead them *into* new ones, *in-ducere*. A mere accumulation of new information in the same field of vision produces narrow minded specialists who will know a great mass of technicalities but will not be able to handle the law as "the speech of the church."

• *Commentaries.* They must be composed with a new attitude of the mind. This can be stated in a negative and in a positive way. Negatively, a purely legal commentary, of the kind we have known before the council, will not do. Positively, the commentaries should present the values the laws intend to serve, and then judge the laws in function of those values. Moreover, when commentaries are reviewed in professional journals, the field of vision of the authors should be an essential element in assessing their worth. Thus the doctrine of horizon can become a reliable tool for critical assessments. Such a method could contribute greatly to a new flowering of canonical science.[17]

• *An objection: the project is too idealistic.* It seems that the project is too idealistic on two counts. First, one cannot expect canon lawyers to be specialists in theology, philosophy and other subjects; even if it is desirable it is simply not feasible for ordinary human beings. Second, canon law is studied and practiced by many civil lawyers who have never had any training in theology; in fact, in many European universities canon law is taught in civil law schools and is handled within the horizon of civil legal science only.

In response to the first difficulty, one must say that the project could not be more realistic: it is built on the perception of the real organic connection of sciences. Canon law flows from Christian beliefs and from theological reflections on them. Therefore, to study it without theology would be like surveying a river and neglecting its source. Or it would be like trying to understand the laws of Islam without any reference to Islamic beliefs.[18] Once this much is made clear, it should be admitted that the task can appear daunting and demanding. But we have no alternative that is intellectually acceptable and respectable; *mutatis mutandis* the *logion* from the Scripture is applicable: "What God has joined together, man should not put asunder." If God wanted a church, he wanted its beliefs and norms of action joined together.

In response to the second difficulty, we have to admit that in the future there may well be two distinct ways of approaching canon law. One will seek to understand it with the help of theology, another will handle it on the pattern of civil legal science. Such division will not be new; to some extent it has existed in the past. There was always

17. It is quite possible to write a commentary on the new Code with an old habit of mind; that is, handling the law of 1983 within the horizon in which the Code of 1917 was conceived. In fact, such commentaries have already appeared and, undoubtedly, more of them can be expected. The authors usually insist that they move "within the juridical order"—meaning a horizon that includes law, nothing more. Even teachers of civil law try to do better nowadays, by becoming aware that their law cannot be taught well without presenting it within its historical, economic and social background.

18. Or like trying to understand the legislation of a communist state without reference to the political doctrine that has inspired it. The law was necessary to serve "socialist" values, and for no other purpose.

When in a number of countries belief in those values collapsed, the foundations were pulled out from under the laws—and they crumpled as well.

a certain difference between the approach to canon law in the civil law schools of Europe and in the ecclesiastical universities. Without denying the contribution made from within the horizon of civil law, for the internal use of the church the theological horizon is indispensable.[19]

A remark

When dialogues flounder. When two persons operating at a different level of consciousness within the same horizon, or when two persons (or groups, for that matter) are operating in different horizons, mutual understanding cannot be achieved by an exchange of information or by an explanation of diverging opinions, because a transition from one into the other is accomplished through a movement by the whole person. Such movement requires much more than the convincing power of a syllogism. This is why so often the "perfect arguments" in the religious controversies after the Reformation failed to bring about conversions. That is why Catholic fundamentalists after Vatican Council II are unable to accept its reforms. In truth, they are unable to step out of the enclave of their narrow horizon. For them, such a move would be like stepping out of the warmth of the old house where they grew up into the unknown quarters of some modern construction; they cannot bear the burden of the change.

Conclusion

A deceptively simple theory. As we arrive at the end of our reflections and are about to sum up the results, we have to take a last and strong look at the doctrine of horizon. It has two sides. On the one hand, as a theory, it appears simple; even the philosophically uneducated can understand that each human person or, for that matter, every human community has a field of vision which marks and influences all their thoughts and actions. On the other hand, in practice, a change of horizon can be a near intractable issue: both universal history and

---

19. Paul VI stated in an allocution on December 13, 1972:
    Wherefore, it is clear from both revelation and the practice of law which is observed among the apostles, that canon law is a sacred law, altogether distinct from civil law. It is, to be sure, a law of a special kind—hierarchical—and that by the very will of Christ. It is totally woven into the salvific action whereby the Church continues the work of redemption. Since it is so, the juridical institutes of civil society cannot be transferred to the church without risk. (CLD 7: 70-71)

our own experience can bear witness to the fact that to move from one horizon into another can be a catharsis for persons and communities.[20]

The theory is deceptive because once it is articulated and we have grasped it, it blends harmoniously with our own experience; there is nothing jarring about it. Yet many ancient and modern philosophers failed to notice how all our concepts and judgments are influenced by the extent of our horizon, and consequently were not able to give a full account of the process of knowing. Nor could they explain why so many intellectual disputes and conflicts never produced satisfactory results. They thought it should be a matter of more explanations of concepts and judgments; they did not realize it was a conflict of horizons.

To reach a concordance of discordant horizons, or to expand the existing horizons, is indeed a complex issue; it is complex because the move involves the whole person or, as the case may be, the whole community. The change in prospect may well appear as a threat because it uproots a person before it allows him or her to strike roots in a new environment. In the process of transition too much of what a person may treasure and which contributes to a person's identity has to be reassessed.

It follows that the authentic development of the legal life of the church is not just a matter of acquiring new concepts and marshalling them in a different way; it is a matter of persons being able to lift the operations of their spirit to a higher level, and to move into a broader field of vision. It follows that the future of the legal life of the church will depend much more on the quality of persons than the quantity of knowledge that they may accumulate. It will depend on persons who live and work by a new attitude of mind, a *novus habitus mentis*.

---

20. A most recent example: Archbishop Lefèvbre could not bring himself to enter into the horizon of Vatican Council II. No amount of conceptual explanation (undoubtedly given by many) could bring him around; only a radical conversion could have disposed him to accept the council.

This brings up an interesting question: how should one approach those who are separated from us by different horizons? What else should we do, beyond conceptual and propositional dialogues, to achieve unity? To my knowledge, no specific study has ever been done on this issue.

3

Interpretation:
The Law and Its Interpreters

Introduction

The subject matter of our inquiry is the interpretation of laws. Instinctively, we all would like to reach out immediately for the precise definition of "interpretation," according to the venerable rules of scholastic methodology, so that we would know right from the start what it is. Yet, since we are in the field of jurisprudence, it is wiser to follow the tradition of the Roman *jurisprudentes* and avoid a precise definition. After all, we do have a clear enough conception of what interpretation should be. It is a clarification of the meaning of the law by diverse means and by various persons. Such a description, general as it is, should be satisfactory as a point of departure.[1]

In fact, the art of interpretation is not new; it has been around as far back as the memory of the human family runs. The serpent practiced interpretation in the garden of Eden when it approached the first couple and cunningly distorted the meaning of the law of God. They accepted its fallacies uncritically, and disaster followed for the whole human race. In contrast, much later, when the fullness of time came,

---

1. Philosophers, to advance, must seek definitions; lawyers, to let the community progress, must often shun definitions. Compare the attitude of Socrates with that of the Roman *jurisprudentes*. He was eager to determine what the virtue of justice was; they avoided even describing the meaning of natural justice, yet they practiced it to a remarkable degree. A good definition in philosophical enquiry moves the reflection forward; in law, it can become a straitjacket hampering development. Once a concept is firmly circumscribed in law, there is little room for evolution. Thus some vagueness in fundamental concepts in the field of law is not only pardonable but desirable, *pace* Socrates!

Jesus of Nazareth gave a new meaning to the old law and freed his disciples from the slavery of mindless legalism.[2]

Indeed, the art of interpretation is a delicate instrument. It can make human persons captive to falsehoods; it can bring them the experience of freedom.[3] Ordinarily, the interpretation of our canons will have no such cosmic impact. Yet, in many subtle ways, the pronouncements of our legislators, the decisions of our judges, the decrees of our administrators, the insights of our teachers, and the way our people observe the laws become part of the fabric of the church. If such contributions are ill conceived, they weaken the social body; if they are well conceived they strengthen it. Every act of interpretation is important, as the precise chiseling of every stone is important if it is destined to become a part of the delicate structure of a cathedral.

There is a special reason, however, why the sustained study of the science and art of interpretation is so necessary in canon law. Briefly, it is this. Ecclesiastical laws are mostly the products of human effort and ingenuity. As such, they are marked by the limitations of our human nature. Interpretation can help to perfect them.

The church is helped by the Holy Spirit to remain faithful to the evangelical message; it cannot lose, destroy, or substantially distort the word of God. But the church is not helped by the Holy Spirit to create the best legal system or to enact the wisest laws all the time. It needs the intelligence and the prudence, the learning and the competence of Christian persons to make good laws, to interpret them correctly, and to do away with them when they have fulfilled their pur-

---

2. The Gospels speak about Jesus as supremely concerned to restore the right hierarchy of values in the interpretation of the laws. His disputes with the Pharisees about the observance of the Sabbath are a good example of his approach; see Matt 12:1-8: Jesus defends the disciples who are plucking ears of grain and eating them on the Sabbath; also Matt 12:9-14: after having healed a man on the Sabbath, he defends himself against the accusation of breaking the laws.

Among the apostles, Paul, the "last born," may have been the first to grasp fully the teaching of the Master; his quick understanding enabled him not only to oppose firmly the application of the law of circumcision to converts from paganism, but also to justify his stand on theological grounds.

The New Testament as a whole contains more directions for the interpretation of laws than we may be aware of. Note also that the problems in interpretation which Jesus encountered concerned not so much the immediate meaning of the terms in their text and context as the subtle reversal of the right order of values in the application of the laws.

3. The immense power the Supreme Court of the United States exercises over the lives of individual citizens, and over the nation as a whole, comes to the judges through their constitutional power to interpret the laws.

pose. Exaggerated as the following statement may be, it contains a grain of truth: the church depends more on human contribution in developing a good system of laws than in preserving the deposit of revelation. Part of this contribution is interpretation.

The method of our inquiry is determined by its scope. A short study, like this, cannot be all-embracing and exhaustive. But it can single out some topical and substantive issues, explain them, and show how new insights and new discoveries can advance the old science and art of interpreting canon law.

PART ONE: THE LAW

What is law?

The question, "What is law?" has occupied the minds of philosophers ever since Socrates, or so Plato tells us. This innocuous-looking question has provoked so many answers that they could fill a library—with some shelves empty because the end of the dispute is not yet in sight! Indeed, Adamson Hoebel, best known for his research on the role of law in primitive societies, has concluded that to "seek a definition of the legal is like the quest for the Holy Grail." The despair of locating the mythical object led Max Radin, an American jurisprudent, to exclaim, "Those of us who have learned humility have given over the attempt to define law."[4]

Such counsel of despair, however, goes too far. It is possible to reach a good understanding of what law is, but we should realize from the first moment of the search that the conclusion will flow from the premises; that is, the answer given at the end will depend on how the question was raised in the beginning. There is a great variety of definitions because the issues can be raised in many different ways. We do not need, however, to examine them all. Let us focus just on two radically different ways of initiating the inquiry.

In the abstract order. The question "What is law?" can be raised in the abstract world of essences, and there alone. "What is law?"—that is, "What is the very essence of a binding norm given to a community, irrespective of whether the community lives by it?" That is how

---

4. *See* Steven Vago, *Law and Society* (Englewood Cliffs, N.J.: Prentice Hall, 1981) 7. For extended comments and bibliographical references see the chapter on "Conceptualization of Law," ibid. 6–10.

38 Interpretation: The Law and Its Interpreters

Aquinas raised the question, and he reached his answer accordingly. The following "definition" is not word for word from him but it is a faithful collection of the essential elements of the law as he presents them:

> law is *ordinatio* of reason
> [*ordinatio*—from *ordinare*: action to create order—is not equivalent to the English "ordinance" which means a command]
> by the one who is in charge of the community
> for the sake of the common good
> promulgated (cf. *Summa theologiae,* Prima secundae, q. 90, art. 1-4).

This definition holds in the abstract world of essences. That is, it holds in a world that abstracts from any historical reality, in which no question is raised about the actual use of the norm by the community.

In the existential order. The question, "What is law?" can be raised within the context of the existing order, in the order of *esse.* "What is law?"—that is, "What is the normative element in the mind and heart of people which actually, *actu,* moves them to act?" Then the question concerns a norm which has a working efficacy in the existential world. The answer is that the norm is the law, accepted and acted upon by a community of intelligent and free persons.

Thus, law is an analogous concept. Each definition of it is valid, but each in its own realm only. Those who assume, probably more subconsciously than reflectively, that law is a univocal concept will continue to search for its one and exclusive meaning. Those who know that the human mind is able to construe an abstract world (nonexistent but having great logical coherence) and that the same mind is able to know the real world (existent but not so coherent) will find no difficulty in admitting that the term "law" can have two different meanings, each being valid in its own world. Thus, the point of departure of the inquiry determines the outcome.[5]

---

5. Even the use of the word "law" in ordinary language should warn us that it is an analogous term with several related (partly identical, partly different) meanings. We speak of good laws and bad laws; we speak of laws on the book, even if not observed, and of laws even if they have never been formally enacted but emerged from customs.

Those who accept Aquinas' way of raising the question cannot come to any other answer than Aquinas did. But both the question and the answer remain in the realm of essences; they do not speak of the existing world. For them, if the law is not observed at all, it is still law; if the community really lives by another

These reflections are not idle flights of fancy. Stress on the first type of understanding has led, often enough, to the making of laws which were intellectually attractive but unsuitable for a given community, and to the neglect of the role of the community in understanding the laws and implementing them. Canon law, in particular, has suffered and is still suffering from this essentialist approach.[6]

norm, that norm is not the law. This is the inevitable consequence of taking the word "law" as a univocal term. The evolution of ideas usually consists in a movement from univocal to analogous concepts. Both the enacted but not observed norm and the non-enacted but observed norm are laws, but in an analogous, that is, partly identical, partly different, sense of the term "law."

The Code of Canon Law of 1917 accepted the Thomistic definition and drew the consequences with faultless logic. For example: if the term "law" meant the enacted and promulgated norm, no interpretation could add or take away anything of its meaning; it had to be there fully at the moment of its promulgation. Therefore that Code allowed two types of interpretation only, one that declared the meaning of the law which was *in se certa* in the first place (i.e., clearly evidenced in the text), another which extended or restricted its original meaning. This second type of "interpretation," said the Code, should be handled as new legislation. But how could interpretation ever be identical with legislation?

Futher, the same Code took away any intrinsic force from customs; their binding force had to come from the legislator, too, *ab eo qui curam communitatis habet*.

But real life cannot be ignored without penalty. In silent contrast to the above theories, volumes of interpretations by ecclesiastical courts and offices are continually published, interpretations which clearly go beyond simply declaring what was *in se certa* in the law. Further, custom is recognized as the "best" interpreter of the law, which clearly it could not be if the meaning of the law had been fixed at the time of its promulgation. Custom can operate only in the existential order.

6. The issue of distinguishing the concept of law in the abstract order from that in the existential order should not be confused with the issue of distinguishing good law from bad law.

In the scholastic tradition, only good law can be law, since only good law can be *ordinatio rationis*. Hence, a norm which is not grounded in right reason (that is, which is not upholding the right values) is no law at all. It has no binding force.

When I try to broaden the traditional idea of law and propose that the reception of the law by the community should be included in its definition, I do not imply that a norm with evil purposes becomes acceptable once observed. Since the element of *ordinatio rationis*, as explained, has been missing from the beginning, the norm remains deficient throughout. The legislator and the community simply made and accepted a bad decision; they are in pursuit of false values. But the fact cannot be denied: they are moved by a norm; that norm exists.

Civil lawyers tend to call such bad norms "laws"; so do we all in ordinary speech. But more alert people add the qualification "bad" or "immoral," or something similar. It follows that before a discussion on the meaning of law can begin, a careful semantic analysis of the term is imperative.

The life of the law

For a more comprehensive and balanced understanding of what law is, let us describe the "life of the law" in the midst of a community. Every human law has its own preordained stages of life:

- it is conceived,
- it is born,
- it lives,
- it dies or fades away.

These stages of life are not mere metaphors. We can genuinely speak of the life of the law, and within its life span of different stages of existence, as well as of transition from one stage to another. The law's life span (human law's, that is) can be divided into two great periods. The first extends from its conception by the legislator to the moment when it gains full binding force. It concludes when a law is proposed, with authority, to the community for observance and has legal validity. The second great period comprises the time of the reception of the law by the community and the adjustment of the community to the new norm. During this period the law obtains existential validity in the sense that it becomes a living guide and vital force for the community; the life and the operations of the community are shaped by it.

Interpretation belongs to the second period. But in order to understand its role, it is necessary to survey how a law is conceived, how it is born, how it prospers, and how it dies.

The first period

• *Conception: formulation.* The first movement toward the creation of a law is in the convergence of three judgments within the legislator. First he must assess the nature of the community and its needs. Then he must determine the values which can fill those needs. Finally, he must ascertain that the community has the concrete capacity to work for and obtain those values. Something can be most desirable, most needed, and yet not practical, in the sense that the community does not have the moral strength to live up to it.

At the conception of any good law, these three judgments play their part. First, the legislator must make a judgment about the good to be obtained. Then, he must make a judgment, a somewhat abstract one, about the need of the community to pursue that good. Finally, he must assess the capacity of the community to pursue that value in the concrete order. All three converge toward inspiring a norm: "The community ought to do this or that."

The design of a law that exists only in the mind of the legislator must take flesh in a text. Meanings must be clothed with technical expressions. Such a process takes place at the time of the drafting of the law. Highly specialized terms and idioms are taken from tradition. The intended rule is balanced against, and brought into harmony with, existing rules: gradually, the law takes shape. This process can take a shorter or longer time, depending on the extent of the issues the norm intends to cover. Eventually, the text is ready.

• *Birth: promulgation.* Through the act of promulgation the law comes into existence. It is born. The act of promulgation also becomes the legal proof for the existence of the law.

As a rule, the law does not bind immediately after it comes into existence. Time is given to the community to get acquainted with the new rule. This time is called *vacation*. Its length is determined either by general legislation or by the individual law that has been promulgated.

• *Full vigor.* The law comes of age, it obtains full vigor, it binds the community and its members. Nothing more can be added to it on the part of the legislator.

Thus the first great period ends. The law has reached the state of full vigor, it is *lex vigens*. We can call it a valid law. The expression means that the legislator completed the constitutional process of providing a norm for the community. It does not and cannot mean, at this point, that the community lives by the law. This statement will be important when the issue of acceptance is raised.

The second period

We are in a different field now. We consider law in the midst of the community; or, we consider the community as guided by the law. We are interested not in abstract concepts, but in the concrete situation as it develops when the group for which the law was intended begins to appropriate it.

We are speaking of the acceptance of the law by the community, not in the notional but in the existential sense.

• *Living reality: reception, implementation, interpretation.* The community consists of intelligent and free human beings. The law is not and cannot be received by them existentially, unless they understand it and act on it.

The process toward the construction of the true meaning of the law consists of several steps. Light does not come all at once. The text of the law must be ascertained on the basis of some official act. In the church, this usually means turning to the text printed in the *Acta Apostolicae Sedis*. Then, it is necessary to bring to bear all the rules of interpretation on the text. Various options should be considered in searching for the authentic meaning. Each hypothesis should be weighed and pondered according to the evidence available from the text of the new law and the content of its native environment. Eventually, one answer may impose itself as the true one. If that happens, the interpreter must surrender the freedom he or she enjoyed while inquiring and accept the truth as it is.

Such is the process of interpretation, reduced to its bare elements.

The implementation of the law is ultimately a personal act. No matter who does it, an administrator, a judge, or an ordinary citizen, it is worthy of its name only if it is done freely. Implementation could mean doing what the law prescribes, or abstaining from what it proscribes. In either case it has value only if it is done freely. Clearly, implementation happens in the concrete world; it cannot happen anywhere else. When it happens, either the shape of the world is changed for the better, or a value is preserved against eroding forces. In either case, the law shapes the life of the community through the action or attitude of the individual.

• *Death: the demise of the law.* We mention the demise of the law for the sake of completeness. When it is suppressed officially, canon law has technical terms for it. It speaks of *obrogatio, abrogatio, derogatio*. According to the context, they can mean full or partial extinction of the law, either because it has served its purpose, or because the whole matter has had to be legislated all over again. When it is abandoned by custom, we speak of *desuetudo*: the people of God judged it and found it unnecessary.

Thus the life of a law comes to an end.

As described here, the law is a norm of action in the existing world, adopted and used by a community of free and intelligent persons in order to build well balanced social structures. Such orderly structures are needed by everyone to grow peacefully in grace and wisdom. Note the specific terms *adopted* and *used*; both are in the order of *esse*, beyond the stage of promulgation. I went one step further than Aquinas.[7]

---

7. At this point, we are touching on a sensitive philosophical and theological issue: the transition from the abstract order into the world of existence.

There is a difference between a creature in God's mind only, and a creature moving on the ground here and new. There is a difference between an automobile on the drawing board only, and one rolling off the production line.

What does all this have to do with interpretation? A great deal. It determines its scope. The law is there to be interpreted throughout its life, from its birth to its demise. It follows that genuine interpretation, by its very nature, must be more than the declaration of a meaning which was there, clear and certain, *in se certa*, at the time of its promulgation.[8] It is a creative process.

The balancing role of *epieikeia*

A systematic study of the science and art of interpretation of laws would be incomplete and structurally imbalanced without giving due place to Aristotle's *epieikeia*. There are few legal institutions as clear and simple in their conception as that one, yet there are hardly any over which so many layers of theories and explanations have accumulated. I intend to do no more than to restate, as far as I can, the Philosopher's proposition in its original form; once understood, I trust, its soundness will be enough to prove its enduring validity.

Aristotle introduces the idea of *epieikeia* in the context of his reflections on the virtue of justice in the *Nichomachean Ethics*.[9] *To epieikes*,

In the Thomistic tradition, the difference is that between *essence* and *existence*, which is a lot of difference.

In the case of law, there is even more. First, there is the norm conceived and promulgated; second, there is the norm which has become a source of action for a large group of people. In the first case, the norm exerts no force (which is not to say that it is not binding). In the second case, the norm actually exerts an influence; the community is moving.

8. Although the reception of the law will be the topic of Chapter Five, in order to avoid any misunderstanding let the reader be warned that when I affirm the need for the reception of the laws, I do not imply that there is no duty to obey them.

The very nature of a community composed of intelligent and free persons requires that every law, every "ordinance of reason," should be given to the community in circumstances respecting human nature, which is intelligent and free. The community should be given the opportunity to see the values the legislator intends to uphold, and it should be expected to obey out of the depth of its freedom.

The very fact of belonging to the church requires obedience to its laws. But still, the church member should implement those laws as befits a person: intelligently and freely.

9. See Aristotle, *Nichomachean Ethics* 1137ª32-1138ª39; in English translation, Richard McKeon, ed., *The Basic Works of Aristotle* (New York: Random House, 1941), 1019-1020. See also two outstanding commentaries published recently: Abraham Edel, *Aristotle and His Philosophy* (Chapel Hill: University of North Carolina, 1982), p. 301 on *epieikeia*; W. K. C. Guthrie, *Aristotle: An Encounter. A History of Greek Philosophy*, Vol. 6 (Cambridge: Cambridge University Press, 1981) 375-376 on *epieikeia*.

usually translated somewhat misleadingly as *equity*, is really an act of justice; its scope is to balance, or correct, or complete the application of law, whenever it is so warranted. In other terms, the very nature of every law is such that, in some cases, it may grant imperfect justice only, or no justice at all. Then *epieikeia* must enter. "The reason is that all law is universal, but about some things it is not possible to make a universal statement which shall be correct" (NE 1137^b 12-14). "For when the thing is indefinite, the rule also is indefinite" (28-29).

There is the empirically-minded Philosopher, the faithful observer of nature, in this case of the nature of the norms serving a political body. He sees that real life is more complex than any set of rules which the human mind can conceive. Hence, an *ad hoc* corrective is necessary. It must originate in the same source as the laws, that is, in the virtue of justice.

Aristotle's *epieikeia* is not equivalent to the *equitable law* of the Romans, which was a new, flexible legal system distinct from the old, rigid civil law; a flexible system, too, may need the corrective of *epieikeia*. But his theory comes close to the practice of the English chancellor who used to grant "equity" when the literal observance of the law led to injustice. Modern English "equity," however, is like the Romans' equitable law; judicial precedents have produced a fixed set of norms.

Traditionally, canon law acknowledged the right to use *epieikeia*, even if the explanations of it varied greatly. To conceive it again in its original simplicity may enhance its scope. To confine it to extreme cases only, such as filling the gap in the case of a *lacuna legis* (there is no law *and* there should be one) would be to restrict it too much, virtually making it useless.

In Aristotle's mind, *epieikeia* is an integral and indispensable component of every legal system. It goes hand in hand with statutory law. Justice for all can be achieved only through the subtle and judicious dialectics of imposing the law in most cases and letting *epieikeia* prevail in some.

Legal positivism, which holds many modern civil systems in captivity, of course cannot accept the idea of *epieikeia*, since it would make the validity of a decision depend on the virtue of justice. But such prejudice should not operate in the field of canon law. It *should* not, I say, because there have been periods in the history of canon law when *epieikeia* has been forgotten, in the sense that it played no serious role. For such neglect there was a penalty, flowing directly from the nature of things: as the application of *epieikeia* receded, legalism raised its ugly head.

Legalism is a sickness in the system; it places greater value on the observance of formalities than on the granting of true justice. When it is rampant, it erodes the strength of laws from the inside, and it brings them into bad repute on the outside. The best prevention against such disease is the faithful application of the laws in general and the vigorous invocation of Aristotle's *epieikeia* in particular.

Reception

In earlier ages, the dispute about the need for the law to be received by the community used to flare up with some regularity, but in recent times it has been rather quiescent.

Again, the way the question is put determines the answer. If I ask, "Is reception, in the sense of ratification, necessary for a law to be validly enacted?" the answer is negative. Ratification is not required for validity. Indeed, as long as Aquinas' definition of law is used, the answer must be negative.

But if I ask, "Is reception necessary for the law to become a vital force in the community?" the answer must be affirmative. Since the question is about something in the existing world, the response must come from there, too. In the existing world, the law must be received in order to be a vital force in the community. Once received, it can shape its structures, it can govern its actions. A law not received is as good as nonexistent. Before its reception, *actu*, the law is no more than an abstract norm which has not touched the life of the community.

There are, however, requirements for the correct reception of the law. First, the community and its members must understand the value the law intends to uphold. Then, they must decide freely to follow the norm. A Christian community cannot act according to its own innate dignity unless it acts with intelligence and freedom.[10]

---

10. This statement is clearly against blind obedience in the community of the faithful, and rightly so. If our redemption means that light has come to shine in the darkness, light should shine, above all, in the minds and hearts of the people.

When a law is promulgated, mere insistence on obedience cannot be enough. Precisely to obey well, an intelligent person ought to grasp the value toward which his or her action is directed; if not, he or she is not obedient, but is acting as a mindless automaton. In the case of natural values, it should not be too difficult to achieve such clarity; at least, not among persons of common sense and some degree of education. In the case of values known through faith only, no one may be able to grasp the value fully because it is wrapped up in a mystery, yet the legislator can still show that our faith postulates that a given value should be pursued by the community.

Ideally, there is no other type of legislation in the Christian community than

It follows that the legislator must promulgate the laws with due respect for the dignity of his subjects. A significant part of his duty is to explain the need for the law and the values it intends to uphold. Otherwise, how could he obtain the intelligent and free cooperation of those for whom the law is intended?! I am not speaking of a legal obligation; I am stressing a moral duty of the legislator, be it towards the civic community, or the members of the Christian *communio*.[11]

A well informed community, aware of the respect the legislator has for its role in giving life to the law, is likely to become a good interpreter. The opposite is true, too: an uninformed community, on whom an abstract norm is imposed, will not be a good interpreter.

To make the law a vital force in the community is the common task of all those who make the law and all those for whom it is made.

PART TWO: THE INTERPRETERS

Who are the interpreters?

The question "Who are the interpreters?" again can be raised either in the realm of the abstract or expanded into the realm of the concrete. If the essence of the law is completed with the act of promulgation, no one other than the one who conceived it, drafted it, and promulgated it can interpret it correctly. If the law takes on a new dimension with its acceptance by the community, its meaning can be shaped by those who live by it.

As I have given an account of the stages of the life of the law, I shall now enumerate the interpreters, as they operate in the existing

---

the one based on service. Promulgation of a law is not simply the imposition of a norm of action from above, but rather the communication of a vision concerning the life of the community. This is communication with power, surely, but we should recall that to act with power, *en dynamei*, is a biblical expression, always with the connotation that the strength of the Spirit is there.

Not until the twelfth century did "power" become synonymous with "jurisdiction." When it did, its traditional and rich theological significance was lost, and it became a legal term, used not very differently in canon and civil law.

11. There is nothing wrong with saying that the legislator should account (not in the legal sense) to the community for the law that he intends to impose on them. While it is customary to speak about "superiors" and "subjects" in the church, it is more correct (and more biblically minded) to speak about a close *communio* between the legislator and the rest of the membership. They are all one body.

world. They are many; moreover, they divide into distinct groups, each with a different task.

• *The legislator.* The legislator has the advantage and the disadvantage of being close to his own law. He made it; therefore he is in a position to dispel any doubt that may arise about its meaning by simply repeating the meaning that he intended to put into the law. To be able to do that is certainly an advantage. Canon 16 calls it the authentic interpretation of the law. As a matter of fact, there is very little interpretation, in the ordinary sense, in such a declaration; it is really a repetitive act. It reaffirms, perhaps in different terms, what the legislator intended to say.

Under another aspect, the legislator is not necessarily the best interpreter. Since he drafted the law, he is so close to it that he may not perceive its limitations and ambiguities. There he is at a disadvantage. He may not be able to see a discrepancy between what he intended and what he said; that is, between his original intention and the text of the law. He may be tempted to force an interpretation on the text that does not necessarily follow from it. Such a danger may well be the reason why, in civil law, those who hold the power to legislate do not hold the power to interpret.[12] The parliament makes the law, the courts determine its meaning. Once the law is born, its parent must leave it alone. The courts take care of its development. This is not to

---

12. In constitutional democracies there is a balanced division among the three branches of power: legislative, judicial, and executive. The task of interpreting the laws is given to the courts, which are autonomous and apolitical. The members of the legislature and the executive officers of the government, as representatives of political parties, are not suited for detached interpretation. They could be tempted to interpret the laws to their own political advantage. In totalitarian societies the courts rarely, if ever, have the power to pronounce on the objective meaning of the law; such power rests with the ruling party: the law must mean what it wants the law to mean.

The church is not a political society. At the highest level of its government, there is only one undivided power, a fullness of spiritual strength, *dynamis en pneumati,* which flows out into external government, to be used for the edification (building up) of the community.

There is no reason, however, why the church, on less than the highest level, could not use some of the practical wisdom of well ordered civil societies and grant some power to its courts to interpret the laws. In fact, the tribunals of the Holy See are separated from its administrative offices; they already interpret the law autonomously whenever it is to be applied to a case. It would require very little to extend this power and give the Rota or the Signatura the right to issue judicial declarations concerning the meaning of the law.

48 Interpretation: The Law and Its Interpreters

take the power of the legislator away; he can always intervene by means of a new legislative act.

• *The courts.* The ordinary duty of the courts is to resolve a conflict concerning a right and duty situation. Their task can be conceived as purely mechanical. On the basis of the law, they should determine with precision the original meaning intended by the legislator. Then they should consider the facts. Once all the elements are in place, the conflict can be resolved in the same way as a mathematical problem is resolved, by inserting the proper factors into the right equation. But in real life, the courts work differently.

First of all, the text of the law is never so clear as a mathematical axiom. Litigations and conflicts arise, often enough, because the text of the law admits several constructions. If that is the case, the courts will choose one and apply it to the individual case before them. That is an act of creative interpretation. They make law at least for the parties who are seeking justice. At the courts, law and life meet. There the abstract rules of the legislator confront the concrete needs of the community. When this happens, the judges must often make adjustments; the abstract, general and impersonal norm does not always respond well to the demands of a concrete, particular and personal situation. The judges must keep the right balance between the world of the law and the postulates of justice. Effectively, they make law through interpretation.

Finally, in some legal systems the courts are granted the power to interpret the law authentically, that is, authoritatively. To give them such authority helps to uphold the "rule of law" against the "rule of man." It can also save the members of the community from lengthy and costly litigations. Qualified persons or organs can address a question to the court about the meaning of a specific norm. The answer may settle a dispute. English common law grants such power to the courts. Canon law does not. Moreover, courts can receive even greater power when the interpretation of the fundamental law of the country, usually known as a constitution, is entrusted to them. They can pronounce whether or not secondary laws correspond to the principles laid down in the foundational document of the country. Needless to say, courts have no such power in the church.

Indeed, canon law restricts the competency of the courts in canon 16, § 3 to making binding pronouncements in individual cases only. The strength of their decision does not extend beyond the parties who happen to be before the judges. Yet as we all know, this is more theory than practice. The decisions of the Roman Rota are carefully recorded, catalogued, and printed to help lower tribunals make the right decision. Our practice goes beyond our theory.[13]

• *The executors of the law, or the administrators.* In canon law, as in civil law, there are persons in charge of administrative offices. In fulfilling their task they must know and interpret the law.

Such interpretation can take place when, e.g., a Roman Congregation issues an instruction, or more simply when it grants a favor. There are many lower office holders, too, who are interpreters of the law in their daily work.

• *The doctors.* The doctors are those who do not hold an office with power attached to it such as legislators, judges and administrators do. They are usually teachers or writers. Their task is to find the meaning of the law through the critical criteria of scientific research. They service all the other groups.

The task of the doctors should not, however, be only to construe the meaning of existing laws. Their horizon should be broad enough to allow them to survey and understand the needs of the community. Then they should examine critically whether or not a given structure or a specific norm takes care of those needs. On the basis of such assessment they should be able to suggest new legislation or new ways of applying the existing laws to individual cases.

• *The people of God.* We did not say laity on purpose, because we want to include all Christian persons, lay or not. Through their understanding, acceptance, and practice of the law, they become interpreters. Canon 27 acknowledges this when it says: "Custom is the best interpreter of laws." Naturally enough, such interpretative practice requires a large measure of intelligence and freedom in the community.

This requirement leads us to point to a deep social problem in the church, certainly present, but rarely mentioned. Our legal traditions developed in an age when the standard of general education was much lower than today and, as a rule, there was no cultural equality between the legislator and his subjects. In more blunt terms, the educated and learned legislated for the masses who were uneducated and ignorant. In such circumstances it may have been right to stress obedience to the law and to assume that the members of the community had little

---

13. In theory, canon law does not give any scope to the accumulated wisdom of judges; ideally each judgment should be a fresh departure from the text of the law. Thus an inexperienced judge of the lowest court can ignore the precedents set by the judges of the highest court. In practice, the impact of the jurisprudence of the supreme courts (the Rota and the Apostolic Signatura) on diocesan tribunals is significant well beyond what the theory would allow.

capacity to contribute to the legislative process. Today we live in a different world. The standard of education is high in many countries and rapidly developing in many others. The Christian community at large is more and more capable of making its contribution to the creation and interpretation of laws. Such a development is bound to have an impact on the world of canon law.

It would be wrong to ask an intelligent and free person to perform an act, even in obedience to a law, if he or she had not reached a personal judgment that the act was in pursuance of a true value and decided freely to do it.

Today it is no longer fitting to promulgate the law without any explanation and then to urge the people to obey. The legislator has the duty of clarifying the value that the law intends to uphold, or the good effect that the law is meant to achieve. By doing this, he recognizes that the church is a gathering of intelligent and free persons.

So, to the question "Who are the interpreters?" the answer is that in the concrete order there are many. Each meets the law in a specific way: some reading it in the official books, others applying it with calm detachment in a case to third parties, others again experiencing its impact in their very bones.

APPENDIX

Qualities of the Interpreters

The task of the interpreters is to find the truth of the law. That is, they must find out the objective significance of the law. They must conceive and generate a *meaning* on the basis of the text, in its doctrinal and cultural context.

This task demands not only a capacity to read a sentence and construe its meaning out of internal evidence, but also the ability to put that sentence into the much broader context of the entire body of the law. Then all the significance that emerges should be collocated in the still larger environment of the Christian faith and human culture, where it all has originated.

1. The interpreters should be aware that their interpretation is a historical event in two ways: they describe the law at a specific point of evolution, and their capacity to know is at a specific point of development.

This principle does not relativize all knowledge, but it brings an element of relativity into all knowledge, including the interpretation of laws. We have spoken many times of the evolutionary character of the laws. It is, therefore, not surprising to hear that the content of every interpretation must consist in the determination of the point which the law has reached in its process of evolution. The interpreters, however, do not stand still in the universal flow of history either. They too are developing all the time. Their capacity to perceive, understand, and judge data will depend on how far they have progressed in this vital process of development.

2. The broader the horizon of the interpreters, the closer their interpretation is to truth.

Horizon here means the extent of the field that the sight of the researchers can embrace. The more extensive it is, the better they can understand the role that a legal institution or norm can play in the real world.

Canon lawyers who are *merely* lawyers will never grasp the full meaning of ecclesiastical laws. To be enclosed in a mere legal horizon is to operate within a narrow field where meanings are distorted. Since the whole world of canon law is rooted in the world of Christian doctrine and its systematic understanding, for the construction of the right legal meaning the interpreters need to return to those roots.

Further, religion is rooted in human nature. Therefore, not even Christian faith can be well understood if it is not put into the context of those sciences that inquire about human nature, such as philosophy (on a more abstract level), psychology, anthropology and sociology (on a more concrete level). Values recognized by Christian doctrine or sound philosophies must play their part in the understanding of the laws of the Christian church.

Horizon, ultimately, means not only intellectual knowledge of different fields but also a capacity to assimilate existentially the world, religious and human, in which the law exists. If that experience is not present, the interpretation will always be one-sided and limited, often distorted and harmful.

3. The interpreters who can approach the law with more sophisticated categories are more likely to find the right meaning.

By categories we mean key concepts through which the law can be understood. The more the interpreters have of those instruments, the more sophisticated their interpretation will become. We are not talking of legal categories only, but of others, too, from the fields of various sciences that are helpful for the understanding of laws.

The law concerning non-Catholic Christians can serve as an illustration. The Code knows only limited categories to classify those Christians who are not in full communion with the See of Rome: they are either heretics or schismatics; hence, deprived of favors and subject to penalties. But recent theology has given us a more sophisticated approach: they are "separated brethren"; that is, they are both united with us and divided from us. Moreover, there are degrees in communion; the proportion between division and union may shift and change.

Canon law does not have, as yet, sophisticated enough categories to handle these developments. Before, the law saw every Christian as being either fully in or fully out of the visible church. Now, the law should see them as being inside and outside at the same time. How can we express such a situation in legal terms? Insightful and creative interpreters may help us to find the necessary new categories.

Questions raised by the science of hermeneutics have hardly penetrated the field of canon law as yet. There are no systematic treatises on the science of interpretation, still less on the required qualities of the interpreter. Canon law has been a sheltered science. The great intellectual movements of our times have hardly touched it; at times this has been for the better, at times for the worse. But such a state of things cannot last for long, nor should it. The foundations of our laws are strong enough to resist corrosive influences. They are vital enough to profit from new insights and discoveries.

If canon lawyers want to learn about epistemological issues and hermeneutics, they must look for help in the fields of other sciences which have encountered similar problems connected with interpretation and are at least in the process of learning how to solve them, such as biblical studies, theology, or civil law. Their questions are important for us. The answers they give illustrate, in other subject matter, how scientific progress can be made. We must raise similar questions but find our own answers.

4

Interpretation: Guiding Principles

Literary forms in the book of laws

The Code carries the message of the legislator to those for whom the law was made. To understand the meaning of the message correctly, the subjects should know that they do not have in hand a document with an even tone and tenor throughout. Rather, they have a collection of small literary pieces widely differing from each other in nature. To catch the meaning of each, the nature of each must be determined. The literary form of a given text is part of the meaning of that text.

If an analogy is needed, there is a good one from the field of biblical sciences. We know that the Bible is not a uniform literary product from the beginning to the end, but rather a collection of many pieces each having its own literary form. To find the correct meaning of each one we must start by determining its nature. *Mutatis mutandis,* we must take a similar approach in interpreting the Code, since it contains several differing types of utterances by the legislator.

In the Code we can find the following literary forms:

• *Dogmatic statements.* There are statements of belief, virtually amounting to a profession of faith. Usually, such statements are there to introduce practical dispositions, e.g., about the government of the church, or the administration of the sacraments. In those statements, the church remembers God's mighty deeds, the *gesta Dei.* A good argument could be made for not putting such anamneses into a book of law, but once it has happened, they must be taken for what they are: articulations of belief. They must not be interpreted as laws are; they are not subject to juridical methodology. To find their meaning, the interpreter must leave the world of law and enter the world of dogma. Christian doctrine is not proper subject matter for disciplinary legislation, nor should we assume that the legislator wanted to make it so. Therefore, even if a point of doctrine appears in our book of laws, it has not become a law. It should be interpreted from theological sources and with theological methodology.[1]

• *Theological opinions.* There are theological statements which do not represent any article of faith, but are historically conditioned opinions of a theological school. As such, they have no right to demand universal assent.

While it could be argued that such opinions should not be in a book of laws, the laws which flow from them are not necessarily out of place. Often enough, the need for an ordered and peaceful life in the community postulates a practical norm for action long before there is a theoretical consensus among theologians. Then, the legislator may well feel compelled to use one of the accepted theological opinions as his point of departure. But such opinions have no standing before the courts, and the laws flowing from them can be interpreted more broadly than the seemingly "canonized" opinion would allow.[2]

1. In recent years, while the work was progressing on the new Code, many theologians and canon lawyers expressed their concern about the insertion of statements taken from Vatican II into the schemata. Since the conciliar texts appeared in a new context, they were effectively given a new meaning, or so many thought. They believed there was a danger that the doctrine of the council was being changed through legislation.

There are indeed statements in the new Code taken from Vatican II. But they should not cause any worry. Their meaning does not depend at all on the new legal context; it depends exclusively and entirely on the original theological context from which they were taken and to which they continue to belong. There is no need to be concerned about the danger of "canonical texts restricting the council." On the contrary, they are more likely to broaden the law, provided they are interpreted according to the doctrine of literary forms, that is, with the help of theological sources, and are not allowed to become law.

2. For instance, there are different theological opinions concerning the capacity of a lay person to participate in the jurisdictional activity of the church, and the possible extent of this participation. The issue is still under debate, yet some practical rules had to be given. Thus, the new Code allows a lay person to function as a judge in diocesan courts in well defined and limited circumstances.

Let this be added by way of an *obiter dictum*:

Clearly the debate is not concluded. Good arguments are being brought forward for much broader participation. After all, the norm of the Code of 1917 was that only clerics could exercise jurisdiction, but to be a cleric meant merely to be tonsured (cf. canons 108 and 118). In other terms, a purely ecclesiastical ceremony,

- *Statements of morality.* There are canons which touch on issues of morality. Their wording may lead an interpreter into concluding that the intrinsic quality of the act, its levity or gravity, has been determined by the legislator. Yet the levity or gravity of an act, or its morality, is a matter of doctrine, too. Hence, before such a statement can be interpreted correctly, it must be restored to its natural environment, which is the field of moral theology. This may be a complex task. It may lead, in some cases, to uncertain results, but nothing is wrong with that. It is not the business of the law to give final answers on disputed ethical issues.[3]
- *Spiritual exhortations.* Some canons are exhortations pure and simple. They express what the legislator desires, but they do not create right and duty situations. An interpreter who does not grasp the literary form of such pieces will change their character and transform them into binding obligations.
- *Theories borrowed from philosophers.* There are canons with a metaphysical content. They offer the insights of philosophers to solve canonical problems. In interpreting such canons, the unbroken tradition of the ecumenical councils should be kept in mind: the church has never committed itself to any school of philosophy. Hence, the interpreter is on secure ground if he or she assumes that the legislator uses the metaphysical principles and categories as useful tools in handling and solving some canonical problems but does not really vouch for their ultimate correctness.

Further, when philosophical theories are built into the legal system, they should not have the stability of the system but should be subject to the normal development that takes place in the field of philosophy. They should not be interpreted as if they were legal norms but according to what their nature is, which is philosophy. By doing this we could keep the law free from a metaphysical rigidity which can ultimately do a great deal of harm.

---

with no foundation in divine law, could make any layman capable of receiving and exercising jurisdiction.

Then there is the issue of the participation of women in the power of jurisdiction. Historically, there is no doubt that *Abbesses nullius* performed acts which for all intents and purposes displayed the signs of jurisdictional power; they did so with the tacit or explicit support of the Holy See.

3. In general, it should never be assumed that the church wants to exercise its full teaching authority in matters of dogma through disciplinary legislation. At most, the legislative act can be a part in a much broader process of development of doctrine.

• *Affirmations borrowed from empirical sciences.* There are canons which contain scientific statements, e.g., from the field of psychology or psychiatry. They should be interpreted according to scientific criteria, taking into account the evolutionary nature of these sciences. In other terms, if a canon speaks of the effect of mental diseases, it should be interpreted according to the latest advances in medicine and not according to the state of information of the legislator at the time of the promulgation of the law.

• *Canons creating right and duty situations.* The true legislative pieces are the canons which deal with right and duty situations. To interpret them, the sources and resources of law must be brought into play. Some of these canons are directly concerned with establishing certain structures and keeping them intact; others are primarily norms of action imposed on all or some members of the community. The difference between norms for structures and norms for action is more nominal than real because, even in the case of structures, the law is concerned with actions that will either create or support them.

This list should not be taken as exhaustive. Besides, even in the same category there can be nuances; the weight of one canon can be greater than that of another, e.g., a canon introducing a new chapter or a new topic in the Code can contain an important clue for the interpretation of all other canons in the same group.[4]

The application of the doctrine of literary forms to the laws of the church is new. But it is a sound doctrine, well tested elsewhere. When judiciously used, it can throw new light on our canons.[5]

---

4. I wish to thank Prof. Francis Morrisey, St. Paul University, Ottawa, for drawing my attention to the particular genre of "leading canon," which may determine the meaning of several others to follow.

5. The canons on marriage in the Code of 1983 offer ample material for illustrating the different literary forms:

• *dogmatic statements:*
—marriage is a sacrament: 1055, no. 1;
—a sacramental consummated marriage cannot be dissolved by any human power: 1141;

• *theological opinion:*
—the matrimonial contract among baptized persons is always *ipso facto* a sacrament: 1055, no. 2;

• *statements on morality:*
—they who have pastoral offices have serious duties concerning the preparation of the couple, and concerning the welfare of those who are married: 1063–1072;
—the spouses are bound to common life: 1151;
—the parents have a grave duty to give an all-round education to their children: physical, social and cultural, moral and religious: 1136;

Interpretation: Guiding Principles 57

Sometimes the objection is raised that the application of the doctrine of literary forms can destroy the unity of our laws. Besides, who would be competent to decide the genre of a legal text with any authority?

The first and obvious answer is that if the ecclesiastical legislator has decided to gather different genres of texts into one Code, we have to handle that Code as it is; that is, as composed of a multiplicity of literary forms. This is no more than respecting the data given to us, and refraining from any ideologizing for the sake of a preconceived unity.

The second and less obvious answer is to request the objicient to consider carefully the consequences of the opposite position. If there are no literary forms in the Code, every dogmatic statement (and there are plenty of them) must be taken as a piece of legislation, its meaning determined from legal sources; in other terms, it must be cut off from its nourishing roots which are the scriptures, patristic writings, the church praying, and so forth. An absurd enough position. Theological opinions would have to be regarded as disciplinary decrees; moral

- *exhortation:*
—the couple is urged to receive the sacraments of confirmation, penance, and eucharist before the celebration of their marriage; again, the canons on pastoral care provide examples: 1063–1072;
- *philosophical theories:*
—the matrimonial consent is an act of the will: the statement relies on Aristotle's metaphysical psychology: 1057;
—all the canons that refer to the interplay of mind and will in the chapter of consent: 1096–1101;
- *empirical psychology* built into canon law:
—those who do not have the required degree of the use of reason, those who do not have the necessary discretion of judgment, and those who suffer from a psychological disorder that hampers them from fulfilling their marital obligations cannot validly marry: 1095;
- *creation of strict legal rights and duties:*
—most of the canons throughout the title on Marriage; the chapter on the canonical form contains virtually no other genre of canons than those which establish legal rights and duties: 1108–1123.

When a canon contains several affirmations, more than one literary form may have to be invoked to explain its full meaning. E.g., canon 1055, no. 1 contains a dogmatic statement, a theological opinion, and a statement on the history of dogma; no. 2 includes a statement of belief, a theological opinion; canon 1056 is a philosophical statement about the nature of marriage in general, and a theological affirmation about Christian marriage in particular. For a detailed analysis of these canons and others in function of their literary forms, see Ladislas Örsy, *Marriage in Canon Law* (Wilmington, Del.: Glazier, 1986).

duties would be classified as legal obligations subject to the jurisdiction of the courts and tribunals. Exhortations inviting the faithful to generous giving would be degraded to burdensome ordinances, those who fail to live up to them exposed to unnamed penalties. The truth of a philosophical assertion would not be decided by critical intelligence but by the *fiat* of the legislator. Psychological disorders and deficiencies could be defined only as far as they have been determined legally; no medical knowledge should influence their meaning. Legalism would reign supreme.

Once the fact that there are literary forms in the Code is accepted, it has a liberating impact on the understanding of the role of law in the Christian community. It eliminates the fear that the law may strangle the mysteries.

The hierarchy of values and the laws

The question can be raised whether all laws, even when determining rights and duties, have the same weight of authority; that is, have the same binding force, or is there a variation among them in this respect?

In civil law, the question is hardly ever asked. It is assumed that since all laws come from the same source (the Congress, the Parliament), they all have the same binding force. Even if there is legislation by delegation (e.g., executive orders), they are binding in the same way. Sanctions for nonobservance may vary, but that is all.

In canon law, the supreme legislative power for the universal church is vested in an ecumenical council or the pope. If, on that universal level, we consider the source alone, all laws bind with the same authority. In that sense, canon law is not different from civil law.

But there is another aspect to the issue. Canon law originates with and remains tightly bound to a hierarchy of values, human and religious. The values promoted and supported by the laws are not equal; there is a genuine hierarchy among them. Clearly a law concerned with some fundamental value must have greater weight and more authority than another which is about secondary values, or even lesser matters.

The hierarchy of values should be taken into account in the interpretation of canon law. In the case of conflict between two norms, the one upholding the greater value should prevail. In the case of conflict between a fundamental but not codified value, and another protected by a positive text only, the former should prevail.

Admittedly, we are moving in a delicate field not lacking in pitfalls. Alert judges, reflective administrators, and wise commentators are better placed to find the right solution in concrete cases than someone who argues only from abstract rules. After all, values exist in the concrete world, too.

But a short general remark is in order:

Nonobservance of the law can be either in the form of underrating a value or overrating it. Underrating would occur when, e.g., a fundamental value is subordinated to a rule of procedure; overrating when, e.g., the observance of some law which has become a burden to the community is urged without discretion. Authentic obedience does not mean attributing the same force to all laws; rather it supposes a capacity to weigh the laws and to discriminate wisely.

Often there is the difficulty that the text of the law must be related to a value not defined in the legal system, precise words versus somewhat vague theological or philosophical ideas. The temptation to rely on what is in print and clear and not on what is merely mentally and sometimes confusedly apprehended can be a serious one.[6]

Civil law could hardly ever enter into such exercises, because in modern pluralistic states, as virtually all states which respect the free-

---

6. Administrators and *jurisprudentes* are often called on today to determine the correct order of values in connection with laws concerning ecumenical issues. The Code of 1917 clearly put the value of the Catholic education of the child above that of a harmonious marriage; the Code of 1983 conveys the message that the issue of religious education should not put an undue strain on the marital relationship. Before Vatican II, priority was given to protecting the faith of the Catholic; hence the prohibition of *communicatio in sacris* was extended as widely as possible. Today cordial relationships with other Christian communities are recognized as supremely important; hence the prohibition is reduced as much as feasible without compromising the Catholic faith.

Some of these and similar changes came by decree; much is still coming via benevolent administrators and perceptive interpreters.

Obiter dictum: In the field of ecumenics the law has become an inadequate instrument for two reasons. First, the complexity of the theological situation cannot be expressed in legal concepts. "Separated brethren" means both to be divided and to be united. The law can easily handle the one or the other (excommunicated or member), but we have no legal concepts for partial *communio*. Second, the pace of development in ecumenism is too fast for legislation. Often enough, the best a canon lawyer can do is to weigh the values and see how the law can be adjusted to the legitimate postulates of the life of Christian churches. The letter of the law should never become an impediment to the gift of unity, if God wants to grant it.

Needless to say, anybody doing this "weighing" and "adjusting" should be no less competent in ecclesiology than in canon law! A felicitous combination, if it can be found!

dom of citizens are, there is no agreement about any hierarchy of values. The fragmentation of society in this respect is very much a fact of life. Therefore, civil lawyers have to rely much more on the positive text of the law. But canon law must always remain fully integrated with, and dependent on, religious and human values.[7]

Authentic Equity

Equity has been used, and at times abused, ever since in the third century B.C. in the city of Rome the magistrates and lawyers began to invoke it on a larger scale. It has more than proved its value in bringing new life into an aging system of law, in bringing flexibility into rigid structures. But, no doubt, it has been invoked many times, also, to justify illegitimate excursions into otherwise forbidden territory. We should do all we can to open the door to authentic equity, while keeping it closed to illegalities.[8]

---

7. Since Latin has no definite article, the expression *optima interpres* can be translated into English as "the best interpreter" or as "one of the best interpreters." I know of nothing in canonical tradition which would tell us which of the two is "the correct" translation.

8. There is a not-so-subtle inconsistency in both the Code of 1917 and that of 1983. On the one hand, both clearly hold that the meaning of the law is fixed at the time of its promulgation and, on the other hand, firmly state that custom is the best interpreter of the laws. But if the meaning of the law is fixed at the moment of promulgation, how can any interpretation by custom, which can take place only after the law has been promulgated and received by the community, add anything to that original meaning?

The root of this inconsistency is in the historical development of canon law. Until the 1917 Code, much of it was based on custom, and, surely, custom was the best interpreter of earlier precedents. The Code changed the very foundation of the system; custom had no authority any more, unless, of course, it was approved by the legislator. But the rule that custom is the best interpreter was too venerable to be left out. Thus the inconsistency.

Note that any interpretation by custom can be described also as a way of receiving the law. But if such reception can modify the meaning of the law, reception is more important than it appears in the Code. Is there an implicit recognition of the role of the community in the process of making the law?

I think honest discussions on the issue of the reception of the laws have been bedeviled by the tacit assumption that reception means legal ratification. As long as that ghost is not exorcised, there is no likelihood of progress. Why not use rather the parable of the sower who went out to sow the good seed? The seed must be received in the soil, otherwise it cannot grow. The lawgiver should find the right seed for the soil, should go out and sow it with care; the soil must take it, shelter it, feed the latent life in it, and give growth to it. If this parable can describe the

As at many times, history is our best teacher. There is no doubt that equity brought powerful transformations into both the Roman and English systems of laws. The fruit of its influence has been excellent; therefore, in these systems we must be able to find an authentic expression of it.

But before we do so, let us say clearly that equity is not the same as *epieikeia*. The latter is part of the virtue of justice. With its attention to particular cases, it balances out the generality of legal norms; *nomos* (law) and *epieikeia* belong to the same category. Not so with law and equity, as we shall see.

Nor is equity to be equated with economy, *oikonomia*, which will be described later in this chapter. The latter is a hidden power in the church, undefinable, to come into play in rare and insoluble cases, through the ministry of the *oikonomoi*, the bishops. There is nothing hidden about equity, and it may well come into play quite frequently. But let us return to Roman law.

The origins of Roman law are in the norms of the Twelve Tables, composed in the fifth century before Christ. They gave birth and development to a strict system of laws interpreted with literal exactness. Eventually, the shortcomings of such structures began to work to the disadvantage of the citizens whom they were supposed to help and protect. Moreover, the system proved insufficient to handle the needs of many non-citizens who either came to Rome or over whom the power of Rome was extended.

To provide for the needs of strangers and aliens, in 242 B.C. a special magistrate was appointed, the *praetor peregrinus*. Since he did not administer justice for the citizens, he was not bound by their laws. He was free to appeal to the ideals of natural justice, the demands of human nature, the image of a good head of the family, the ways of a reasonable man, and to administer justice accordingly. Gradually, the *praetores*, succeeding each other, developed a new system of laws which did not depend on the Twelve Tables anymore, but rather on the ethical ideas of the Roman people.

There we find equity at work. The *praetor peregrinus* found the existing legal system all too narrow to accommodate the demands of life.

---

spreading of the Word of God, why could it not enlighten us about the creation and implementation of practical norms in the church?

We have no difficulty in recognizing that the reception of doctrine is necessary for the *sensus fidelium* to play its part in doctrinal development; we should not have difficulty, either, admitting that the reception of a law is necessary in order to let the *sensus fidelium* play its role in developing the legal system.

Hence, he went out of the field of law, entered into the field of ethical principles, and with their help construed new legal norms. Equity in Rome meant to invoke higher principles than the law could provide, and with the help of those principles to give a balanced solution to legal problems. Thus, harmony between moral and legal values was reestablished.[9]

The enterprise was so successful that, eventually, the equitable system of laws superseded most civil laws, and was applied to all, aliens and citizens alike.

The history of the entry of equity into the legal system of England was not all that different. There, too, the common law of the king, from the late Middle Ages onward, proved insufficient to remedy naturally unjust situations which found shelter behind the rigid rules of common law. The chancellor, who was the keeper of the conscience of the king and had enough power at his disposal to intervene, began to distribute justice in his own way. Since, during the formative years of equity, the chancellors were always bishops, they distributed justice according to the principles of Christian morality. The common law continued to operate through the king's courts; but if natural justice was defeated through its application, there was recourse to the chancellor's court. He, like the praetor, in reaching a sentence, took his inspiration from outside the field of law, invoked a higher principle, and gave justice accordingly.

The pattern of development in England was not really different from the pattern that evolved in Rome. In both cases, the shortcomings of the legal system were recognized, and, through the agency of an official person, a correction was brought into the law out of the field of morality, based on the needs of human nature or the dictates of Christian conscience.

---

9. Most of the devotional and penitential practices such as the observance of Sunday as the Lord's day, the Lenten fast, Friday abstinence and others, were created by the community as signs of its dedication and generosity. But eventually the law entered the scene and made the voluntary observances into binding precepts and thus into occasions of sin. It is tempting to speculate how Paul would have judged such developments.

After Vatican II, however, there was a trend to return to our ancient traditions and lift the devotional and penitential practices out of the realm of law, and consequently out of the realm of sin (see, e.g., the Apostolic Constitution *Paenitemini*, AAS, 58 (1966) 177–198; cf. CLD, 6: 675–678). Unfortunately, for many, such a "new" initiative is hard to understand, and they continue to ask persistently what is now the precise obligation "under sin." The right answer is that the church would like to operate on the field of generosity where sin has no place at all.

We are now in a position to understand how authentic equity arose and developed in history. Here is the pattern: there is a legal system, but it is not able to protect an important value or give redress when injustice has been inflicted. Then, the value is upheld on ethical or religious grounds, and the law is sentenced (so to say) to pay respect to that value and accommodate itself to it. Authentic equity, therefore, comes into play when the law is unable to uphold a value important for the community. The community then turns to another (non-legal) system of ideas to justify a departure from the legal system. It lets the value prosper intact and it brings the law into the service of that value.

No legal system is perfect, not even canon law. Ecclesiastical laws are human creations; consequently, they too may prove themselves unable to protect a certain value in the Christian community or to provide a remedy for an injustice suffered. In that case, in canon law too, there must be recourse to authentic equity. Whoever is in charge of the issue, whoever it is who must give speedy justice, is entitled to invoke higher principles of morality and state that the law must cease to operate, and, through necessary accommodations, must become a servant of the value which must be safeguarded.

Thus, there is no magic in equity. There is no fuzziness either. The life of human communities is regulated by various norms, legal, philosophical, religious. Each group of norms has its own built-in limits. When, in concrete life, a case arises which cannot be justly resolved by law, it is right that the community should turn to philosophy or religion and let them prevail over the positive law. When this happens, there is authentic equity.

Interpretation in an evolutionary context

The church is an evolving community. About that fact there can be no doubt. The synoptics refer to the kingdom of God as a tender plant growing from the smallest of seeds into the largest of trees (cf. Mark 4:31). John reports the Lord's saying, "I have yet many things to say to you, but you cannot bear them now. When the Spirit of truth comes, he will guide you into all the truth" (John 16:12-13). We are a social body growing in understanding. The point is in the movement. If the whole group, and every member of it, is growing, there cannot be any other correct interpretation, even of seemingly rigid laws, than the one which takes the evolutionary process into account.

The issues lead us to one of the foundational principles of intelligent interpretation. An evolving community cannot be ruled by immovable laws. Either the laws will break the community or the community will break the laws. This is another reason why Aquinas' definition of law is unsatisfactory; if the law is complete at the time of its promulgation, it is an immovable law. Laws destined to guide a community are more complex. They should bring stability to the social body, yet they should evolve with the same body.

Only practical wisdom can supply the answer. Both stability and mobility are needed. The right balance is somewhere between the two.

To some extent, nature itself takes care of this need. We speak of the meaning of a canon. But meanings are not bricks laid down and preserved intact from one age to another. Meanings are in the land of the living. They are conceived by the legislator; they are in his mind. Better still, they are he, the legislator, conceiving the law. Now the legislator himself changes with the passage of time. Nature does it to him. With him, the meaning of law undergoes a change.

Those who receive the law are living persons, too, growing in understanding, shaped by a changing world around them. As they interpret the law, they bring into its meaning new elements out of their own historical situation, according to their capabilities. All this is an evolutionary process.

It might help the interpreters greatly if they realize that they, too, are part of this ongoing historical process. They are not outside of the community on an immovable platform from which they can take an objective look at what is happening. No; good interpreters themselves are evolving beings. Their interpretation of ten years ago may not be that of today, even if the text of the law has remained the same.

The interpretation of every human law must be governed by the theory of relativity: the whole universe is in motion and we are moving with it. But this is not an invitation to relativize all truth; on the contrary. As the theory of relativity has led to a better knowledge of the true state of the universe, so the principles of evolving interpretation should lead us to a better understanding of our laws.[10]

---

10. Evolutionary interpretation can be found wherever there is an evolving jurisprudence, that is, in the decisions of the tribunals and in the practice of executive offices. Every book written on the jurisprudence of the Rota, or a Roman Congregation, is written on the underlying assumption that in the course of events something new emerged through the judgments and acts of those institutions, something which was not *in se certa*, clear and certain, in the text of the law.

If the fact of evolution is not recognized, or if evolutionary interpretation is disapproved by the judges, administrators, and interpreters, they will often go to extraordinary (and inordinate) lengths to explain that there is nothing new in their interpretation, that they are merely proclaiming a meaning which was there, unchanged, ever since the promulgation. They are impelled to cover their tracks by

The significance of "horizon studies"

The doctrine of horizon is explained in the second chapter of this book. Here, I wish to do no more than, first, to recall it in a summary way and reinforce it with a thought experiment, second, to illustrate it by an example taken from real life and show how the extent of the horizons of the judges of our tribunals can influence their decisions—even if they are not aware of it.

First: The doctrine of horizon completes and corrects the traditional conviction that knowledge increases through the acquisition of new ideas only. That position asserts that the more ideas we possess, the richer we are. Of course, to be operational, the ideas must be well organized and neatly arranged according to the direction of the first principles, such as the principles of identity, contradiction, causation, and so forth. At a final count, however, those two elements, ideas and principles, make up the basic furnishings of the human mind. That is the clue to the understanding of "how we understand."

The doctrine of horizon proposes that there is another element which plays a capital role in our acquisition of, and progress in, knowledge. This other element is the field of vision of the mind, or the mental horizon, in which all ideas and principles are located. We all live and operate within our horizon, even if we are not aware of it. Aristotle did not advert to its existence, nor did Aquinas give any consideration to it. Yet they too lived and worked within its limits. So do we. So do all the interpreters.

A thought experiment may help to understand this phenomenon better.

Imagine a room, tastefully furnished. All objects on the floor and on the walls balance each other artistically, so that the room speaks of the cultured mind of the owner to every perceptive person who enters.

One day, however, a magician comes around and, with a turn of his wand, makes the room expand in all four directions. He moves the walls, but keeps every piece of furniture in place. The room is now much larger, but otherwise nothing has changed.

The perceptive person, who has seen the room before, comes back and looks at it in its new shape. What does he or she see? Not just the expanded walls, but a functional disorder: everything in the room

---

making such excuses since they are not able to admit the evolutionary nature of this universe. Their explanations, in the long run, bring the law into bad repute and, more seriously, widen the gap between law and life.

is out of place. The internal harmony is destroyed, the pleasing balances disturbed, the quiet message of a cultured mind jumbled. To restore the artistic structures, every piece of furniture should be given a new place in relation to the new position of the walls. Then, the room would be elegant, as before.

From this simple example, I turn back to the theory. Our capacity to know and understand does not depend on ideas and principles only but on the extent of the space in which our mind operates. This "space" is a figurative word for the mental horizon of the person.

Let us go further and speak more concretely. Through Vatican Council II, we have achieved a broader understanding of the church. It is a *communio* of the people of God. This perception has replaced many others: the church as primarily a hierarchical organization, or principally a perfect society, set above kings and princes, and so forth. The new understanding expanded our horizons; the walls which used to limit our perception were pushed outward. In consequence, every structure, from the parish to the papacy, must now be reinterpreted in a broader context. Legal institutions cannot remain in their old places and play their old roles; they do not fit anymore. They must be redesigned and rearranged to be in harmony with the new "space."[11]

Moreover, it should be recalled that horizons themselves are not static structures like the firmament of the sky as ancient peoples conceived it. Rather, they are part of living persons. Therefore, they can expand, they can contract, they can change.

Besides, as every person has his or her horizon, so has every community. This, too, can be expanded or, as the case may be, restricted. As Christians achieve a better understanding of who they are, what their community is, what the role of their community is in this large world, their horizon expands. Then every word of the message they received earlier needs to be reinterpreted within a broader field of vision. Such development has its repercussions on our legal system, and our laws, too, ought to be reinterpreted accordingly.[12]

---

11. In the future, historians of canon law will have to cope with a significant (somewhat abrupt, but not to the point of overall discontinuity) change in the meaning of legal concepts after Vatican Council II, precisely because the traditional words appear now in a significantly altered context. They will have to report on deep changes in the meanings: changes which do not originate in the intrinsic nature of the ancient institutions but in the newly expanded horizons surrounding them.

12. Some more examples of movements into broader horizons:
• Our horizon in understanding a human person has expanded due to developments in the study of the human psyche; the legal repercussions can be found in the expanded grounds for nullity in marriage cases; in fact, much of the law

Second: an illustration from the operation of our tribunals.[13]

The evidence gathered in a matrimonial case consists of fragments which by themselves appear like the pieces of a jigsaw puzzle. They must be put together to reveal their meaning. This "putting together," however, is only the first step toward the final decision.

There is a difference between the image that emerges from the pieces of a puzzle and the interpretation that attributes a meaning to the evidence. The pieces of the puzzle can produce only one image, which will be the same no matter who looks at it. The interpretation can bring forth several meanings, which are the creation of the inquiring minds pondering the evidence. In other terms, the material image emerges automatically and uniformly when the pieces of the puzzle are put together; the judicial decision is the result of the insight of the judges into the facts presented to them.

Here the doctrine of horizon enters, and an important doctrine it is. It dispels the illusion that cases based on similar evidence will lead to similar decisions; it shows the virtual inevitability of different conclusions, which become different decisions. Let me explain.

All judges operate within their own mental horizons. When the evidence is presented to their court, their horizons play an integral role in finding its meaning, which leads to their decision. To demonstrate this, let us look at six judicial colleges, each with an increasingly broader horizon. (Whatever we say of a college can be easily transferred to an individual judge.)

concerning the capacity of a person to make an irrevocable commitment is in the process of being reinterpreted.

• Formerly, authentic apostolic work was conceived as done "in the name of" or "by the mandate of" the hierarchy, a conception which strongly inspired the structures of the Catholic Action movement, *Actio Catholica*. Now, we see that baptism itself conveys to every Christian the right and duty to proclaim the gospel; hence, we are reassessing the state and work of the laity in the church.

• We have a broader perception of what the church is, and we know that there are degrees of communion; therefore, we are both united with and divided from non-Catholic Christians. Our respective laws have been revised, or are being revised, or ought to be revised, or must be reinterpreted accordingly. Those who once were called "heretics and schismatics" have now become our "separated brethren."

Examples abound. The room has been enlarged and every piece of furniture must be rearranged.

13. This illustration is taken from my essay, "Questions Concerning the Matrimonial Tribunals and the Annulment Process," *see* William P. Roberts, ed., *Divorce and Remarriage: Religious and Psychological Perspectives* (Kansas City, Mo.: Sheed and Ward, 1990) 145–147. The text is slightly altered.

68 *Interpretation: Guiding Principles*

The horizon of the first college extends to pastoral care only; their deliberations are not subject to the normative rule of canon law. Accordingly, their decisions will be dictated by compassion and fairly immediate practical experience. (Did the church operate in this way during the first millennium when there was no tribunal system?)

The second college is moved by pastoral considerations but they let canon law play its part too. Their decisions in a number of cases will be different from those of the first group; since they operate in a broader horizon, they can give a different meaning to the same facts. (Was this the way of the tribunals before the discoveries of modern psychology?)

The third college is familiar with theology and understands that legal norms are to protect and promote theological values. Inevitably, theological principles and categories will enter into their deliberations. (Should our tribunals be open to such theological consideration?)

The fourth college's horizon extends beyond those mentioned to the field of psychology and psychiatry; their additional expertise will often determine their judgments. (Is it correct to say that the tribunals came to a new life, especially in the U.S., when judges began to pay attention to psychological factors, and to create new *capita nullitatis*?)

The fifth college has an additional sensitivity to cultural differences; in sifting the evidence, they may find a meaning that none of the previous groups could have detected. (Can a tribunal take into account ethnic differences?)

The sixth college understands well the corrective factors to the rigidity of the law: equity, *epieikeia, oikonomia* and *lacuna,* and they are able to apply them judiciously to the facts of the case. They may see convincing evidence for nullity where the others could not have discovered it. Such variations are not deviations; they are part of our human condition. They occur at every level of the tribunal system, and no amount of legislation can eliminate them. Although many studies exist on judicial decisions, to my best knowledge no study exists that would show how the horizon of the justices influences their sentences.

The doctrine of horizon cannot be neglected.

The significance of the modern science of hermeneutics

The oldest work on the science and art of interpretation is found in Aristotle's *Organon,* the collection of his logical treatises. It is short, about twenty-five pages in an ordinary textbook.[14]

14. Aristotle: *Organon* 16^{a}1-24^{b}9; cf. Richard McKeon, ed., *The Basic Works of Aristotle* (New York: Random House, 1941) 38–61.

In modern times, the new science of hermeneutics has blossomed out of the old roots and produced a great deal of good fruit. It has given a new direction to historical literary criticism. It has helped us to find new meanings in ancient conciliar texts. Above all, the books of the Bible have yielded a new wealth of information as our scholars read them again with the help of hermeneutical principles.

Admittedly, when it comes to the question of what exactly modern hermeneutics is, we can easily find ourselves lost in a maze of definitions, descriptions, and clarifications, sighing with Dante:

> Midway in the journey of our life
> I found myself in a dark wood,
> for the straight way was lost (Inferno 1: 1-3).

I am not sure I can show the straight way, but through a brief explanation I hope to bring a little light into the darkness of the wood.

A warning: my explanation will touch on one limited aspect of hermeneutics only; there is much more to this science than I am going to expound here and now.

This one aspect is that the study of hermeneutics makes the interpreter aware that *there is more to a text than its conceptual and logical content.*

Truly, human speech is an amazing texture of words woven together in systematic patterns. But when living persons speak, or write, for that matter, they are influenced by many existential factors. They are moved by their feelings; they may be calm or angry, or inspired by joy. They may state the conclusions of their abstract reasoning, or speak out of their concrete experience. In any case, they always communicate within a vast cultural context where many things are taken for granted but are not articulated.

The canonical legislator is also a living human being, or a collectivity formed by living human beings. He, too, is influenced by all sorts of existential factors. In making a law, he may be calmly building a new social structure, or angrily reacting to an extreme situation, or enthusiastically promoting a good cause.[15] All such dispositions, seemingly so "external" to legislation, leave their mark on the final text and give a new shade to the meaning of the law.

Further, a legislator with experience is bound to speak differently from another who has only conceptual knowledge of the problem at

---

15. Was the Apostolic Constitution *Veterum Sapientia* (1962) of John XXIII inspired by such enthusiasm? Do we have in this case a law duly promulgated but not received?

hand. Someone who has practiced as an advocate is better qualified to reform the law of procedure than another who has never met a client.

Moreover, human speech is understandable only in a vast cultural context. We usually do not advert to that because we converse with persons who live in the same "frame of reference" as we do. The legislator, too, lives in a culture that colors everything he says. The science of hermeneutics tells us to replant the text into the culture from which it comes and interpret it in that context.

The best proof that modern hermeneutics is a well-grounded science, in spite of all the obscurities that still plague it, is the fact that it gives importance to down-to-earth situations which leave their mark on our mental activities.

Hermeneutics may be a new science, but it is mature enough to encounter our venerable canonical texts and throw new light on them.[16]

The relevance of the Gospel

In the learned commentaries on the Code, hardly ever is there a reference to the Gospel; even in the rare cases where there is one, the evangelical rule is not likely to be invoked to determine the meaning of a canon. Yet, ever since Vatican II, we hear again and again that the church should keep examining itself "in the mirror of the Gospel"

---

16. The most significant hermeneutical issue in canonical science is the understanding of the same law in many different cultural contexts. Some facts can be usefully recalled:

—canon law has been and, to a large extent, is being created in the context of European culture, and especially in an Italian environment;

—canon law is meant for Christians all over the world, living in different cultures;

—there is a significant difference from one culture to another in the perception of the role of law in a human society and in its application to daily life.

I know of no secure and universal guidelines which could tell the interpreter how the transition of a law from one culture to another can best be made; I know only that persons at home in both cultures (where the law originates and where it is to be applied) can do a great deal to facilitate the transition.

By way of concrete example, the difference between the spirit of English common law and European civil law can be invoked. This difference in spirit also implies that the attitude of the citizens toward the law is different. But can Christians in different places have differing attitudes toward the universal law of the church? As a matter of fact, they do, and as long as human nature is with us, they will continue to do so. Intelligent interpretation can alleviate such differences, which in the concrete order may well mean alleviating the burden, too.

See the excellent article by John Huels, "Interpreting Canon Law in Diverse Cultures," JUR 47 (1987) 249–293.

and thus work for its own ongoing reformation. This reformation refers, of course, not to the meaning of dogmas but to certain structural matters and practical policies. The consequence is that canon law, mostly an expression of the humanity of the church, should steadily be examined in the mirror of the Gospel, perhaps more than any other aspect of the life of the church. Besides, arid legalism is an ever-present danger for any organized religious group, Christians not exempted. Only the repeated confrontation of the laws with the spirit of the Gospel can protect the community from succumbing to this temptation.

Let us begin with the obvious: no interpretation of the law that goes against the spirit of the Gospel can be correct. The overriding duty of the church is to proclaim the good news. No law may ever contradict that message. In the practical order, whenever a conflict seems to arise, the Gospel must prevail, if necessary through the application of *epieikeia* or equity or any other of those devices which are there to temper the severity or tame the excesses of the law.[17]

Clear contradictions, however, are not likely to happen often. There is a more subtle and far more serious danger: the complexity of the system of laws may overshadow and obscure the clarity and simplicity of the evangelical message. Let me explain by two examples, both within the realm of our recent experience.

At one time or another, we have all entered an old church building, expecting to see its clear and simple structures, but, once inside, we found only a confusing accumulation of ill-fitting additions. It may

---

17. Examples for such an exercise are easy to find:
• The Gospel requires that the ministers should minister; that is, the servants of the people should serve the people. If our laws were to stress the role of power more than the value of service, if they were more insistent on the first places than on the last ones, then the laws might be in need of revision.
• If a person asking for justice must go through a labyrinth of rules and regulations even to be heard, let alone to obtain redress, there might be a discrepancy between the original message and the legal structures we imposed on it.
• When our people make their generous offerings to God by way of celebrating the eucharist or by fasting and abstaining, they are obeying the law of the Spirit (cf. Rom 1–8). If the law then enters and transforms their spontaneous giving into a complex system of obligations with appropriate sanctions, the law can be guilty again for having come in to "increase the trespass" (Rom 5:20).

The honest task of the interpreter is to point out clearly when a law is too much of a burden on the community and, if it is so warranted, to lighten the burden by interpretation. Besides, the community itself should be aware of its capacity to evaluate the law and to respond to it by customs legitimately initiated. If the *sensus fidelium* has a role to play in determining doctrine (and it does), it must have an even greater role to play in recognizing and receiving wise laws!

have been an old basilica which was made into a receptacle of paintings and statues, vaults and arches, to such a degree that the luminous beauty of the original was gone. Our eyes just wandered in bewilderment, and our mind became oppressed by the sheer weight of the intrusion of foreign matter, put there to satisfy the taste or devotion of another age. Perhaps we have heard that an effort is being made now to clear out the latter accumulations and restore the basilica to its original splendor. We approve.

Or let us look at the liturgy of the Latin rite. In the beginning there was a translucent simplicity in it, evidenced by the canon of St. Hippolytus or the lapidary sentences of many ancient prayers. Then additions began to accumulate everywhere, in the prayers, in the ceremonies, in the calendar, until the burden became too much to bear. Rightly, the last council opted for a return to greater simplicity, and now we are all experiencing the benefits of a liturgical reform; prayers are shortened and more to the point, ceremonies are simpler and more telling, and in the calendar the great Christ-event is not overshadowed by the multitude of his saints. We approve.

Even if we knew nothing of the history of canon law, we should be alert to the possibility that a similar pattern of accumulation could have occurred there, too. After all, why would Christians have acted in a different way in constructing their legal system than they did in erecting their buildings and formulating their liturgies? As a matter of fact, they did not. The history of canon law is also the history of accumulations. One has only to think of the development of the complex structure of dispensations reserved to the Holy See in all sorts of matters, great and small, the nearly inextricable web of some marriage impediments, the maze of the privileges "communicated" among religious orders, the pitfalls and delays of lengthy procedures, and, last but not least, the intricacies of penal law. Statutory legislation after the last council has done much to trim off outdated structures; the new Code does away with more. But let us be frank; there is still much that should be eliminated to let the clear and simple structures of the church appear in their beauty.

The trimming back of a legal system, however, is easier said than done. Laws are not like old statues which can just be carted out, nor like prayers which can be marked "to be omitted." Laws tend to cling tenaciously to the books. It takes time and expert hands to do away with them when, by their sheer volume, they obscure the evangelical message. No wonder the reform of canon law is a slower process than the clearing of a basilica or the restoration of the Easter Vigil. No wonder the reform of our laws is still far from being completed.

The critical interpretation of laws, which must include their evaluation "in the mirror of the Gospel," can do much to bring out into the open the beauty and simplicity of the structures of the church. It demands, however, interpreters who are well versed in church history and ecclesiology and have not succumbed to any subtle temptation to legal positivism.

Indeed, the spirit of the Gospel should be behind, or in, every interpretation. I am not suggesting that the genuine complexity of a case should be reduced to an artificial simplicity. Yet in interpreting our laws and implementing them, the evangelical injunction about simple speech, "Let what you say be simply 'yes' or 'no'" (Matt 5:37), remains a guideline. It puts a limit to sophisticated casuistry in canon law. There are somersaults in legal logic which are clearly incompatible with the way of thinking and the style of speaking of the Teacher from Nazareth.

In general, from time to time, it is necessary to take our book of laws and place it side-by-side with the New Testament and let the comparison speak for itself.

On the meaning of *oikonomia*

In our days theologians and canonists of the Latin church have expressed an increased interest in the *oikonomia*, "economy" in somewhat poor English transliteration, of the Orthodox church. It seems to belong to the science of jurisprudence; it can solve seemingly insoluble problems. Yet it appears also to be a device which is invoked from somewhere other than the realm of law, since it is more powerful than the law can ever be. Be that as it may, it is certainly used in the Orthodox, especially the Greek Orthodox, churches, and there is a desire to introduce it into our Latin jurisprudence, if at all possible. After all, we too have insoluble cases.

There are many explanations of *oikonomia* in our Western literature; few of them are faithful to the Eastern original, many of them are projections of the Western legal mind. Here, I intend to do no more than to discard some misconceptions and point out the direction in which the right understanding can be found. Of course, being of the Latin rite, I do it with some trepidation.

Oikonomia is not an Eastern version of some Latin legal institutions which are meant to temper the severity of the laws, such as dispensation, *sanatio in radice*, canonical equity and others. *Oikonomia* is not part of the legal system of the Orthodox church, although its application has legal effects.

74 *Interpretation: Guiding Principles*

Oikonomia is not equivalent to the *epieikeia* of Aristotle; it is not even akin to the equity of the Romans. Its origins are not in any philosophical theory, nor in some pragmatic wisdom. A good way of progressing towards the understanding of the Orthodox mind which created or discovered *oikonomia* is to think of the origins of the Christian community.

It emerged as a community turned toward a transcendental person: Christ, the Risen One. He held them all together; they were at his service. This orientation was so strong in the group that for a long time they did not feel the need for any elaborate legal system; in fact, a really elaborate legal system developed in the West only, due perhaps just as much to the general culture of the Middle Ages as to the needs of the church.

The early communities believed that the Spirit of Christ held them together; in their need they had to turn to him. Now, what happens in the case of *oikonomia* is that the bishop, the *oikonomos* of the house of God, turns to the Risen One and brings the insoluble situation before him. Through an *analogia fidei*, he searches and seeks how the Lord in his power would heal a wound, would redress an injustice, would bring peace where it is needed. Then, because the church has the power to "bind and loose," the *oikonomos* himself (never less than a bishop, or a synod of bishops) brings redemption into the situation where everything seemed to be amiss.

Thus, *oikonomia* is indeed more than the law can offer. It can never be summed up in a legal maxim, nor can a precise description be given as to how it operates. It is rooted in the power of Christ, which is present in the community, and which never, absolutely never, can adequately be defined by laws. This power cannot be invoked by anyone else than a sacramentally ordained bishop, or possibly by a synod of bishops. The bishop is the trustee of the forgiving and healing strength of Christ in the church. Thus, *oikonomia* is not arbitrary, in the sense that anyone at any time could demand it.

Clearly, we have nothing like this in the Latin church. Yet it would be difficult to refute the theological judgment of the Orthodox church in upholding the practice of *oikonomia*, without ever wanting to define it. The Latin mind is easily repelled by such vagueness; it senses danger in the lack of precision. The Eastern mind is attracted by the mystery and senses the healing strength of it.

May the ecumenical movement progress to the point where we Latins can be enriched by the great traditions of our sister churches.[18]

18. The different meanings of *oikonomia* were discussed at the meeting of the

Interpretation: a summing up

In my introduction to Chapter Three I refused to give a definition of the science and art of interpretation. I still have no intention of offering one. But I am now in a better position to gather some scattered insights together and give a more coherent, although summary, description of the science and art of interpretation. Clearly, here, I look beyond the "authentic" interpretation of the legislator.

- *The first stage* is always the gathering of information, from the text, from the context, from all available sources. The language of the law is a kind of coded language, concise, even cryptic, to the uninitiated. The real meaning of the terms can be understood only if their history is known and their relationship with the whole fabric of law and the whole structure of our beliefs is perceived.

- *The second stage* is the conception of insights. Once the interpreter is in possession of all the information available from the sources, "from the outside," he or she must conceive the meaning of the law "from the inside," that is, from his or her own resources. Let us pause here for a moment, because the "essence" of correct interpretation is usually understood as simply finding a meaning which was always there, like a treasure hidden in the ground, waiting to be found. Not really. The original meaning was in the mind of the legislator. He could not give that to anybody. He could only communicate it through intelligible signs, leaving it to others to conceive a meaning as close to the original as possible. There is an element of discovery, and there is a need for creativity.

But no matter how close the mind of the interpreter comes to that of the legislator, the truth is that there are cases where the interpreter must go beyond the pristine intention of the legislator. It cannot be any other way, since the inexorable law of life is change and development. The wise interpreter knows how to combine the historical interpretation of the mind of the legislator with the demands of a social body which lives, moves, and grows.

- *At the third stage*, the interpreter should pronounce on the truth of the law; he or she must state what the law is. This is a final judgment, perhaps after doubts, hesitations and tentative hypotheses. The interpreter may find the decision unpalatable, but this may be precisely

Eastern Canon Law Society in Thessaloniki, 1981; several diverging opinions were expressed. See my article, "In search of the Meaning of *oikonomia*: Report on a Convention," TS 43 (1982) 312-319. Above, I tried to give an account of the idea which seems to be most widely held in the Eastern churches.

the sign that he or she has surrendered to an objective state of affairs instead of construing a personal norm for the community. Such surrender must be based on solid evidence and critically acceptable insights. Often enough, it is possible to put all sorts of constructions on a text, to rationalize loopholes or outlandish actions. But there is no truth in such exercises; they only give a bad reputation to the law and to lawyers.[19]

- *The fourth stage* is assuming responsibility. The task of the interpreter cannot, must not and does not end with the pronouncement on the truth of the law. The law must be presented to the community, and with authority; not the authority that comes from jurisdiction, but that which comes from reflective intelligence.

As the standard of education is rising in the whole world, the attitude of subjects to the law is undergoing a thorough change in both the civic society and the Christian community. They want to understand the law; they want to implement it freely. In ages past, when the legislator was in a culturally advantageous position and in privileged possession of a great deal of information, while many of his subjects were culturally disadvantaged and lacking in education, perhaps the social body was best governed by clear cut ordinances accompanied by an appeal for loyalty. Not so today. The citizens and the faithful are much more aware of their innate dignity. They want to know why the law is there; they want to act with responsible freedom. We have heard many times that the law ought to be the "teacher" or the "educator" of the community. It cannot really be that. By its very nature, the law is impersonal. But the interpreter of the law can be an enlightened teacher and educator.

By way of conclusion: a proposition.

We have a new Code of Canon Law. But the Catholic community needs more than the bare bones of new canons. They need to know

19. Let me note here that the scholarly interpreter of canon law must accept a significant limitation. His or her conclusions may be unshakable by scientific criteria, yet they can be overruled by the pronouncements of the legislator (a rare case), or by the decisions of the judges (not a frequent occurrence), or by the accumulated actions of the administrators (a practice to be reckoned with). They may bypass, or even turn against, the meaning established through rigorous scholarly work and impose with authority another one, usually as a matter of policy.

(The same situation does not quite arise in civil law. There, once the law is enacted, it has a life of its own. The legislator cannot determine its meaning authentically, although the courts can. In canon law, the legislator can keep his hand on the law, and protect it from going astray!)

and appropriate the values the law intends to uphold; they need to decide and to act freely in its implementation.

To be practical about such lofty ideas, let us say simply: the community needs assistance in the reception of the law. Such assistance should come through a new type of commentary. The project can best be conceived on the model of the critical commentaries on the books of the Holy Scriptures. These were landmarks in the history of exegesis; through the relentless application of scientific criteria, they uncovered new meanings in the old texts and gradually led the whole Christian community to a better understanding of the word of God.

Canon law is not the word of God. But by placing the practical norms in their theological context, from which they originated anyway, and by distinguishing the essentials which are needed to protect the mystery from the accidentals which are no more than historical accretions, the house of God can regain something of its pristine beauty.[20]

This is not to suggest that the interpreters can or should do away with the laws. No, they are not lawmakers. But it is to say that interpreters can do much to lead the people to see the mysteries that the rules meant to serve, and thus they can contribute a little to the fulfillment of that great promise: "that they may have life, and have it abundantly" (John 10:10).

APPENDIX

Rules of Interpretation

The inspiration for the following rules comes from the well known *regulae iuris* of Boniface VIII. The present rules, too, are meant to be

---

20. A last *obiter dictum*, but certainly not the least important one: the image of God prevalent in the community has always had a strong impact on the making of the laws, their implementation, and their interpretation.

Historically it could be shown that in the church there has always been a close affinity between the prevalent image of God and the conception of the laws. For instance, the image of a severe God who, in the concrete order at least, offered no salvation to those who either were not baptized or broke away from the unity of faith, inspired laws of extreme severity towards infidels, heretics and schismatics. Or, the image of God as a meticulous judge led to meticulous laws concerning religious observances, to the point that many in the community experienced more fear of damnation than joy of salvation.

When such aberrations enter the legal system, it cannot be reformed from the inside; the image of God needs to be broadened. Better laws can come only from better understanding of the personality of our God.

legal proverbs, each containing a grain of truth but never the full truth. None of them should be applied literally or exclusively. They overlap and balance each other: they must be used with due discretion and in conjunction with one another. Together, they can serve also as a checklist for interpreters: they speak of many factors which should be considered before the meaning of a legal text is finally determined.

1. Every legal norm is a child of history.

Some norms have more, some have less history. Be it much or little, their history must be known in order to construe their meaning accurately. If there has been a development, a shift, or perhaps a radical change in their meaning, the transformation should be critically exposed. As a rule, one can say that living law can hardly ever be reduced to its primitive intent (the crucible of life tends to shape the law); yet, living law does not tolerate easily a radical break with the tradition either. For instance, the norms concerning the "cooperation" of the faithful with the power of the hierarchy cannot be well understood, appreciated and evaluated without the knowledge of many historical facts, in particular how far the "laity" have participated in the "jurisdictional acts" of the hierarchy in the course of Christian history.

2. The meaning of a norm depends on its literary form.

Every single norm in the great corpus of canon law is embedded in a context that has its own specific literary form which contributes to the determination of the meaning of that norm. This context by and large is legal, that is, determining rights and duties, but there are many cases when it is not legal; hence, overall caution is wise. To interpret in the same way the laws concerning the financial assets of the church and the norms encouraging the faithful to receive the sacraments would be a misguided undertaking.

3. When the origin of a law is in a theory, to understand the meaning of that law, it is necessary to go back to the theory.

Theory, here, means some kind of doctrine that inspired the law. It could be theological (dogmatic or moral), philosophical, legal, or of another kind. In the course of the life of the law such theoretical foundations can be forgotten, and the original intent can become twisted or lost. For instance, the Roman contractual theory inspired much of our marriage legislation. The discovery that such a theory is not part of the ancient tradition of the church can offer great freedom for the revision of marriage laws; a freedom that could hardly be deduced from the canonical texts.

4. The legislator cannot speak except within his own cultural context.

"Legislator" should be taken in a broad sense here. It means, obviously, someone legislating with authority. But in our context it can also mean the community creating customary norms for its own use. This rule is virtually absolute: no less than any other human achievement, the law always reflects the cultural milieu in which it was made. No wonder, therefore, that there is a relative element in every law, since it represents the cultural mentality of the legislator and the impact of his environment. To understand a law that originated in the Middle Ages, it is necessary to know something of the culture of that time. To understand a law that originated in Italy, it is necessary to be familiar with the Italian way of life. To think that any legislator can speak independently from his own internal and external worlds is just as much an illusion as to think that natural phenomena can take place outside of a field of gravitation. The meaning of the law is affected by the cultural circumstances of the legislator. Our procedural law is a good example: it is of Roman or continental inspiration, and is significantly different from common law procedures.

5. As the mission of the church is to be light to the nations, so the laws of the church should show forth the wisdom of the church to all peoples.

Since the church is "light to the nations," its laws should reflect light for all nations to see. Hence, among all possible meanings of a rule, those must be chosen which display more visibly the Christian virtues, in particular justice and mercy. Should there ever be an ecclesiastical law that by omission does not uphold (say) justice and mercy, it should be considered seriously defective, and a responsible interpreter would have the duty to say so.

6. Universal laws are meant for the universal church.

This rule sounds like a tautology. It is not. It means that when the meaning of the universal law is construed, it should be understood in such a way that it can have universal application. In other terms, the very nature of a universal law postulates that it should make good sense all over the earth. It must be universally applicable. If it can be applied in particular places only, then the law cannot be universal; it is in need of revision or revocation. By way of example, if a universal law determining the rights and duties of Catholic universities were not applicable to a significant number of the same universities because of their cultural and legal circumstances, the law would fall short of being a universal law; it would be in need of revision or revocation.

7. Every law in a Christian community intends to uphold the dignity of human persons.

It follows that whenever the text of the law is broad enough to allow several interpretations, that one must be chosen which more effectively upholds the dignity of human persons, inside and outside of the church. If canon law prescribes a "just wage" for those employed by the church, it is legitimate to construe the norm as meaning, in the case of married persons, a wage that is enough to provide for the physical, emotional and spiritual well being of a family.

8. Canon law is there to uphold Christian values.

It cannot be any other way. Canon law must promote faith, hope and charity, and it must create a friendly environment for God's grace. If any law allows several legitimate interpretations, the one that most upholds Christian values should be chosen. For instance, the greatest Christian value in the administration of the sacrament of penance is the manifestation and granting of God's mercy: all norms, therefore, concerning that sacrament should be interpreted with a predilection for mercy.

9. Law in the Christian community aims for supporting a value; the moment it becomes sheer formality, it collapses and ceases to exist.

To support a theological or human value is the purpose of every ecclesiastical law; such intention belongs to the very substance of each of them. The value supported can be in the structure set up by the law, in the duties to be performed, or even in the restraint imposed by the legislator. Be that as it may, in every instance, the law must be concerned with a substantial matter, and not with introducing an empty ritual. The reason for this requirement (that can be considered absolute) was already given by Paul: we have been freed from the formalities of the Mosaic law. Meaningless observances should not be brought back in the Christian era by legislation or custom; to do so would destroy the people's freedom in Christ. All interpretation, therefore, that is not able to point to a value to be supported becomes a questionable interpretation.

10. Every rule has its own authority.

At the first reading, this rule may seem incorrect. After all, the universal laws of the church are promulgated by the authority of those who have full, supreme and universal power in the church, which has been granted only to the episcopal college and to its head, the pope.

The Code of Canon Law has been published with the one and all pervading authority of the pope. Yet, even within such a unified system, it is still necessary to examine the binding force of every single rule because the legislator himself did not intend to put the same weight behind every single regulation. There is a hierarchy of obligations because there is a hierarchy of values supported by the laws.

11. The meaning of a single norm must be understood in the context of the whole system.

The legal system of a nation, or the legal system of the church for that matter, is like a carefully designed building: it stands there because it has internal cohesion and unity. Although a single rule can be read and interpreted separately from the rest, its full significance cannot be grasped and explained otherwise than in the context of the whole system. Every single part plays a role in upholding the whole edifice, and the structure of the whole gives meaning to the individual parts. The canons on the teaching office of the bishop ought to be balanced by those on the teaching office of the pope, and vice versa. Further, both teaching authorities need to take into account the *sensus fidelium*.

12. Meanings do not stand still; they, too, are part of an evolving universe.

This rule looks like an attack on the stability of the legal system. In reality, it simply states a fact of life. Words and sentences are no more than signs. Meanings exist in minds, and minds do evolve. As generation follows generation, each reads the same statements. Yet each interprets them in a new way because each generation is composed of living persons who are part of an evolving universe. An interpretation that does not take into account this evolutionary nature of the meanings cannot be a true interpretation of laws meant for a human community. Still less can it be the true rendition of the meaning of laws conceived to guide a community animated by the living Spirit who continuously "recreates the face of the earth," *renovat faciem terrae*, which must include the renovation of the legal system as well.

13. The core meaning of a norm is more enduring than the rest of it.

A system of laws is intended to bring stability into the life of the community. This is not possible unless there are some enduring elements in the rules. Such permanency should be conceived in harmony with their evolving character. The balance is not always easy to find, but at least it must be sought. For instance, in the matter of marriage, the idea of *consortium totius vitae* is more enduring than the contractual theory, and hence it must be much more protected.

14. Law is communication: to grasp its message, it is necessary to have a good knowledge of the world of the legislator.

Every law is an act of communication between the legislator and the subjects. But this communication is not mechanical. It is not like transmitting electronic signals from one station to another. Why? Because the meanings that the words and sentences carry exist in the minds of living persons who perceive and understand everything in the context of their own universe. The universe of the lawmaker is not the same as the universe of the subjects: a message communicated to another is received in a different world. By necessity it receives new shades of meaning.

15. A law can be a dialectical response to a contemporary problem.

There is no need to be a Hegelian to see that humanity in general, and human institutions in particular, often develop dialectically; that is, not through uniform steady growth but by first going too far in one direction and then by moving in the opposite one. When an authoritarian regime goes too far and people revolt, the worst form of chaotic democracy may follow; conversely, when anarchy gains ground, tyranny is likely to arise. Progress is often through theses and antitheses.

There are analogous phenomena in the history of the church: for instance, centrifugal forces in particular churches have often provoked increased centralization in the universal church; the time of the Reformation and its aftermath can offer an example.

Law can be instrumental in the bringing about, or in the strengthening, of such dialectical movements. When this happens, the full import of the law can be understood only within its dialectical context. For instance, many of the disciplinary decrees of the Council of Trent were dialectical responses to corrupt practices in the church, or to the excesses of the Reformation; their purpose was to restore the correct balance in practice and doctrine. Once the balance is restored, there is bound to be a subtle shift in the meaning of those decrees.

5

Implementation Through Reception

The new Code of Canon Law entered into force on November 27, 1983. The process of its implementation has been going on ever since.

But the Code was not the last piece of legislation; in the church there is a steady flow of new laws; hence, there is also a non-ending process of implementation.

In the previous chapters we discussed interpretation; we should turn our attention now to implementation.

But what is implementation?

It will not help us to know with precision what the law is if we do not have the right understanding of what it means to implement it. Does it mean to receive the law and let it shape the life of the community, with no questions raised; or does it mean to receive the law and let it also be shaped by the forces of life?

Such questions are legitimate, since today "implementation" is a household word in the church. At times, one has the impression that it is used in the same sense as "completion" is used for an edifice under construction. All things must be done according to a previous design, every piece must go to its assigned location, so that the building can rise and stand and withstand the corrosive forces of nature. Similarly, the new Code is conceived as the master plan for new and better structures in the community, each canon taking care of a detail, so that when all of them are implemented, a new order arises, and finally the work initiated by Vatican Council II is completed. Clearly, if implementation is conceived in this way, the best contribution the subjects of the law can offer is to obey the norms. Any deviation from the original plan would be a risk; it could compromise the integrity of the edifice.

But a student, any student, of the Dogmatic Constitution on the Church, *Lumen gentium*, may find this understanding of implementing the Code one-sided. It assigns all the active roles in the process to those who have legislative or executive or judicial power in the church; it compels the rest of the people to remain in a passive state. Yet according to Peter they all together are "a chosen race, a royal priesthood, a holy nation, God's own people" (1 Pet 2:9) and according to the council they all together form a "messianic people" (*Lumen gentium* no. 9, *passim*). Once so endowed, surely they must have a positive role to play, a contribution to make. If so, it is just plain good sense that we should give scope to their talents and energies. But to do so, the right environment must be created. Some crippling assumptions should be discarded and some freeing propositions should be accepted.

Implementation

A good starting point in this operation of "discarding and accepting" is to take a critical look once again at the classical definition of law, based on Aquinas' texts, since that definition has become *the* philosophical assumption which inspires and permeates virtually all legal activities in the church. It says that *law is reason bringing order into the life of the community, enacted by the one who is in charge, for the sake of the common good, properly promulgated.* Please note that while this definition is a faithful rendering of the meaning of law as it is defined in the relevant passages in the *Summa Theologiae* (cf. I-II, 90ff.), it is not a literal translation of any one passage found there.

The definition contains saving and enduring insights. If a norm does not spring from reason, it is not law, hence it binds not. If it is not for the common good, it is no good at all. If it has not been duly promulgated, people should pay no attention to it. This is quite a protection for common people against the excesses of tyranny!

But some other elements in it are not reassuring. Taken narrowly or literally (there is no need to assume that Aquinas himself would have taken it so), they can lead to attitudes and actions which are in marked contrast with the rich understanding of the people of God as it comes to us from the earliest (cf. 1 Peter) and the latest (cf. Vatican Council II) expressions of our Christian traditions.

The definition states that the rightful author of the law is always the one who is in charge of the community, a conception that has its roots in the theories of Plato and Aristotle. Both stressed the theory that the king or prince should be chosen from among the wisest, since his principal task is to give wise laws to the people. From there, it is easy (although plainly illogical) to come to the conclusion that only those who are "in charge" can give wise laws. Once that conclusion is reached, virtually no room is left for the wisdom of the ordinary people. The author of laws must be, exclusively, the one who rules. The community at large is not called to contribute to the creation of binding norms.

Yet history offers abundant proofs to the contrary. Some of the best legal systems, such as the law of the ancient Romans, or the common law of England, or the structures and the discipline of the early Christian church, came into existence and were developed not so much by statutory legislation as through customs, to which all made their contribution: the rulers, the magistrates, *and* the people.

It follows that the definition should be emended on the basis of the experience of the human family. Balanced structures and wise norms can be created by the cooperation of a whole community, civic or religious. The wisdom of ordinary people can play a capital part in the process.

Further, the definition implies that the law is all made and ready, and there is really nothing to add to it once it has been promulgated.[1] In other terms, once enacted, the law is assumed to be in the state of accomplished perfection.

But it stands to reason that no matter how well the law was conceived and composed, as long as it is only on the books, it is *not* a vital force in the community. It is a blueprint, bidding people to build their life accordingly. As yet, the existential element is missing.

Reception

Indeed, another amendment should be added to the classical definition: law is what has been promulgated *and received*. The inclusion of the existential element is indispensable for the correct understanding of what the fullness of law is. Law in theory and law in action are not the same, not even by the classical scholastic criteria. The one is on the way to becoming a vital force, the other has become one. The contribution of the subjects must come precisely on the existential level; their impact must be felt while the law is being applied. Thus, *reception by the community belongs to the fullness of the law*. To avoid any misunderstanding, by "reception" we do not mean an act of formal ratification through some kind of a plebiscite; but we do mean the intelli-

---

1. No wonder, therefore, that even the new Code of Canon Law insists that an authentic interpretation of the text can come from the legislator only; and when it comes, in many cases it does no more than state again what was already there, "in itself certain," even if it had been misunderstood by many (cf. canon 16)!

gent and responsible accommodation of the law, an abstract norm, to the demands of concretely obtainable values.[2]

To receive the law well, some preliminary conditions must be fulfilled.

That a human person is an intelligent and free being has its own demands. Such demands reach out into the field of law making, they bind the legislators themselves. Whenever a new norm of action is proposed to intelligent and free beings, respect due to them postulates that the why and the wherefore of the norm, *that is, the values the law intends to uphold,* should be explained to them. Then, and only then, will they be able to understand the need for the norm and receive it as befits their nature.

Such understanding of the law is a preliminary condition for intelligent obedience in freedom. Those so disposed will act primarily not because of an external constraint, but out of an internal dedication to the world of values. Such an attitude is the best protection against the permanent temptation of legalism.

Then the scene is set for the contribution of the subjects to the process of implementation. When the law is first applied, it is put to an exacting test. The abstractly conceived norm meets the demands of concrete life. The most qualified witnesses to this encounter are those who are involved in it, especially the bishops and people of the local churches. There are no others who could tell if such a meeting, when it happens, brings peace or provokes undue conflict. Their experience can help and guide them in judging if the law should be simply accepted, or correctly adjusted, or prudently interpreted—as the case may be—so that it should not become an unnecessary burden or an empty formality, but should be what it was intended to be, a promoter of values. There is no proper reception and correct implementation without critical and creative intelligence.

There is, however, more to it. Let us move to a more theological level.

The Dogmatic Constitution on the Church, *Lumen gentium,* speaks at some length of the *sensus fidei* (cf. no. 12), that capacity in our people which enables them to perceive and recognize God's mighty words

---

2. For a historical and systematic exposition of the idea of "reception" of both doctrine and laws *see* Yves Congar, "La 'reception' comme réalité ecclésiologique," *Droit ancien et structures ecclésiales* (London: Variorum Reprints, 1982) XI, 369–403. This "reality" is an integral part of our Tradition, with capital T. As such, it cannot be lost: the Spirit will take care of that. But it can be obscured or neglected by our lack of attentiveness.

and deeds. This is a divine gift; through it the church may come into the possession of infallible knowledge. Now if the *sensus fidei* can work so powerfully in doctrinal matters, surely it can help us in making practical decisions! Hence the question: how much scope does our legal system give to this precious endowment? The answer is disturbing: virtually none. That is, we have a source of immense energy, offering wisdom and strength to the people, yet in the practical life of the church we hardly ever allow it to be used. We all are the poorer for it.

The new Code, of course, grants official recognition to customs arising in the community, but with such restrictions that in practice it strangles them. They can have binding force only if they are approved by the legislator. Moreover, the community has no right to this approval, no matter how suitable the customs may be, no matter how much the people want them. No wonder the young churches of today in Asia and Africa are not able to develop their own way of life, as the young churches did in the early centuries. More often than not, they are called on "to implement" the law, with no questions allowed. The irony of history is that the emergence of a distinctly Roman rite and discipline was greatly facilitated by the respect of the other churches for the ways of the Romans.

Further, is it not of the greatest importance in this ecumenical age that we, the Roman Catholic church, should convey forcefully to other Christian churches and ecclesial communities that we have nothing but the deepest respect for their ancient and legitimate customs? Is there a better way of conveying this message than by showing respect in our legislation for the diverse manifestations of life in our own household? Such deeds can take us further on the road to reunion than many discussions.

Be that as it may, if the gift of *sensus fidei* means anything, it must play a role in the implementation of the laws. Thus the concept of reception includes not only the understanding of the values involved, but also the judicious use of this instinct of faith. Every part of the body, head and members, has a role to play.

In the practical order this may well mean that to some laws in the new Code even greater scope will be given than was intended by the legislator; from others, power will be taken away because they interfere with a delicate balance of values; others still will be given new meanings mainly through quiet interpretation. Thus life shapes the law.

Future policy

The implementation of the new Code of Canon Law cannot mean simple passive acceptance of the norms and their uncritical imposition and application. Such an approach would be less than respectful to those whom God has endowed with intelligence and freedom; also, it would exclude all the good initiatives that may spring from the *sensus fidei* of the faithful. No one can say it better than the council did: "For by this sense of faith which is aroused and sustained by the Spirit of truth, God's people accepts not the word of man but the very word of God . . . penetrates it more deeply by accurate insights, and applies it more thoroughly to life" (*Lumen gentium* 12; trans. Abbott and Gallagher). It follows that by this sense of faith, God's people can penetrate the laws by accurate insights and apply them correctly to life. When this happens, the law is received in the community.

Finally, a word about implementing not the Code but Vatican Council II. The process can be conceived in two distinct ways. One is that the council has given us a body of doctrine to be appropriated, a number of guidelines to be followed. When that teaching is fully accepted, when those guidelines are loyally followed, the implementation comes to completion. The church can be at rest.

Another is that the council brought the church out of seclusion and created in it an intense movement to search for new horizons, new understandings, new ways of action, all for bringing the Good News to the whole human family, no nation, no person excepted. In doing this, the church cannot rest.

If the second sense of implementation is the correct one—and who could doubt that it is?—to implement the council means to enter wholeheartedly into the movement that the council initiated and then to do what the council did: to raise new questions and search for new answers, so as to keep the gospel ever fresh for this world of ours. Paradoxically, to implement the council means to go beyond the council. To stand still is to break with the council.

The clue to the understanding of the reception of the new Code of Canon Law and any new law is in the correct understanding of the implementation of the council.

6

Values and Laws

The question

The question which this inquiry, philosophical and theological in scope,[1] intends to answer is, "What is the ideal relationship between values and laws?" In other terms, what the relationship between the two *ought* to be; not what actually, in one system or another, it happens to be.[2] But our goal is not purely theoretical; as we progress in our reflections, we hope to find also some practical guidelines for bringing and keeping the world of values and the world of laws together—guidelines of interest to those who are entrusted with the task of making, interpreting and implementing the laws.

Although we often use the word "community" in a general sense, our main interest lies in the Christian community, that is, the church. Consequently, the relevant values for us are the ones which the Christian community can call its own (be they divine or human), and the pertinent laws are the ones by which the same community operates. So, a more specific way of raising the question is, "What should the

---

1. Indeed, my inquiry throughout will be both philosophical and theological since it deals with values in the communities of human persons who have a share in divine nature. Neither aspect can be left out. In my reflections I may focus more at times on the needs of our human nature, at times on the correct response to divine gifts. The ideal is the harmony of the two.

2. This is not an empirical study. It sets out an ideal that we can strive for but never quite reach. But the ideal presented is nothing else than correctly measured balances in the community. Such an ideal can prove most useful in the concrete order because it gives a norm for the assessment of the life of the community. A thorough comparison between how the community lives and how it ought to live can confirm that the group is in good health but it can also bring to the surface the symptoms of a latent illness.

90 *Values and Laws*

relationship be between the values proper to the church and the valid laws of the church?"

What are values?

Values can exist only in relation to intelligent and free beings. They are "good things" which contribute to the development of persons.[3]

To understand the role of values we must begin with a foundational proposition: all human beings have been created imperfect;[4] therefore, they all must progress. They do so by appropriating good things for themselves, or by creating good things within themselves.[5]

They can appropriate good things on a biological level: nourishment contributes to their physical well being. They can do the same on a psychological level: a friendly emotional environment lets the child blossom. Or, on an intellectual level: instructions received in school can make a person rich in knowledge. Or, on a spiritual level: openness to grace is the key to heavenly wisdom. In all these processes, the pattern is the same: intelligent and free persons appropriate good things, and when a symbiosis between persons and good things takes place, the persons are enriched; to a small degree, they may become perfect.

Now it is easier to see what a value is: a good thing, not in itself alone, but in its relationship to human persons. That is, the concept of value always includes two elements: it signifies a thing and its capacity to contribute to the perfection of human beings.[6]

The most fundamental values are discovered by an innate attraction: we instinctively favor life over death. Other values can be found

---

3. Aristotle said, and so did Aquinas and all their followers, that "all things are good," *omne ens bonum*. The concept of value goes one step further: it signifies those "things" (to use an everyday expression, although "being" may be more correct in rendering *ens*) which can contribute to the perfection of intelligent and free persons.

4. In the sense of being "unfinished" or "incomplete." They can reach their completeness only in time; they are historical beings.

5. There is a value not only in what I receive at the different levels of being, such as food, instruction, supernatural revelation, but also in what I can create in myself, such as penetrating insights, responsible decisions, humble openness to grace. Some values come from the outside, some originate inside.

6. When we speak of "value judgment" we mean precisely a judgment about the suitability of an object to perfect human beings. Values exist in the objective order, but not every value is suitable for every person. Many thinkers have postulated a special faculty for the perception of values.

through philosophical reflection; Socrates was an expert at it. Specifically Christian values are studied by moral theologians; their task is to speak of good things and good deeds that can keep a person in God's grace. The values canon law is interested in are those which have a social significance; that is, which are needed to build a Christian community and are necessary to sustain its life.[7]

But no human being is an island; we are all social animals, in the noblest sense of the term. We need a community for our progress on any level, biological, emotional, intellectual or spiritual. We need it so much that without it our personality is likely to become undernourished and distorted even to the point where life is destroyed. We need to belong.

Thus, to form communities is natural for human beings. The life and operation of their communities are not very different from those of individual persons. They are not perfect; they are all perfectible. It follows that they, too, need to appropriate good things in order to live, to grow, to become whole.

Communities have their physical needs, such as a place to meet. They have their psychological needs: without a friendly environment they cannot exist; indifference can kill them. They ought to progress intellectually: a common mind can be built only through knowledge shared by many. And, if they are a Christian community, they must also progress in grace and wisdom. Indeed, communities are like individual persons: they live and grow by reaching out for good things, by appropriating values.

---

7. There is little doubt that the proper field of secular law is the field of external social relations. Its field does not extend into the internal world of human persons. In traditional scholastic language secular law operates on the external forum only (the forum of the courts), not in the internal forum (the forum of God, or the forum of the conscience where God judges a human person). This is not to deny, of course, that our conscience can bind us to obey a secular law; it can. There is a difference between a law trying to regulate from the outside our internal acts, and our conscience telling us from the inside to obey an external rule.

The issue of what is the proper field of operation of canon law is disputed. On the one hand, no human law can ever reach and take cognizance of the internal acts of the human spirit; the most it can do is observe their external manifestations and draw appropriate conclusions on the basis of previously built assumptions (or presumptions, in canonical language). On the other hand, our modern canon law speaks and behaves as if it were capable of knowing what is happening in the depth of the spirit of human persons; this is particularly evident whenever the law is meant to judge an "intention," as in the case of matrimonial consent.

The opinion which holds that the proper field of the operation of all ecclesiastical laws is the external forum is better grounded.

What are laws?

Laws are norms of action for the community, set by legitimate authority, for the appropriation of values by the community.[8] They are instruments of life, growth and perfection because they point to needed values and prompt the community to reach out for them.[9] Laws here are to be taken in a broad sense, so as to include legally binding customs as well. They express a judgment concerning the desirability of certain values and convey (impose) a decision to reach out for them.

But how can the community know about the suitability of a given value; how can it make a decision to reach for it? A seemingly simple answer is that to create good norms and implement them the community must become of one mind and one heart. In truth, it is the only answer. But how can this unity of minds and hearts be created?

There is no one way of creating it. The community, depending on its particular constitution, may accept the judgment of its own delegates or representatives, or, if so inspired, it may take directions from its own religious leaders.

In any case, to determine what values are suitable for the community two questions must be raised, one more in the abstract, the other entirely in the concrete order. The somewhat abstract question is, what specific values are suitable for this type of community? The answer

---

8. Let me call this definition a tentative one since I am not sure that it is a comprehensive one. But it brings out the dynamic character of the law: *a norm of action*, leading and prompting the community to the *appropriation of a value*. Aquinas' famous definition "a norm of reason" *(ordinatio rationis)*, can carry (and probably did) a static meaning: through the instrumentality of the law reason was bringing order into a society; with order came peace, and then the group was at rest—a concept akin to happiness, the Aristotelian *eudaimonia*.

Neither Aristotle nor Aquinas had an adequate understanding of the evolutionary character of our universe; they understood all beings through the doctrine of eternal and immutable essences, allowing for accidental changes only. Influenced by such a world view, lawyers came quite naturally to hold that change in the law was "odious," *mutatio legis odiosa*. To this day the church does not have the machinery for letting the law develop with a normal rhythm; changes are often brought about by tensions, agitations and conflicts—not always an edifying spectacle to the world. Our legal system progresses rather by dramatic leaps than through an on-going organic development; consider the total absence of any provision in the Code for changes in the laws, notwithstanding that new needs continually emerge in the church and postulate changes.

9. I am speaking of good laws, of what the role of laws ought to be. Unless we are aware of the ideal (which may never exist in its purity) we have no norm to judge the real.

will tend to describe an ideal situation: a model parish must have a dynamic priest, a shrewd council, a steady source of income, etc. The concrete question is, what is the capacity of this community to appropriate the envisaged values? Something may be suitable but not obtainable. If the community has no ability to provide and support what is necessary for a model parish, those values are not for them. The values that they cannot use must not be imposed on them.[10]

The answers to these questions, however, do not take the community beyond the mere identification of the needed values. To obtain the benefit they can bring, action is necessary to appropriate them. Such appropriation can take place with or without the help of legal norms.

For instance, the whole community may want a value because of their common religious or moral conviction, or because of their common cultural tradition. Such a unity in action based on unwritten traditions, however, precious as it can be, is never quite enough. To keep the societal life of the community on an even keel, the help of some well defined legal norms is needed.

Such legal norms have a double function: they point to values and "order" (direct) the community to take action to obtain them. Here we can see where the roots of good laws are: in an objective system of values that is judged suitable for the community. Here we can see what the laws are for: to be instrumental in promoting the appropriation of needed values.[11]

10. If those who are in charge of making laws raise the first question but neglect the second, they will create laws which are suitable for Utopia. When such laws are imposed on a flesh-and-blood society, a tension develops between the laws and the demands of life; eventually a breakdown of the public order is likely to follow. The American experiment of Prohibition could well serve as a typical case for the study of utopian legislation and its unwanted consequences. In the church the utopian temptation can come in the form of trying to impose the same laws in the same way on all nations and peoples. Ideally the values represented may be suitable for the church universal, but concretely some particular churches may not have the capacity to appropriate those values. Marriage tribunals can be valuable institutions; yet in the better part of the Catholic church they cannot and do not function properly for lack of funds, personnel—or even lack of passable roads.

11. Once this understanding of the laws is adopted a broad new field opens up for investigation: the identification of values behind the laws. To be quite practical about it, in canon law a whole series of doctoral dissertations could be started. A study could begin with the presently valid law, e.g., concerning ecumenism; then it could continue by identifying the values which the law actually supports; further, by identifying the values that the law should support but does not; and finally it could conclude with appropriate suggestions for the future. Or a study

An integrated community

We speak of an integrated person when someone possesses a harmony between the mind and the heart, a continuity from the perception of values to their appropriation. We say that a person is integrated when he or she acts out of conviction.

The term "integrated" can be applied to a community as well. An integrated community is one that has the capacity to know the values it needs, and the strength to obtain them. As we have seen, the legal life of the community plays an important role in building up this common integrity. The norms point to a value that is needed and instruct the community to reach out for it. There is a fundamental wholeness in the community that is contented with its laws and lives by them.

This integrity can be achieved only when the world of values and the world of laws blend into each other so that there is a smooth transition from one to the other, when there is an organic and dynamic unity between them. In our imperfect world, however, a fully integrated community is just as difficult to find as a fully integrated person—perhaps even more so. Distortions of the ideal, at varying degrees, are of common occurrence. When such distortions happen, they harm the community; they take away something of the wholeness of the social body. Sooner or later the symptoms of an internal illness appear.

• *One type of distortion occurs* when the world of laws moves away from the world of values. Laws begin to reign supreme; they can even present themselves as objects of a religious cult, gently leading the community toward a kind of "worship of the law," *nomolatria*. They no longer appear as servants of values; they justify their existence with the fact that they exist. They tend to claim authority and demand compliance on the ground alone that "this is the law" and "the subject owes allegiance to the law." When this happens, the symptoms of a sickness are present. Laws have become autonomous values, independent of genuine ontological values.

The result is an internal illness in the community. The legislator himself may become inattentive to the objective order of values, to their

could begin by identifying the values in a theological institution, e.g., in the episcopal college, continue by examining how far the presently valid laws support those values, and finally, if so warranted, it could conclude by showing how the laws should be improved.

There is hardly any part of the Code of Canon Law that would not benefit from such an examination. Such studies, in their own unobtrusive way, could mean an objective and detached evaluation of canon law *in its roots,* and could lead to a radical renewal of the legal life of the church.

hierarchy. The interpreters of the law (who can be judges, administrators, teachers) may not feel compelled any more to refer back to the values in which the laws should be rooted, so they produce a somewhat sterile exegesis of the text. Their main concern is to declare the mind of the legislator, though that may in fact be their own construction.

The name of this sickness is *legalism*. No one has given a better description of the havoc that it can cause, especially in religious communities, than Paul. The problem, of course, had been identified by Jesus who showed dramatically how the right order was reversed: in the understanding of the priests and lawyers, the law of sabbath became a value in itself and displaced the very value that it was meant to support in the first place.

The consequences of legalism can reach far and wide and cause various disorders in the community. The subjects sooner or later perceive the discrepancy between the world of values and that of the law. Such perception is usually prompted and sharpened by the increasing burden that the law is trying to impose on them. They notice a certain emptiness in the law, a cult of formalities; they begin to lose their respect for it. Evasions, non-observance, at times plain defiance can follow. A vicious spiral may start as well: the legislator, disturbed by such phenomena, tries to stop them by making even more laws, "in order to close the loopholes." But, in truth, there is no other solution than to bring the laws back to where they belong: the humble service of values.

• *Another type of distortion is* the neglect of values on the part of the laws. The community is in need of "good things," and it could obtain them if properly directed, yet no help is forthcoming from the legislator. The result is a reduced vitality, a kind of social anemia. Such a situation can be a prelude to the fatal disease of anarchy. But even if it does not go so far, it can cause serious breakdowns in the life of the group.[12]

The name of this disease is *lawlessness*. When it is all-pervading it is anarchy. It can be also partial, affecting only certain fields of operation. For instance, if there are no good rules for the courts, there will be a "lawlessness" in the administration of justice. A pertinent example in the new Code is the absence of effective provisions for the

---

12. Canon law knows about this particular danger and has an institution to prevent it from doing harm. Whenever there is no law applicable in a situation that cries out for justice, a *lacuna legis* can be invoked, and a judge or an administrator can make provisions which will have the strength of law.

96 *Values and Laws*

judicial protection of the fundamental rights of the faithful. Or, whenever there are sources of energy in the church yet the law does not provide adequate outlets for their use to the benefit of the community, to that extent there is "lawlessness." For example, there are few adequate laws to open the door for an effective participation of the laity in the life of the church; the control over their initiatives by the clergy is so far reaching that it can be stifling.[13]

The testimony of history

No matter how correct a theory may sound, if it can be confirmed by facts its credibility increases. The theory of a necessary and organic link between values and laws can be confirmed by facts—in our case, since we are interested in canon law, from the history of the church. Let us look at two periods, one that was initiated by the Council of Trent, another that had its beginnings with Vatican Council II.

The Council of Trent and its aftermath

In the period after the Council of Trent a severe distancing occurred between the world of values and the world of laws.[14] The principal aim of the council and the popes who took charge of its implementation was to restore the unity of the church, a most urgent need at the time. But in promoting this one value they lost sight of some other values needed for the wholeness of the community, and the result was an imbalance. Instead of the law being in the service of authentic values, the service of the law became a value in itself. A few examples can tell the story better than long explanations.

In the sixteenth century, with the renaissance of classical studies, an intense interest in the original texts of the Bible developed. But there was a danger: discordant translations could put into jeopardy the unity

---

13. There are several other rich and unused sources of energy in the church; for instance, there are no adequate structures that would assure that the laity is heard by the hierarchy; apart from an ecumenical council, there are no structures to support the effective exercise of episcopal collegiality; the legal system offers little help, if any, to particular churches to develop their own personality.

14. For a more detailed analysis of the "legal nominalism" introduced into the life of the church in the wake of the Council of Trent *see* the address given to the French canon lawyers by Gérard Fransen (to whom I am indebted), Professor of Canon Law at Louvain-la-Neuve, published under the title "L'application des décrets du Concile de Trente. Les débuts d'un nominalisme canonique," in *L'année canonique*, 27 (1983) 5-16.

of explanations. The council therefore made one translation into Latin the official one, known under the name *Vulgate*. Preachers and teachers were ordered to use it, and forbidden to go beyond it. It was to be known as the "authentic" text of the Scriptures.

The problem is that the *Vulgate* was not really the authentic (in the sense of genuine) text of the Scriptures; the council substituted a legal authenticity for a natural one. With such an act the council introduced a subtle nominalism into the operations of the church. The genuine could not be considered authentic, and the authentic was not genuine. This was nominalism, even if no one has called it by its true name, or conceivably, no one has recognized it.

The council wanted an "authentic" text of the *Corpus Iuris Canonici* as well, not necessarily identical with the genuine one. The so called "Roman correctors," *correctores Romani*, were charged with revising and adapting the original text to new circumstances. But that *Corpus* was an original creation; the rules contained in it were developed in function of values—vital for an evolving legal system. Gratian in his *Concordance of Discordant Canons* always sought a reasoned resolution of conflicting claims, and so did the popes often enough in their decretal letters. For them, to know the *why* of a law (that is, to know the value behind it) was necessary for the understanding and (presumably) for the observance of that law.

It had to be different in the future. The *why* of the laws had to be sought in their very existence; the search for values had to end there. The laws were binding because they were there, not because they served the community in the appropriation of values. The scene was set for a new mentality which saw the laws as ultimate values and exalted obedience as the highest of virtues. An inquiring mind that tried to go beyond the obvious sense of a text was easily regarded as a disloyal mind. The task of canon lawyers was no longer to seek harmony in dissonance (which would have meant a return to values) but to find meaning in the norms without asking why they were there in the first place. In such circumstances the science of canon law (science, in the sense of inquiring into ultimate causes) was doomed. The best and the most a canon lawyer could do was to write elaborate paraphrases of the existing texts, to go into fine distinctions, or to construe imaginary cases and solve them. A new phenomenon arose: canon law was acquiring an increasingly bad reputation among God's people.[15]

15. No wonder the very definition of law inherited from Aquinas underwent a radical transformation. Aquinas put the emphasis on *reason* bringing order into the community: *ordinatio rationis;* Suarez (the best expositor of the post-Tridentine

But more important than anything else was the bull of confirmation of the Council of Trent, *Benedictus Deus,* promulgated by Pius IV in 1564. He decreed:

> To avoid any perversion and confusion, which could arise if it were permitted to anyone who so wished to publish his own comments and interpretations on the decrees of the council, with apostolic authority we order that . . . no one must publish, in any way whatsoever, without our authorization commentaries, glossaries, annotations, *scholia,* or interpretations of any kind concerning the council's decrees; or to state anything in anybody's name about them, not even with the aim of giving greater strength to them, or promoting their implementation.[16]

The pope decreed also that in case of any doubt concerning the meaning of a conciliar text, the Apostolic See alone was competent to resolve the doubt.[17] This bull set the course of theology and canon law for centuries, not only by proscribing genuine scientific investigation into the council but also by introducing a mentality which saw the solution of virtually all problems in a response from some higher authority. In other terms, intellectual problems had to be solved by legal decrees.[18]

From the point of view of canon law, any critical inquiry into the connection between the world of values and the laws was excluded. In ecclesiastical sciences a sort of subtle nominalism took the place of the robust realism of the Middle Ages. The imprint of this mentality

---

understanding of the law) put the stress on the law being the will of the legislator: *voluntas principis.* Suarez's legal philosophy has become the hermeneutical guide for canon lawyers; the manuals in use before Vatican Council II bring ample testimony to it. Even Cardinal Felici, while directing the revision of the Code, repeatedly stated that the commission had no intention of looking into doctrinal issues. At times such an attitude could have been sound; at other times not so because it could have been a refusal to examine the relationship of laws to values.

16. *See* DS: 1849.

17. It has been reported also that the Pope ordered the Acts of the Council to be kept under lock and key at Castel Sant'Angelo to prevent anyone not properly authorized from having access to them. Moreover, for a long time the interpretation of the decrees was reserved to the Congregation of the Council (charged with the implementation of the council), which made any scholarly research virtually useless. The "authentic" meaning of the text had to be what the congregation wanted it to be. Since there was little scope for research and creative thought, theology and canon law entered a long period of starvation and stagnation.

18. This is probably the origin of the modern habit of sending questions to Rome even when there are ways and means of finding the answers locally.

can be found in the canonical literature which has seen the light during the centuries following the Council of Trent.[19]

Contemporary events: Vatican Council II and after

Vatican Council II was truly a new point of departure in the history of the church, probably more than we can realize now. The fact that its impact is not diminishing but steadily increasing shows that it was not a passing event. Even those who have never quite accepted it take refuge behind its vocabulary.

The reason for the exceptional importance of this council is that it has given a new direction to the life of the church, as the Council of Trent did in its own way. Vatican II enjoined us to return to the sources of our traditions. We are bound therefore to go beyond any text, even the texts of Vatican II, back to our origins. It follows that there cannot be any authentic commentary, glossary, annotation, scholion or interpretation of this last council, or of any council for that matter, or of any other document that has recorded our Christian beliefs, without relating them to the authentic (that is, genuine) values by which the church has lived so long.[20]

Ideally, the revision of the Code of Canon Law should have proceeded by first clarifying the values that the future law was meant to uphold. This should have been done by a fully interdisciplinary committee of theologians and lawyers, neither side prevailing over the other. After the completion of such a preliminary study the lawyers could have taken over, but not without giving a voice to their colleagues in theology. In truth, to ask for such a procedure would have been too much. The revision was a very pragmatic process, probably the only one possible in the aftermath of the council.

Nonetheless, the Tridentine spell was broken by Vatican II. The drafters of the new canons brought the law closer to genuine values

19. It would be an interesting study to see if there are still traces of a subtle nominalism in our contemporary church. For instance, when a diocesan bishop is said to be the vicar of Christ in his diocese (as Vatican Council II repeatedly affirmed) yet has only a minimum of discretionary power in his territory, is he the vicar of Christ more in name than in reality? Or when freedom of research is affirmed in the law but the controls over the researchers are excessively strict, is the grant of freedom real or nominal?

20. This should not be interpreted as advocating a revival of those customs and usages of the primitive church which are not suitable for our age. It does mean though that later development should be critically examined, and historical accretions which do not belong to the core of Christian tradition should be discarded if they have outlived their usefulness.

than it has been for centuries. The fundamental rights of the faithful are named and recognized by the law, even if as yet no practical and effective remedy is offered to protect the values enshrined by the declaration of those rights. The dignity of the episcopal office is clearly brought to the fore, even if little scope is given to the value of collegiality. The law makes a great effort to uphold the religious values in marriage, notwithstanding that it still uses the secular language of contracts. The results may be partial, but a new departure is real. Progress may be slow, but there are achievements to show. As the values and laws are brought closer, there is a decline in legalism. As values are gaining more recognition, the laws show a better disposition to protect and support them; the result is less "lawlessness."[21]

A community of mature persons

As the community perceives that laws ought to be in the service of values, it becomes necessary to re-model the legislative process. To promulgate a norm of action and then to expect "blind obedience" from those who have been called "the children of light" does not make good sense. For obedience to be intelligent and free, it is necessary that it be informed. Information means communication on the part of the lawgiver not only of what a legal norm is but also of what the value is that the norm intends to uphold. The subjects are exercising their full personhood only when they make an effort to understand that value and decide to reach out for it. There is the true "reception" of the law.[22]

Such a cooperation on the part of the subjects can greatly enhance the quality of the laws. The subjects are the witnesses to what happens when the abstract legal rule meets the concrete demands of life. They can report back to the legislator how the values survive in that

---

21. The new law of marriage can serve as an example of where genuine progress has been made away from legalism and toward greater dependence of the law on values, but where much remains to be done. See Ladislas Örsy, *Marriage in Canon Law: Texts and Comments, Reflections and Questions* (Wilmington, Del.: Glazier, 1986). Throughout the book I tried to interpret and "evaluate" the canons in function of the values that they are meant to serve.

22. This does not mean that all the subjects must understand the reasons for every single paragraph in a law. It means a reasonable effort on the part of the legislator to put out substantial information, and similar effort on the part of the subjects to learn about the values that the law intends to uphold. Technicalities can be left to technicians.

encounter.[23] A mature community is one that steadily tends toward this ideal. The church envisaged by Vatican Council II is a mature community—even if in practice we are still far from the ideal.[24]

By way of conclusion: the beauty of the laws

To speak of "the beauty of the laws" could be an invitation for sarcastic comments; rarely does a legal system awake any kind of aesthetic interest! Yet there is a genuine beauty in the ideal we have described: laws in the service of values, nothing more, nothing less. Harmonious proportions always delight the senses; when such proportions happen to be in a world that is above the senses, they delight the human spirit. Harmony between values and laws can indeed be delightful. Ultimately it is the same kind of harmony that we see in an integrated person who is led by a clear vision and acts with a firm determination.

The closer the life of the community is to this ideal, the greater will be their progress in appropriating "good things." In the Christian order more can be added. The values that the church is seeking are not only what is fitting for our human nature but also what brings eternal life. Therefore, laws in the church have the task of ministering (imperfectly, no doubt) in the distribution of divine gifts. It follows that the more our canon law conforms to the humanity of our God, the more its specific beauty will be revealed.

---

23. It should be the task of canon lawyers to assist the people in this process. This brings up the problem of the training of lawyers in the church. If they are not trained to recognize values and judge their relationship to the law, they will only perpetuate the legal nominalism of post-Tridentine centuries. It is gratifying to see that many places of instruction are aware of this danger and are making an effort to awake an inquiring spirit in the students.

24. There has been much turmoil in the church after Vatican II. This was inevitable. When two powerful rivers meet, there is turbulence in the waters. The Council of Trent and Vatican Council II initiated powerful movements, both within the Christian tradition but still very different. In these "turbulent" post-Vatican II years we are witnessing the confluence of two currents, one carrying the weight of centuries, the other propelled by youthful energies. In nature when we see the powerful play of torrents when they meet, we know that there are immense energies at work; nature is very much alive. This image can tell us something about the state of the church today: it is alive.

7

Integrated Interpretation
or
The Role of Theology in Interpretation

Introduction by way of a summary

To give the summary of a chapter by way of introduction is unusual, but in this case it may well be justified. The issues we are going to face range far and wide. A first look at the field we want to cover, an indication of the path we want to walk, and some pointers toward the goal we wish to reach can be of some help in understanding the successive steps we are going to take. In other terms, a brief description of the journey before it begins can be a useful guide.

The principal question which this chapter intends to answer is: *How far can or must theological positions and ideas govern the interpretation of the canonical texts?* Further down the road this one question will lead to some more specific queries, such as *How far does theology determine the overall purpose of the law in the church?* and *How far is theology relevant or competent to give guidance for the construction of legal norms applicable to particular institutions?*[1]

---

1. The reader should be warned not to identify too readily the laws of the church with the Code of Canon Law, old or new. Not only because there are laws outside of the Code but also because many canons in the Code do not qualify as legal rules since they do not deal with right and duty situations.

Ideally, it would be better to have a strictly legal code with those rules which create right and duty situations (e.g., laws referring to offices, property, etc.); then, another book containing a description of our devotional practices (e.g., Sundays, holy days, penitential days) created and sustained by the generosity of our people. The task of an interpreter would be greatly facilitated. Although such an arrangement is certainly an ideal worthy of consideration, it could hardly be the object of a realistic expectation, at least in the near future.

Integrated Interpretation or The Role of Theology in Interpretation 103

Initially, let us define theology somewhat broadly as "our knowledge concerning the transcendental mysteries," or, faith seeking understanding; canon law as "a system of norms of action in the service of mysteries," or, faith seeking action. Clearly, the conceptual world of understanding is not the same as the decisive world of action, yet to one point they converge, and at one point they meet: both are concerned with values. On the issue of values, they are bonded and blended together: *theology provides the community with an overall vision and definition of Christian values, while canon law provides norms of action for the appropriation of those values which are meant to serve the common good.*[2] This unifying and living contact I intend to affirm, clarify and describe.

Indeed, in every human community, as in every human person, there must be an organic unity between the discovery of authentic values and the effort of reaching out for them. Hence, the church itself cannot have internal harmony and operational integrity unless its perception of values through theology is followed by practical effort to appropriate them. The precept to uphold this unity can be rightly called "the principle of integration." If it should ever be missing, the internal life of the church would be fragmented and its capacity to witness to the beauty of the evangelical message would be impaired.[3]

History tells us that legal rules in the church were born from theology: values discovered by faith became the objects of legal norms.[4] In the Middle Ages, however, as a full fledged system of laws developed, a shift took place and the two disciplines, theology and canon law, became separated from each other to a degree that was not good for either of them. In fact, mutual estrangement would be a better term to describe what happened![5] Eventually, especially after the sixteenth

---

2. Norms of action for the appropriation of values are provided also by moral theology. Canon law is primarily interested in values which foster the life of the community as such.

3. We realize today that the church cannot preach justice to the world without practicing it within its community. If our words were contradicted by our deeds, the effectiveness of our preaching would be undermined and the world would rightly convict us of a lack of integrity.

4. A typical example could be found in the history of the sacraments. They were celebrated and played a life-giving role in the community long before any laws were made about them. Another example would be in the history of the ecumenical councils. They interpreted the word of God with authority for the community long before their convocation and operation were regulated by any law.

5. In the practical order one reason for such a separation (and estrangement)

century, laws were perceived not so much as instruments for appropriating values identified by faith and reason as the expression of the sovereign will of the legislator. As a consequence, they were less subject to critical examination than those statements concerning our beliefs.[6]

The main thesis of this chapter (and its plea) is that in order to have integrity in the life of the church theology must play an overriding hermeneutical role in the interpretation of canonical norms; so much so that without the integration of theological elements, no authentic legal interpretation can arise. The term "authentic" is used here not in the technical sense which it has in canon 16, which calls an official interpretation *authentica*, but in the sense of "genuine," reached through objective scientific criteria.[7]

---

may have been the establishment of separate "faculties" of theology and canon law.

Another reason may have been the fact that the medieval canon lawyers took their inspiration from Roman law and eventually adopted it as *the* model of canon law. They were so satisfied with it that they did not feel the need to look any further and thus became locked into the horizons of a legal system which was secular through and through. The canonists of today who are reluctant to admit the dependence of canon law on theology, and are stressing the autonomy of canon law, are the heirs to this tradition.

6. It is undeniable that the doctrine of legal positivism had a subtle impact on canon law. This should not be surprising. As the law became increasingly viewed as the expression of the will of the legislator, *ordinatio legislatoris,* the inquiry (logically enough) tended to stop with ascertaining the mind (the intention) of the legislator. An investigation into the relationship of the law to values appeared irrelevant and unnecessary; at most it was the business of the legislator to take them into account. He had to be trusted, not examined: a subtle taint of positivism.

On the other hand, when law is regarded as *ordinatio rationis ad bonum commune,* that is, reason bringing order into the life of the community, all critical inquiry into the law will focus on the *bonum,* value, which makes the *ordinatio,* the ordering, reasonable, because the goodness of the law is essentially dependent on the objective order of values. Hence, not a shadow of positivism.

Further, when law is perceived as being primarily the expression of the will of the legislator, the freedom and independence of the science of canon law is imperiled because any critical assessment of the law in function of values can be seen as undue criticism of the personal judgment of the legislator.

See the interesting chapter on "The Language of Law" in *The Making of Moral Theology* by John Mahoney (Oxford: Clarendon Press, 1987), 224–258. Although he is concerned with the impact of the language of the law on moral theology, it is obvious that much of the undesirable impact has come from a voluntaristic perception of the law.

7. One should recall that in reality a so-called "authentic" interpretation, according to canon 16, can be (and at times has been) a way of re-writing the law.

So much for the initial summary; let us proceed now to the proper exposition of our theme.

Formulating the question and naming the sources

For an inquiry to be successful in expanding our knowledge, two conditions must be verified right from the beginning. First, we must know what we are looking for. This means that we must not rest until we are able to formulate our question with a precision that leaves little or no room for confusion concerning the object of our research; otherwise we are bound to meander around in unchartered territory for a long time to come.

Second, we must identify the sources where those fragments of information can be found which, once put together, can throw some light on the object of our search and fill the gap in our knowledge.

With regard to the first, our question is: *What is the role of theology in the interpretation of canon law?*

The truth is that we may be in possession of a good deal of theological knowledge, and have a sound store of learning in canon law; but we do not know much about the dynamic relationship between theology and canon law. That is, we search for a better understanding of the movement from theological ideas to legal norms.

The canonical manuals published between the two Codes followed a centuries-old tradition and steadily abstained from any such investigation and reflection. After Vatican Council II the situation began to change. More and more voices were raised, including that of Pope Paul VI, in favor of a new approach; his insistence on the need for a *novus habitus mentis*, a new attitude of mind, is well known. But such voices remained mostly on the level of recognizing a need and stating some principles; only a relatively small number of authors ventured into actually interpreting the norms in function of theological ideas. Old habits are slow to die.[8]

As for the second, there is not any one source that would tell us about the movement from ideas to norms of action. The sources of in-

---

The correct translation into English of the expression *interpretatio authentica* should be "official interpretation," or perhaps "authoritative interpretation."

8. There are authors who continue to insist on the autonomy and inviolability of the "juridical order"—a theory which, when applied to the church, is as questionable as that of the "perfect society." The commission for the revision of the Code of Canon Law often took such a stance; the *Communicationes* kept reporting that it did not wish to get involved in doctrinal questions.

formation are in both fields, theology and canon law. We can learn about the relationship between the two by reflecting on the nature and extent of each. In doing so, we must keep in mind the history of both sciences as well; only by remembering the past shall we keep our study well anchored in our traditions.

Before we embark on such reflections, some clarifications are necessary.

The world of theology, the world of canon law, the point where they meet

In the Middle Ages and after, there has been much talk about theology being the queen of all sciences. All others had to be in its service. Philosophy was granted a task of honor: that of the handmaid. The others followed, according to the dignity of each. Since theology reigned over them all, it had the right and duty to supervise and, when it was warranted, to correct them. Thus, new insights into the works of nature or new discoveries in empirical sciences were evaluated and judged in function of the prevailing theological opinions. Naturally enough, theologians got involved in all kinds of issues, such as the rotation of celestial bodies, or the evolution of the animal species.[9] It was an organic and hierarchical understanding of the entire universe of human knowledge, and quite mistaken at that. It failed to grant due autonomy to the various sciences.

We know today that there is no hierarchical subordination of one science to another but that there is an organic connection among them. There is no queen, there is no handmaid, there are no masters and servants at large. There are only autonomous branches of knowledge, each performing a specific task. Once this much is understood and recognized, it should be added that there is indeed an organic connection among them. The connection however is more horizontal than vertical, if such a physical description can be used.[10]

---

9. It was this hierarchical perception of sciences that led church authorities to get involved with cases of astronomy, natural history, biology, even archaeology.

The same perception (although not expressly professed any more) still makes its impact felt when theologians, or canon lawyers for that matter, attempt to solve problems which rightly belong to the field of another science, such as philosophy, psychology, sociology, economy, medicine, and so forth.

10. There is probably no one who explained this better than Bernard Lonergan. See Frederick Crowe, *The Lonergan Enterprise* (Cambridge, Mass.: Cowley, 1980). Crowe calls Lonergan's work "an Organon for our time."

The world of each of these autonomous sciences consists of a complex structure of meanings formed on the basis of accumulated discoveries and judgments.

The world of theology speaks of what we know about God and his mighty deeds for our salvation. There we hear about God's mysteries; there we try to articulate and explain them and to define our relationship to them. Surely, a world of its own. In this world, we stand in "contemplation": our faith seeks understanding.

The world of canon law is radically different: it is the world where rules for action, for the common good, are formulated, promulgated and imposed. It is outward looking. It is interested not in understanding the mysteries, but in doing something in the service of the same mysteries.

These two worlds meet where the values are. First, theology leads to their discovery, then canon law sets the norms for their appropriation. Theology provides the knowledge necessary for acknowledging them, canon law gives binding norms for acquiring them. The two worlds are linked together by the dynamic movement of the subjects from vision to action.[11]

Understanding the role of values

To understand the role of values in the life of the community is so crucial and foundational that, I venture to say, without it, we cannot have good laws, let alone good rules of interpretation.

To arrive at such an understanding, we need to use an analogy: we should look at the role that values play in the life of human persons.

Human persons are unfinished products both in the order of nature and in the order of grace. Throughout their existence, they must grow and develop. To achieve that, they must know what is good for them, and then reach out for it; they must perceive what is valuable for them and then act on that perception. They must do so on several levels: physical, emotional, intellectual and religious.

We speak of persons as well balanced, "being whole," "well integrated" when they display the signs of internal harmony; that is, when they have a clear vision of what is genuinely good for them and then act on that vision. We find fault with those who see but do not act, or fail to see before they act, or act differently from their vision.

---

11. For a description through concrete examples of this organic connection between theology and canon law see Ladislas Örsy, *From Vision to Legislation: From the Council to a Code of Laws* (Milwaukee: Marquette University Press, 1985).

We speak of such persons as having a fragmented personality, we might accuse them of hypocrisy, or in some extreme cases we may suspect them of being affected by schizophrenia.

Now human communities are not all that different from human persons. All human communities have been created unfinished, including the community of Christians, the church.

Yes, the church has been created unfinished; it must grow in grace and wisdom. This is not to say that certain permanent elements are not there; it is to say the social body as a whole has not reached final perfection.

Therefore the church must grow and develop in history by perceiving what is good for the community and then reaching out for it. In other terms, it must come to the vision of true values and do what is necessary for their appropriation.

Theology has the capacity to identify values, canon law has the capacity to give rules for obtaining them.

Thus the two worlds meet. If they join and work together in harmony, there is a wholeness, an integrity of life in the community, from which peace follows. If they do not work in harmony, the community is divided "in its spirit": there is a split between what it sees and what it does.

On the meaning of interpretation

My intention is not to give a long disquisition on this matter; I have done so above in Chapters Three and Four. Here, I want to do no more than to discard again a misunderstanding and to recall the correct understanding of interpretation.

First, the misconception. Interpretation is not the simple reading of the text and the perception of what was in the mind of the legislator. In other terms, the law is not a photographic representation of the mind of the legislator, to be read and reproduced unchanged by the interpreter.

The law is really a "shorthand" message, sent by living human beings embedded in history and their own culture; a message which is received by other human beings equally rooted in history and their own culture. It is a communication from persons living and operating in one horizon to others who are at home in a different horizon.

Second, the correct conception. Interpretation is a creative act. On the basis of the text, the interpreter recreates the meaning of the law, a meaning which may well aim to be identical to the one intended by the legislator but which in one way or another includes something of the genius of the recipient of the law. The interpretation of the Italians was never quite the same as the interpretation of the Anglo-Saxons.

Now the point I want to make is this: our legislator is embedded in Christian history and he lives and operates within a theological horizon. It follows that the re-creating of the meaning of the law by the interpreter must be inspired by Christian history and must take place within a theological horizon.

This fact carries an important message: even if the legislator did not direct us to do so, we must seek a theological interpretation of canon law. In other words, there is no other legitimate interpretation of canon law than one within a theological horizon.[12]

Pulling the threads together: answering the initial question

The question was: *What is the role of theology in the interpretation of canon law?*

The answer is: theology identifies the Christian values the law is meant to serve. Since canon law has no other purpose than to serve those values, and there is no other science to identify them than theology, there is no wholesome interpretation of canon law without theology.[13]

---

12. Obviously there has to be discretion in interpreting canon law from a theological point of view. Theology will be far less applicable in the matter of property contracts than in that of administering the sacraments.

13. Not all values served by canon law are theological values; hence canon law needs enlightenment (so to speak) from other sciences as well, such as philosophy, anthropology, psychology, sociology, etc.

The doctrine of the "canonization" of civil law is well known; we need to work out an analogous doctrine for "receiving" into canon law concepts (conclusions, findings) from other, especially empirical, sciences. Such "reception" of course has been taking place for a long time (e.g., every time the Roman Rota refers approvingly to a medical handbook) but I do not know of any study that has tried to unravel critically the principles behind it.

Needless to say canon law has every right to reject a scientific concept which is not based on proper research but on some kind of non-Christian philosophy of human nature—no less than it has the right to reject a civil law concept based on (say) racist theories.

There is a need in this matter for critical and foundational studies.

Canon law in a theological horizon

To place canon law into a new horizon is not unlike transferring an old piece of furniture from its old home for which it was made into a new building. Seemingly nothing is changed: the piece remains the same. Yet, everything is changed: the new surroundings will dictate the placing and the use of the old furniture.

Canon law, as it came down to us before the times of Vatican Council II, existed within its well defined and closed legal horizon. Now, without destroying its institutions, canon law must be placed into a broad theological landscape. Everything remains the same—seemingly. In reality, every institution must receive a new meaning, dictated by the new theological environment.

This transformation can be described also as conversion: Lonergan would have used that expression. For him conversion was the passage from a narrower horizon into a broader one. All that is and lives and moves in canon law must now be perceived and judged from a higher point of view: that is, from a theological point of view. Hence the need for a *novus habitus mentis,* a new attitude of mind, that Paul VI kept urging on canon lawyers.

I should correct myself at this point: no conversion takes place in the abstract. One science cannot move into the horizon of another. Only persons can go through the process of conversion, because ultimately only persons live within a horizon and have the capacity to move into a broader one. Hence, only canon lawyers convinced of the importance of theology in the interpretation of canon law can bring new life to our old institutions. Everything will turn on their personal conversion.

Enough of theory. The time has come to move into the field of practical applications and see what happens when theology does indeed play a role in the interpretation of canon law.

A hermeneutical principle of general application

In this section, I intend to give an overall hermeneutical principle, and theological at that, to be used in the interpretation of canon law. But before I do so, a misconception ought to be excluded.

The misconception to be discarded is that canon law exists and operates in a "purely juridical order," and that it is as autonomous there as civil law is independent in its own sphere. In truth, the nature of canon law is radically different from that of civil law because the nature of the church is radically different from that of the state. The church exists for the sake of the redemption of human persons, redemption through the proclamation of the good news of eternal life and through the dispensation of the sacraments. The state exists for the sake of creating order and peace in the community and assuring reasonable freedom and temporal prosperity for the citizens.

Every value that the church promotes must be permeated by its "supernatural" purpose. Or, as the Code puts it, "the salvation of souls must be the supreme law of the church," *salus animarum, quae in ecclesia suprema semper lex esse debet* (cf. canon 1792).

The correct conception of canon law places it in the order of salvation; it sees our whole legal system as part of the redeeming mission of the church. Such a mission is the very *raison d'être* of the church; it is a continuation of the mission of the Word made flesh, *qui propter nos homines et propter nostram salutem descendit de caelis,* "who for us human persons, and for our salvation, came down from heaven."

We often describe the nature and purpose of canon law by saying "it must be pastoral." I myself have used this expression many times.[14] But to say that the laws, all laws in the church, must work for our redemption might be an even better description of their special quality.

Such an approach leads directly to some hermeneutical questions.

For instance: Should laws ever impose acts of worship and devotion under the penalty of sin? Or should such norms be rather regarded as guides leading us to render common homage to God, out of that grace-filled fund of generosity that is present in every Christian community by the action of the Holy Spirit?[15]

Another question: Should we read all our laws concerning the laity in light of the principle that the laws' primary purpose is to liberate their energies for various services and ministries in the church? Will such reading give them a greater role than they enjoy now?

Further: How can we conceive a legal system that will speak more emphatically of the "servant church," merciful and compassionate toward all persons of good faith, be they Catholics or non-Catholics, believers or unbelievers?

14. See in particular "Principles of Interpretation," Section (3) "Pastoral orientation" in *Marriage in Canon Law* (Wilmington, Del.: Glazier, 1986) 43–45.

15. Observances concerning worship and penances were indeed created out of the generosity of the Christian communities, not by any law. It was not until the Middle Ages and later that "Law came in to increase the trespass" (Rom 5:20). But "Behold, the Lord's hand is not shortened" (Isa 59:1); we should not think that the gifts of the Spirit are less present and effective in the communities of today than they were in earlier times. Is it correct to say that in these matters the more we put our trust in the Spirit the less we are inclined to put our trust in sanctions imposed by man-made laws?

112 *Integrated Interpretation or The Role of Theology in Interpretation*

Such questions are not only legitimate, they are compulsory. But admittedly to find the answers, which ought to be wise and measured, much time will be necessary, not to mention the need for enlightenment from above and for intelligence and ingenuity on our part.

Practical applications in particular: interpretation with the help of theology

I want to be very concrete now and show how theology can and must contribute to the interpretation of the laws of particular institutions. To achieve this, I shall quote some canons in which a close connection between theology and canon law is fairly obvious. Thus I hope to demonstrate by a few examples that the use of theological sources in the interpretation of some legal texts is indispensable.

> *Canon 752:*
> No assent of faith
> but religious *obsequium* of mind and will
> must be given to a doctrine
> concerning faith and morals [*mores*] which
> either the pope or the episcopal college affirm
> in the exercise of their authentic teaching office
> even if they do not intend
> to proclaim it with a definitive act;
> the faithful therefore should avoid
> all that is not congruent with it.

The canon speaks of a dialectic: when the pope or the college of bishops exercise their magisterium, the faithful must respond with *obsequium*. Both concepts are very complex. Magisterium can be (usually is) exercised on several levels; accordingly, the doctrine proclaimed can be infallibly defined, or it can be brought close to such definition, or it can be an opinion stated with some force but still subject to correction, or it can be a tentative approach to the solution of a problem, etc. Undoubtedly, the *obsequium* must vary accordingly. But who can tell us about the levels of authority in the proclamation and the appropriate response? Theology, nothing else. A purely legal interpretation would lead us inevitably into a fixed position: whenever there is a magisterial voice, submission is required. Theology will tell us that whenever the magisterium speaks, the subject matter ought to be weighed and *obsequium* given in an appropriate measure. It could be an act of obedience of faith or an act of respectful critical assessment, which in its turn may be a contribution to the development of doctrine.[16]

> *Canon 960:*
> Individual and integral confession and absolution
> constitute the sole ordinary means
> by which a member of the faithful who is conscious of grave sin
> is reconciled with God and with the church. *(CIC-GBI)*

One of the key expressions is "the sole ordinary means." If we turn to canon law alone, it cannot tell us whether or not this statement represents an article of faith or a description of the contemporary practice of the church. If we turn to theological sources, they can enlighten us about the different ways the church has exercised its power to grant pardon in the course of its long history, and consequently help us to put this statement into the correct perspective. The means which is ordinary today was not ordinary in other times, consequently it cannot belong to the permanent core of the sacrament; yet it is one of the several authentic ways the church can grant pardon. An important point for the interpretation of the existing law, and even more for the making of new laws.[17]

> *Canon 1055 § 2:*
> . . . a valid marriage contract cannot exist
> between baptized persons
> without its being by that very fact a sacrament. *(CIC-GBI)*

No amount of laws can tell us whether or not a baptized person who has no faith in Christ has the capacity to receive a sacrament; it is a theological issue. If theology tells us that a baptized unbeliever cannot marry sacramentally, the law cannot do anything about it.[18] Thus with the help of theology (only!) can the interpreter determine that the canon refers only to those who are baptized and have faith. The true meaning of the canon could not be determined without theology.[19]

16. For a more detailed discussion see "The meaning of *obsequium*" in Ladislas Örsy, *The Church: Learning and Teaching* (Wilmington, Del.: Glazier, 1987) 82–89. The canon as it is simplifies a complex theological issue. Without regard to theology, a simplistic (and false) canonical interpretation can arise.

17. For a small sample of integrated exegesis (theological and legal) of some canons on penance see Ladislas Örsy, "The Sacrament of Penance," *Proceedings 1986* (Washington, D.C.: CLSA) 29–45.

18. Obviously "unbeliever" in this context does not mean those who are weak in their faith, but those, and only those, who have no faith at all.

19. *See* the excellent work of John Baptist Sequeira, *Tout mariage entre baptisés est-il nécessairement sacramentel?* (Paris: Cerf, 1985). He shows the vast historical and

Canon 1254 § 1:
The catholic church has the inherent right,
independently of any secular power,
to acquire, retain, administer and alienate temporal goods,
in pursuit of its proper objectives. *(CIC-GBI)*

The meaning of this "inherent right" could not be determined without taking into account the "inherent duty" not to accumulate wealth to the detriment of the common good. Moral theology alone is capable of giving some norms as to how the right balance should be achieved, a balance fitting for a community which professes that the poor are blessed. Had this right been interpreted always theologically, the excessive accumulation of wealth by the church might not have taken place, and in consequence the rightful resentment of the poor against the church and the eventual expropriations might not have followed, as they did at the time of the Reformation, or the French revolution, or the reunification of Italy.[20]

Many other specific canons could be quoted; in fact any canon which is a statement of belief or represents a theological opinion (they abound in Books II, III and IV) would require an interpretation from theological sources. Let me indicate briefly just a few more issues where no good interpretation of the law is feasible without sound theology.

The exercise of ecclesiastical authority can never be understood in a purely legal way: every act of *potestas regiminis*, power to govern or to judge, must be directed toward the redemption of persons.

doctrinal background to this canon. Sequeira holds that not all marriages of baptized persons are sacraments. For another opinion *see* Denis Baudot, *L'inséparabilité entre le contrat et le sacrement de mariage* (Rome, Università Gregoriana, 1987). The International Theological Commission seems to uphold (cautiously) Sequeira's view: ". . . the absence of personal faith compromises the validity of the sacrament." Cf. Michael Sharkey, ed., International Theological Commission: Texts and Documents, 1969-1985 (San Francisco: Ignatius, 1989) 168. When a question is so hotly debated, how could an interpreter find the true meaning of the relevant canon without taking into account the theological positions?

20. As far as I know there is no major work interpreting this canon from a theological point of view. The main question is: In what way do the "proper objectives" of the church determine and limit its rights? The unilateral application of the principle expressed in this canon can lead to an undue accumulation of wealth by ecclesiastical legal persons, as it did many times in the course of history. On the other hand, the church is certainly entitled to use created means to spread the good news. The elements that can lead to a balanced interpretation of the canon are certainly outside the world of law; they should be sought in the field of ecclesiology, or in that part of moral theology which deals with the obligations of the church toward the faithful and the human family.

The rules concerning worship must never be handled in the same way as disciplinary laws since their theological finality is to help the community to perceive and celebrate the presence of a divine mystery.

Penalties and sanctions must always operate in a context that is meant to heal both the wrongdoer and the community that was harmed.

All proceedings in a marriage case should be in the service of the persons who are in need of help, and not in the service of abstract rules and formalities. And so forth. There is certainly an immense field to be explored by those who are looking for dissertation topics![21]

Theological interpretation by the community of the faithful

Let me raise an additional question, closely related to our topic: is this theological interpretation reserved to the experts, or can it be done also, at least in some cases, by the community of the faithful? Do the latter have the capacity to discover values, and then create norms for their appropriation? The answer comes, in quite explicit terms, from Vatican Council II:

> For, by this sense of faith which is aroused and sustained by the Spirit of truth, God's People accepts not the word of men but the very Word of God (cf. 1 Th. 2:13). It clings without fail to the faith once delivered to the saints (cf. Jude 3), penetrates it more deeply by accurate insights, and applies it more thoroughly to life. All this it does under the lead of a sacred teaching authority to which it loyally defers. (*Lumen gentium*, 12 ABBOTT)

That is, the community has the capacity to come to correct insights into the word of God; to insights which then lead them to a thorough

---

21. As a matter of fact I am saying this to encourage our students to do some interdisciplinary studies. The pattern of such a dissertation could be:

first, determine from theology the values a given institution ought to serve (theological part);

second, examine critically the legal norms presently applicable to that institution (canonical part);

third, see how far the norms do or do not support the theological values (critical part: canon law is measured against theology);

fourth, propose norms which would be in full harmony with the values as established by the theological inquiry (creative part).

Such studies done in a quiet and competent way could do immense good to the church and in the long run they would be the best preparation for a third edition of the Code of Canon Law, no matter how distant in time the next revision may be.

application of the same Word to life. In theological terms, the council affirms that the assistance of the Spirit is given to the people of God, all of them, bishops and laity together, to discover Christian values and find the ways and means to reach out for them. This means obviously that there is a power (*dynamis* in biblical speech) in the Christian community to create good laws which can help to usher in the Kingdom.

The history of the church confirms abundantly the theological statement of the council. Many of the rules concerning the structures of the church or the celebration of the sacraments owe their origin not to any kind of central legislation but to the "supernatural instinct" of the community described so competently by the fathers of the council—a fact well known to anyone familiar with our history.

If God grants the assistance of the Spirit to the community (as he does), and if the community has proved that it can indeed act responsibly (as it has), it appears highly reasonable and desirable that the community should be given the practical possibility to create new applications of the word of God to life. If not, the church would be operating below its normal capacity; the assistance of the Spirit would be in vain.

It follows that a legal system which leaves no room for the contribution of the people as described in the conciliar documents but is built nearly entirely on statutory laws is theologically unsatisfactory. By denying any practical scope to the insights reached by the community, it makes the operation of the Spirit ineffective. The very nature of the church postulates that there should be a real and concrete possibility for the people to contribute.

Many of the faithful may not be able to articulate all this in a theological way; nonetheless, many are able with a "supernatural instinct of faith" to perceive the lack of balance and the consequent inadequacies. Should this happen, a resentment against, or an alienation from, the community may follow. Thus, there is wisdom in the old maxim re-stated in canon 27: "Custom is the best interpreter of laws." But there is also a latent irony in the fact that our legal system goes a long way to inhibit the emergence of customs.[22]

Yet, the church cannot be *whole* in the full sense of the term if there is no room for the community to contribute to the discovery of values

22. It is of some importance that the responses of the *Pontifical Council for the Interpretation of Legislative Texts* should not be so extensive and exhaustive that no room is left for any interpretation to develop by custom. If all doubts are decided by decrees, how could the community ever contribute? What would be the purpose of canon 27 at all?

and the building of the norms for their acquisition. "Customs" belong to the integrity of the church.[23]

The overall scope of the principle of integration

The principle of integration is much broader and reaches much further than the interpretation of laws. It ought to regulate the attitude and actions of all those who are in any way the stewards of the legal life of the church.

Before any law is enacted there ought to be a critical assessment of the values it intends to serve, and its suitability to do so. The act of promulgation should be an intelligent act of communication: the link of the law to the values which inspired it should be explained, so that the subjects can make a "reasonable sacrifice" (if a sacrifice it is) by accepting it. The capacity of the faithful to discover values for themselves and to build customary rules for upholding them should be respected.

Twofold conclusion

My conclusion is twofold: first on the level of ideals not easily reachable, second on the level of our fallen world where some significant steps can be taken toward the ideal.

On the level of ideals the next revision of canon law should begin by examining all our institutions, one by one, in order to determine the theological values which the law must uphold and serve. Then it should assess how far the existing norms measure up to the theological demands. If they do not, they should be duly amended. Obviously a dream; although this was the historical process by which our laws were conceived and established in the first place.[24]

On the level of our fallen world (by which I mean a world affected by original sin and its consequences) we can take many small steps toward the ideal. By steadily upholding the organic relationship be-

---

23. Much has been written about the contribution of the faithful to the development of doctrine, for instance the classical work of John Henry Newman, *On the Contribution of the Laity in the Development of Doctrine*. No major study exists, as far as I know, on the contribution of the faithful to the development of our legal system.

24. The last revision of law, of which the fruit is the Code of 1983, did not follow this process.

tween theological concepts and practical norms, we can in our daily work defend and promote the integrity of the church. By integrity I mean an internal harmony and unity, where all norms of action flow from a vision. In this, obviously, we shall never achieve perfection; it ought to be an on-going process.

8

Moral Theology and Canon Law: The Quest for a Sound Relationship

Setting the scene

The problem: alienation. To all the disinterested observers, it is a well known fact that at the present the relationship between canon law and moral theology at best is disturbed, at worst downright nonexistent. Yet, there should be an organic unity between the two; after all, moral theology defines many of the values that canon law is promoting, and canon law creates obligations which have far-reaching consequences in the field of morality. Thus, mutual understanding and a well balanced relationship should be in the interest of both sides.

The origins of this present day alienation are found in the past history of these two sciences. To listen to the moralists, their theology has suffered badly in the hands of the canonists: they tried to make it into a thinly disguised branch of jurisprudence.[1] To listen to the canonists, the nature of their rules and regulations have been mis-

---

1. The historical development of moral theology—certainly in the last four hundred years—was closely tied up with the administration of the sacrament of penance. Its main aim was to give guidance to confessors, specially for the purposes of assessing the right amount of penance. In this situation, theology lost sight of its own scriptural origins, paid relatively little attention to patristic thought and focused more on vices than on virtues. A positive aspect to the so called "crisis of the sacrament of penance" is that there is much less preoccupation with "helping the confessors" and some effort to return to authentic sources. See the excellent study by John Mahoney, *The Making of Moral Theology* (Oxford: Clarendon, 1987). For a complement to Mahoney's book *see* John A. Gallagher, *Time Past, Time Future* (New York: Paulist, 1990); mainly about moral theology in the post-Tridentine period, and its present day struggles.

understood by the moralists: they tended to make them into divine precepts with appropriate sanctions, including eternal damnation.[2]

All such accusations are, of course, simplifications.

None the less, among the unfair generalizations there is a grain of truth. In the post-Tridentine centuries, the two sciences often encroached on each other's field, and by the introduction of an unsuitable methodology confused the issues and contributed to wrong conclusions. To avoid such calamities, an effort should be made to determine their mutual relationship so that each can enjoy its proper autonomy, while providing support for the other.

I said an effort should be made: this is precisely what I intend to do, by raising some foundational questions and proposing a few answers. A full explanation may still remain to be given, but if no effort is made to find some insights, the goal will never be attained.

The question "What is the relationship between moral theology and canon law?" sounds like a simple one. After all, who could not tell the difference? Yet, on reflection, the question reveals itself as pointing to bewilderingly complex issues. The two fields do not lend themselves to any easy comparison. Moral theology speaks of virtues and vices, canon law issues ordinances. The former's field of vision is much broader than the latter's field of action. Also, moral theology likes to ascend to sublime principles while canon law keeps descending to concrete life situations. How can such disparate entities (or disciplines) be compared to each other?[3]

---

2. This happens every time a moral sanction is attached to a legal norm; in the ecclesiastical literature such moral sanction is declared when non-observance is judged sinful. Such judgment normally should come only from moral theology.

It is a historical fact that in post-Tridentine times moral theologians worked by the principle that whenever there was an official rule guiding the Christian community, there had to be a supernatural sanction attached to it in the form of sin. Norms which did not bind under sin were allowed to exist (as far as I know) in the constitutions of some religious communities only. Yet, there is no conceivable reason why the church could not give guidance to the community, to be accepted and followed generously, but never binding under the penalty of sin.

3. The problem of the relationship between morality and laws is not unique to canon law: Socrates already struggled with the same issue, and so do our contemporaries. Legal positivism in its various forms claims full autonomy for the law: it should not depend on any norm or convention of morality. This means that law is not subject to any control: it becomes a norm for itself. If such a theory is accepted by the judges of a nation, all a tyrant need do is to issue laws according to his or her own whim; the courts will feel duty bound to uphold them on the principle that "law is law."

For a good introduction into the problem of the relationship between values

Locating the problem. Indeed, even at first sight it is clear that moral theology and canon law cannot be compared to each other as two branches of the same science, or as two species of the same genus. Their mutual relationship cannot be explained by such categories: it is of a different type. Another approach is needed.

To find it, we must go back to the very source of their existence. This source is in the consciousness of the church.

By "church" I do not mean just the theologians and canonists, nor the hierarchy alone. I mean the whole community of believers, which is an organically structured communion. In it, every organ, the head and the various members, play their appointed role and contribute to the life of the whole. Indeed, at one time or another in Christian history, all made some contribution toward the development of ethical doctrine, as well as toward the building of structures and customs.

When this church articulates its beliefs concerning the Christian way of life and then reflects on them, moral theology is born.[4] When the church perceives itself as an organic community and decides to have rules to uphold order and harmony and binds the faithful to observe those rules, canon law is born.[5] When those who are so bound accept the obligation in conscience and act on it, the law becomes a vital force and shapes and forms the community.

Thus, we are dealing with three logically distinct moments in the consciousness of the church. The relationship, therefore, between moral theology and canon law cannot be grasped in any other way than by turning our attention to those three connected moments; they belong to the rhythm of life of the earthly church.

and laws in secular legal systems, *see* Peter Stein and John Shand, *Legal Values in Western Society* (Edinburgh: University Press, 1974).

4. The term "theology" is used in a rich sense here, as it was by the Greek Fathers. It includes not only reflective study on the data of revelation but also the proclamation of the revealed truth. To speak about Christian morality can be indeed *theo-logia*, God-talk, because it proclaims and explains the thoughts of God about the Way that leads to him.

5. At this point a warning should be sounded: not all laws are in the Code; nor is the Code all laws. Often enough, canon law is understood as "everything that is found in the Code of Canon Law." This assumption is incorrect on two counts. First, there are laws which are not in the Code, e.g., the particular law that governs the operation of the Roman curia is not in the Code. Second, there are many canons in the Code which are anything but law, such as dogmatic statements, theological or philosophical positions, and exhortations—the latter not in small numbers. Of course, there are also numerous canons defining with precision rights and duties enforceable in courts. The Code of Canon Law is a practical manual about the life of the church, mainly but not exclusively in legal terms.

So, the next step in our inquiry should be a brief presentation of those three moments. Before doing so, however, a cautionary remark is in order.

I have no intention of describing in any detail the relationship (or the lack of it), as it exists *de facto* at this point of history, between moral theology and canon law—at which relationship I hinted in my introductory remarks. Such a work would be, of course, perfectly legitimate and possibly desirable, but it would fall outside the scope of this inquiry. What I intend to undertake is a sorely needed study of the ideal, in order to find the normative elements for the real. We cannot even begin to answer the question as to how to establish in practice a sound relationship between moral theology and canon law, if we do not have a well grounded theory as to what that relationship ought to be. For this reason, this work is a normative study.

Three moments

Since both disciplines originate in the consciousness of the church, the initial questions should be What is the church doing, (1) when it is doing moral theology; (2) when it is creating a system of laws; (3) when it receives the laws?

The answers will be found in observing what happens in those three moments.

(1) What is the church doing when it is doing moral theology? By speaking of the church, I shift the inquiry from the positions found in manuals to the operations of the church as I defined it above, the organic communion of believers. This church *is* doing moral theology, and doing it on several levels.

Receiving the Word. The community of the faithful under the guidance of the Spirit receives the word of God. The Word tells them about the Way they must follow in order to enter the kingdom. The community in its turn proclaims the Word, for all generations to come. To hold and to announce what has been revealed is to do theology in the most ancient and fullest sense of the term: it is to speak of things divine.

Reflecting on the Word. The activity of the church, however, does not stop there: faith seeks intelligence, *fides quaerit intellectum*. Reflections on the basic beliefs follow, prompted both by a natural desire to penetrate the Word more thoroughly, and through new questions raised by believers and unbelievers. In this process, professional theologians play a leading role: they gather the relevant data from the usual theological sources and resources, which are the Scriptures, the Fathers, the councils, the various magisterial pronouncements, the consensus of the faithful, and so forth. Thus a systematic exposition of Christian ethics develops, usually with the help of a philosophy, which provides the inquirers with convenient concepts and categories.

All this is well and good, but it seems to apply to any branch of theology. What then is specific in the endeavor of creating a moral theology? This specificity is the fact that the inquiry concentrates on the discovery of values and on the obligation to appropriate them. The object of moral theology is to find out the truth about the good.

It cannot be stressed enough that the proper and primary objects of all ethical inquiries in the Christian church are the positive values and the equally positive acts for their appropriation, not the "disvalues" nor the morally deficient actions. In other terms, moral theology is first and foremost the science of the good and not of the evil; of the virtues and not of the sins. Indirectly and secondarily, of course, it deals with those situations where the absence of good or the omission of an action leaves a vacuum—and consequently improper objects and blameworthy acts enter into the scene.[6]

(2) What is the church doing when it is creating a system of laws? To begin with, the church perceives itself as an organic community; that is, not just a mass of individual believers who happen to be together at this point of space and time, but a body of believers assembled and held together by the Spirit of God, one person in many persons. The church recognizes also that this internal unity must express itself externally; the members must form an organized society.

Once the church has perceived itself as a social body, it must provide for the needs of such a body. It must grow from strength to strength if it is to fulfill its function, which is to gather God's children and nourish them with the Word and the sacraments. In this process the legal norms play an integral role.

Instinctively and reflectively (both!), through the instrumentality of legal rules, the church prompts the faithful to establish good social balances which favor the operations and the growth of each and all. The growth takes place through the appropriation of good things, or values, which contribute to the welfare of the community.

Thus, canon law, too, is in the service of values, but in a way different from moral theology. The values in which it is interested are defined and circumscribed by the needs of the community as community,

---

6. This perception of moral theology is in harmony with the classical definition of evil: it is nothing else than the undue absence (privation) of good.

as an organic social body. Moreover, its interest in these values is on the level of decision and action, not on the level of abstract definitions.

(3) What is the church doing when it receives the laws? When a law is promulgated and enters into force, those who are bound to the community are bound also to observe its law. But each of the members is an intelligent and free person, and they would not live up to their dignity if their obedience to the law would be like the movement of a robot. Their duty is to learn about the value that the law intends to uphold, and then to choose freely to reach out for it. This is to offer a rational sacrifice to God.[7] The authentic reception of the law is an act of obedience born from an intelligent and free conscience.

Indeed, no human law can go any further than to present itself to the conscience of a person. His or her moral convictions will dictate the response. Thus, at the threshold of that luminous space the law asks to be admitted. Inside, the knowledge gathered from moral theology will give the guidance for a response. Ordinarily, this should be the observance of the law; but there will always be situations, perhaps rare and extraordinary, when norms taken from theology will override the claim of the law.[8]

In the crucible of the conscience, moral theology remains the first counsellor.

Continuity

There is a continuity between the three moments, between seeing the morally good, binding the community by laws, and accepting the obligation. In all three, the acting subject is the same: the church.

---

7. Such an ideal, however, is not necessarily diminished or destroyed if a person does not personally inquire about the value that is behind the law; many may well decide to trust the judgment of the legislator.

8. One of the finest essays written on conscience is by René Carpentier, "Conscience," *Dictionnaire de Spiritualité*, vol. 2, part 2 (Paris: Beauchesne, 1953), cols. 1548–1575. A passage, very much to our point, deserves to be quoted:
> Or la loi retentit dans la conscience actuelle. C'est dans les jugements *concrets* de ma conscience que je perçois la loi divine avec son caractère essentiel d'obligation. Sans doute des préceptes divins ont été extérieurement formulés par révélation: le décalogue, les lois évangéliques concernant la charité, les sacrements, l'Eglise. D'autre part, toute loi humaine exige une promulgation explicite et donc une formulation précise. A vrai dire, cependant, toute obligation repose sur la promulgation intérieure de la loi divine élémentaire, laquelle se fait entendre dans la syndérèse, elle-même ne s'actualisant que dans la conscience. (Ibid., col. 1550.)

It is the same *persona mystica* which first finds the definition of certain values in the revealed word of God and proclaims them, then perceives itself as a community in need of binding rules and norms, and finally through the intelligent and free response of the members elevates the law into a vital force for the health and growth of the whole social body.

The primary source of continuity is then in the operating subject: the church who knows, decides and acts. But there is more.

In all three moments the operations of the church revolve around values. Moral theology speaks of the values by which Christian persons must live. A system of laws binds the people to pursue certain values. When the faithful obey those laws they personally accept the obligation to reach out for those values.

Thus, the secondary but no less authentic source of continuity is in the object of the church's activities: they are about values.

Let us turn now more specifically to the differences which appear in the first two moments; that is, between doing moral theology and creating a system of laws.

Diversity

There are differences on several counts: (1) in the very *purpose* of the operations; (2) in the *nature* of those operations; and (3) in the *result* they produce.

(1) Different purposes. In doing moral theology the church is seeking knowledge: *fides quaerens intellectum*. The field of search extends far and wide, to wherever the seeds of truth can be found. It includes all Christian literature, the grace-filled experiences of Christian communities, and all other sources which may be relevant for forming judgments on values and on the actions of persons. It embraces also the realm of some auxiliary sciences, such as philosophy, psychology, anthropology, sociology, as needed in any given investigation. The aim is the critical use of the information that they can offer, in view of forming ethical judgments. But once those judgments are formulated, moral theology does not go any further; its aim to gather knowledge is fulfilled. To act on that knowledge is not the task of scientific inquiry: decisions are made by persons.

In doing canon law, the purpose of the church is action, *fides quaerens actionem*. The initial search is for values, but with a restriction: the legislator is interested in those values only which are necessary or useful for the welfare of the Christian community as community. Thus, while he may well turn his attention to the corpus of knowledge that the moral theologians are able to offer, he will examine it with the view of selecting some values which can be proposed to the community by legislation. His aim is the practical appropriation of those values.

Briefly: in one case the purpose is knowledge, in the other case it is action.

(2) Particular methods. There is a method to reach knowledge, and there is another to lead a community to action. Knowledge is reached by a process which moves step by step from gathering concrete data to the formulation of abstract principles. If all goes well, it ends with a systematically ordered and cohesive body of science. In substance, this is the method of moral theology.

Canon law works differently. Once the legislator is in possession of the necessary information,[9] he makes the decision about binding the community to appropriate certain values. The promulgation of the law is really the communication of this decision; through it the members of the community are bound to action. In brief, this is the method of legislation. The picture is not very different in the case of laws created by custom, except that the decision to have a norm is formulated implicitly and by frequent usage out of the collective wisdom of the group.

To sum up: there is a method for acquiring knowledge, and another for binding people to action.[10]

(3) Varying results. In the case of moral theology, the end result is a body of systematically organized knowledge of the Christian way of life, perhaps all neatly laid out as a treatise. But, no matter how well such an exposition is done, it is not complete, and will never be so. After all, no theologian can ever exhaust the mysteries, and the Way to the kingdom is part of those mysteries. It follows that moral the-

---

9. That information can come only from theology, in many cases from moral theology. Further, since he intends to impose some action on the community, he must be well informed about its capacity to reach out for the value intended; to ask for too much may lead to non-observance.

10. These two paragraphs are no more than brief pointers toward the extensive analyses of the method of reaching knowledge and the method of coming to a decision. I assume that the reader is familiar with some major works on the topic, such as Lonergan's *Insight* and *Method in Theology*, among many others. For an inquiry about the unfolding of a human person through action, an issue closely related to the making and obeying of the laws (although not directly on that subject), see the excellent work by Joseph de Finance, *L'affrontement de l'autre* (Rome: Università Gregoriana, 1973).

ology is open-ended, because the search for the full understanding of the mysteries will never end.

Not so in the case of canon law. Since its goal is to bring God's people to action, in its final formulation it should not contain any mystery; it must be clear, pointing with precision to an action to be performed.[11] When a norm is presented to those whom it intends to bind, it must be simple and direct—even if it handles complicated matters. Those qualities are also prime hermeneutical factors in the interpretation of any law: the interpreter must assume that the legislator intends to communicate a well defined decision. It would be a fallacy to think that the longer and deeper an explanation of the law is, the closer the interpreter comes to its original sense. The opposite may be true: extensive explanations can destroy the directness of the legislator and obscure the action to be performed.

This difference in results can be put in this way, too: in moral theology there will be always more mysteries to unravel and more questions to answer, while in canon law there comes a point when questions must come to a halt and an action must be performed.[12]

11. The penalty for any law which does not reach this ideal is death, nothing less: *lex dubia lex nulla*, a doubtful law is no law at all. The church knows this principle well and honors it.

When I say that at the final stage the law should not contain any mystery, I do not imply that it should not be, or could not be, formulated in a technical language. As a matter of fact every science develops its own language, mostly incomprehensible to the non-initiated. One purpose of the interpretation of the law is to translate the technical expressions into ordinary language, so that the action can be easily understood and performed. A good interpreter always ends up with a clear definition of the action or an admission that the law is not clear, hence there is no law.

If an interpreter treats the law as a mystery (method of theology!) the end product of his or her work is likely to be endless variations on a theme with no clear direction for action: this defeats the very purpose of the law. Clarity, brevity, conciseness, on the model of the great Roman lawyers (e.g., Gaius) are the signs of a competent approach to law—canon law included.

12. In the practical order this means that dedicated moral theologians will never find themselves at the limit of their science: there is always more to learn about faith, hope and love. Not so with canon lawyers: when they define the action to be performed, there is no more to be said about the law; the next step is the action itself.

If canon lawyers trained in theology are not alert to this fact, they may handle canon law as if they had at hand a theological text. The result will be long disquisitions on many possible meanings and hidden significances of the law—and the directness and simplicity of it will be lost in the process. The wisdom of a canon lawyer is in knowing at what point to stop with the explanations.

Theology has priority

We have reached the point where we can return to our quest for the determination of a sound relationship between moral theology and canon law. By simple inference, we have already a foundational principle, not in need of any further demonstration: moral theology occupies a position of priority vis-à-vis canon law. This priority manifests itself in several ways: (1) in defining values, (2) in setting the parameters for the creation of laws in general, (3) in guiding the making of the laws for particular institutions.

(1) Moral theology has priority in determining values. There can be little doubt about this proposition. Moral theology aims for knowledge, canon law aims for decision and action. Now knowledge always ought to precede decision and action. It follows that there is a genuine relationship of dependence between the two disciplines: the ordinances of the law must follow the confirmed insights of moral theology.

(2) Moral theology sets the parameters for law making. Legal norms in the Christian community cannot, and must not, operate independently within some kind of a self-defined order (*ordo iuridicus*). They must be part of the theological life of the community, which means they must sustain and promote a life of faith, hope and love. In the *ecclesia*, the gathering of the faithful, the theological virtues give sense and purpose to every single norm.

This implies a lot: moral theology has a critical role to play vis-à-vis canon law. It can set the parameters for the law makers, it can tell them how far to go or not to go. It can give guidance for those who are implementing and interpreting the law: it can guide them in keeping the law in the service of the theological virtues.

Such guidance is all the more necessary because the prudential actions of the legislators are not protected by the charism of infallibility, or for that matter by the charism of the highest degree of prudence. Hence mistakes can occur and the delicate balances of the community can become disturbed. There could be so much law that it overshadows the theological virtues; or there could be so little that it leads to anarchy. The right measure is found only when absolute priority is given to faith, hope and love—the prime objects of moral theology.

One hears often that the church is not an absolute monarchy but a "constitutional" one, in reference either to the papacy or the episcopacy. The implication is that the pope or a local bishop is bound to respect certain well defined structures laid down by divine law. Rarely is it mentioned that the pope and the local bishops, and everybody else who is entrusted with any power in the church, is bound by a set of moral precepts to use their power the best way they can for the promotion of faith, hope and love. History leaves no illusion that failures are possible, either by not reaching for the greater good, or by omitting action altogether where it is due. Such failures need not be classified as violations of the constitutional structures of the church but as failures to live up to the moral principles which guide the use of a sacred trust.[13]

(3) Moral theology must be the guide in the creation and application of the laws of particular institutions. In Aquinas' theology there is some parallelism between the statutes and the sacraments of the church: both are (although in different ways) the external signs of God's redeeming grace.[14] The laws are not, of course, the grace-filled symbols that the sacraments are; none the less, they play a major part in creating the right environment for them and provide the rules for their administration.

In creating those laws, the legislator appears to be sovereignly free. He is—from a merely legal point of view. From a moral point of view he is not free. He is bound by a trust deed: the deed of our redemption. He has received his power for a purpose, which is to complete the saving work of the Lord: a theological enterprise, if ever there was one! It is good logic to affirm that theology alone is competent to guide him.

So much for a general theory. The question still remains as to how to find this guidance in the case of particular institutions.

There are too many particular institutions in the church to give a solution which would be suitable for each one of them. Yet a pattern of search can be indicated which is powerful enough to guide the legislator toward conceiving and formulating the theologically best grounded laws for them. Such a pattern I do propose, in the form of a structured sequence of questions. Hearing them at first, they may

---

13. To clarify those principles is certainly part of the task of moral theology. Yet, understandably enough, moral theologians have shied away from writing treatises on "The use of the sacred power." Historians, dealing with the past, are bolder and do not hesitate to judge past popes and bishops not only on the basis of their respect for constitutional structures but on their moral standards in using the powers entrusted to them; the *History of the Popes* of Pastor is full of such judgments.

14. On this issue see the remarkable study by Manuel Carretero Useros, "*Statuta Ecclesiae*" y "*Sacramenta Ecclesiae*" *en la Eclesiologia de St. Tomás de Aquino* (Roma: Università Gregoriana, 1962).

sound quite innocent and simple; but their penetrating force will soon be sensed by anyone who tries to answer them.

Collegiality. Here is the pattern of questions, conducive toward theological guidance:
- What are the values that the practice of collegiality (universal and regional, vertical and horizontal) can bring to the community?
- What are the best means (consultations, synods, councils, etc.) to obtain those values to their greatest extent?
- Who is morally bound to promote those means in order to let the whole church benefit from the values of collegial actions?

Once these questions are raised and answered, the legislative project can get under way. This too, may sound simple; in practice it may demand many years of sustained effort.

Ecumenism. The same pattern can be used but with other specifications:
- What are the values that unity can bring to the separated churches and communities?
- By what actions can those values be obtained? (Dialogues, working together for good causes, reducing within our own household practices which unnecessarily alienate others, etc.)
- Who has moral obligation to act?

In the process we may well discover that the theological value of unity is much greater than the preservation of some of our cherished but not essential traditions.

Fundamental rights in the church. This issue is debated far and wide in the religious and secular press; responsible contributions are certainly needed.[15]
- What are the fundamental rights of the faithful? (This question is already answered quite well in the new Code. Note that behind every right there is usually a potential from which the church can benefit.)
- How can those rights (potentials) be given full scope for the common good; how can they be protected if they are hampered or violated? (The Code offers some weak and mostly ineffective measures, as a matter of fact available only to those who can afford to pursue a long and often expensive process.)
- Who are morally bound to protect those rights (by legislation, judicial action, etc.) and what is the degree of their moral obligation? (An unexplored field in moral theology.)

---

15. On this issue we have a well written and tightly reasoned study by Paul Hinder, *Grundrechte in der Kirche* (Freiburg, Switzerland: Universitätsverlag, 1977).

Sacraments, in particular eucharist and penance.
- What are the values that a given sacrament brings to the community? (Nourishment for life; forgiveness and healing.)
- By what means can the church make such values most accessible to those who need them and are fit to receive them?
- Is the church morally bound to make these sacraments as accessible as dogma allows? ("Dogma should never be wronged": a saying from the East expressing our common tradition.)

Ecclesiastical property. This has been a topic for burning questions throughout the history of the church.
- What is the nature of the goods owned by the church? (Sacred, was the answer throughout history, but before the eighth century the prevailing opinion was that since they were sacred, whatever was left over had to be given to the poor; after, since they were sacred, they had to be kept.) What are the values which church property ought to support?
- What are the ways and means of supporting those values? (Law will play a leading role.)
- Who has moral obligations in this field and what are they? (Again, one could envisage an indepth moral treatise on the use of the assets of the church.)

Procedures, in particular marriage annulments.
- What are the values the church is seeking in a judicial procedure? (To redeem and heal the persons who have been hurt, innocently or culpably.)
- What are the best means to achieve such purposes?
- What are the moral duties of the legislator to provide the best means and do away with others, if so warranted?

Enough of the examples: what a program! The same sequence of questions could be repeated for every single institution.[16] My purpose was to show that a fairly simple but searching pattern of questions on

---

16. My questions should not be read as if they were affirmations. In the history of theology, perhaps no-one has raised more questions than St. Thomas Aquinas, and some of his questions were patently absurd, such as "Is there a God?" This was his method of getting at the truth. Canon law undoubtedly suffered from the fact that after the Council of Trent it contained too many affirmations and too few questions—especially fundamental questions. If it is a true science, it can afford questions, any questions. There has never been a better way of setting out to find the truth. Of course, a rational and responsible inquiry must follow.

the part of moral theology could help canon law to fulfill its purpose, which is to remain in the service of theological values.[17]

Service to theology

By now it may look as if canon law altogether depended on theology, but had very little to contribute to the theological enterprise. This is of course not true. Let me just mention two substantial contributions.

One is to help the community through the bond of the law and the light contained in it to appropriate certain moral values; this should be fairly evident from all that has been said before. In fact, in many ways canon law supports the moral life of the community. When a canon says that a just wage should be paid to all employees of the church, the law is imposing with special force on all employers a minimum standard of charity.

Another is that the law can create structures which provide "free space" for those who are doing theological research and reflection, and can restrain others from interfering with this protected territory. Further, it can provide remedies in case of undue interference. This is no mean service.[18]

---

17. Before closing this section, I wish to raise one more question of a somewhat general nature: Would it be profitable to have a critical study of the Code of Canon Law from the point of view of moral theology as a science of the virtues? The point would not be in looking for faults and failures, but to see if our laws correspond in everything to the highest demands of faith, hope and charity.

Please, note here the words "to the highest demands." Obviously the laws and ordinances of the church are born of faith, hope and charity. But the law maker is not divinely guaranteed to act according to the *highest* degree of prudence, or, for that matter, to the *highest* degree of charity. Therefore it is legitimate, even necessary, to examine and re-examine those human acts in the church and expose them to the "mirror of the gospel" in order to ascertain that they correspond indeed "to the highest demands."

A study, as indicated, done by competent persons cannot but be enriching for the church. If at the end the answer is yes, our laws fit the highest demands, we have gained a great deal because we know how to continue. If the answer is no, the knowledge will help us to make the laws better instruments in supporting the theological virtues.

18. The issue is really much bigger than the service done by canon law to moral theology. A substantial study would be needed on the service of law (or "order") to the word of God and to the sacraments. Canon law has a *raison d'être* as far, and only as far, as it is in the service of those two.

The nature of canonical science

The dependence of canon law on theology throws some light on the very nature of the science of canon law. It shows that (1) canon law is an ecclesial science; (2) it can be correctly interpreted in an ecclesial context only; (3) it must be an *ordinatio caritatis*.

(1) Canon law proper is essentially an ecclesial science. Because it is in the service of faith, hope and charity, it takes on a dimension that civil law can never have. The latter remains within the parameters of the temporal welfare of the community; the former has for parameters the theological virtues. It follows that there is an essential difference between the two, and the method of the one cannot be transferred without some substantial accommodations to the other.[19]

---

19. Eugenio Corecco (former Professor of Canon Law at the University of Fribourg, Switzerland, now the bishop of Lugano) distinguishes four stages in the development of the science of canon law: the sapiential, the techno-juridical, the apologetic and the theological.

> Well before the last two decades this science [*canon law*] had indeed already entered upon the fourth stage of its development despite the resistances of many kinds persisting in a doctrinal approach that can still claim justification in various—outdated—elements of the Code [*of 1983*]. This fourth phase is the theological phase and is based on the acceptance of theology as co-essential for the development of a general theory of canon law. It was preceded by the sapiential phase of the first millennium, the techno-juridical phase of the golden age that had its origins in Roman law, and the apologetic phase of the *ius publicum ecclesiasticum* that was based on natural law.

See "Aspects of the Reception of Vatican II in the Code of Canon Law" in *The Reception of Vatican II*, Giuseppe Alberigo, Jean Pierre Jossua, and Joseph A. Komonchak, eds. (Washington, D.C.: The Catholic University, 1987) 295.

In substance I agree with these divisions, although I would describe them somewhat differently. (1) In the first millennium canon law responded pragmatically to problems of order in the church; it was a creature of Christian common sense. As yet it was not a science; also it remained very close to a non-scientific theology. (2) The age of reflection and abstraction began in the twelfth century. Canon law developed as a science on the pattern of classical Roman and later Byzantine jurisprudence; initially theology had a strong impact on it which, however, decreased gradually. (3) The sixteenth century was the beginning of a new age marked by lack of creativity in the traditional body of laws (due mainly to the prohibition to comment on the Tridentine decrees), and by the rise of the "public ecclesiastical law" which was marked strongly by late scholasticism; further, legal writings became verbose to an excess and interested in myriads of minutiae, which led also to burdensome impositions on the faithful: a complex period perhaps best called the post-Tridentine age. (4) After Vatican II canon law no less than other ecclesiastical sciences reached back to its roots, not so much historically as systematically,

(2) The ecclesial context is an essential hermeneutical element for authentic interpretation. As the creation of canon law takes place in an ecclesial context, it follows that its interpretation must move in the same context too. Admittedly, this is not always the case.

The norms can be read by those who are inside the community and their meanings reconstructed in the context in which they were conceived; also, the norms can be read by those who are outside of the community and then given meanings without reference to, or in variance with, the doctrinal context in which they were created. In other terms, the laws of the church can be interpreted within their own religious horizon, or without it. The diverse approaches may then generate different conclusions. Nothing surprising in that: the field of vision of the interpreter clearly affects the significance of the concepts interpreted.

The important thing to remember is that the interpretation in a religious horizon is more likely to be correct since it is within the field where the norm was born. The interpretation within a secular horizon is bound to leave out important elements, or could conceivably project alien elements into the norm.

The same considerations apply to the history of canon law. The norms in the church arose in the context of the Christian mysteries, and they made sense because of the mysteries. It follows that there cannot be a full historical explanation of them, except by taking into account the same factors that brought them into existence in the first place. To recall this is not idle speech.

The mysteries which were the reasons for the creation of a law were usually not written into the text; therefore, when centuries later researchers read it, they may fail to give any thought to the theological doctrine which inspired the very law they are reading! How could anyone, for instance, interpret correctly the *Penitentials* of the early Middle Ages without being familiar with the development of the dogma of forgiveness?[20]

and increasingly realized its necessary dependence on theology. Today there is a strong trend to bring canon law back to where it belongs, but there is perhaps an equally strong effort to keep it in an autonomous "juridical order." It is still too early to name this age the "theological" one in the history of canon law—no matter how much I would like to see it that way. The situation is unsettled.

20. The thesis that for the full understanding of laws the doctrine which inspired them must be taken into account is not peculiar to canon law. Civil laws often reflect the social philosophy of the political party which enacted them. When courts speak of the "intention" of the legislator, they often admit the impact of a philosophy on the meaning of the laws. Historians are usually more explicit in

Since canon law is well known and researched inside and outside the church, we can take it for granted that there will always be two approaches to it, one in a religious context, another in a secular one. They may even produce two sciences, close and distant at the same time.[21] We have to remember that only the one "within" can do full justice to the texts. Of course, no other interpretation should be used for our own pastoral purposes.

In brief, the proper locus of interpretation of our laws is the redeeming church, and inside of it, the overriding truth of redemption must govern the meanings of the norms.

(3) Ordinatio caritatis: a response to Sohm. Rudolph Sohm (1841-1917) was an outstanding scholar in civil and canon law, as well as an eminent historian. He put forward the opinion that there is a contradiction between the concept of law and the essence of the church; the church therefore must be free of laws. According to him, this was the case in the beginning of Christianity, but law began to penetrate the communities at the end of the first century and reached its culmination with the "corporation" law of the medieval canonists. The evangelical church returned to the original purity, but the Roman church continues to be a *Rechtskirche,* a society held together by coercion; that is, by law, in clear contradiction to the evangelical doctrine.[22] His opinion was well received among Protestant divines because it was in har-

---

these matters and they discuss at length the impact of a philosophy on the meaning of the laws.

21. The secular interpretation is found mostly in universities where canon law is taught in the context of civil law. Then both laws are presented as being part of the same juridical order; from there it is a small step to the applying of the principles and methods of civil jurisprudence to canon law. This effect on the science of canon law can never be avoided; it remains a living demonstration of what happens when the same norms are put into two different horizons, one sacred, another secular, and interpreted accordingly.

22. Sohm's doctrine is easy to understand if his concepts of church and law are recalled. For him, the church of Christ is invisible. Law means a coercive norm. Law is the instrument of order in an autonomous, visible society, such as the state. Obviously, starting from such premises, there must be a contradiction between the very essence of law and that of the church.

Sohm has re-interpreted the whole history of the church in the light of these dogmatic premises.

For references in general *see* the article "Sohm" in *Die Religion in Geschichte und Gegenwart,* 3d ed., vol. 6 (Tübingen: Mohr, 1962) cols. 116-117. For references to publications in English *see* "Sohm" in *The Encyclopedia of Religion,* vol. 13 (New York: Macmillan, 1986) 405.

136 *Moral Theology and Canon Law: The Quest for a Sound Relationship*

mony with Luther's ideas, but it was rejected by Catholic theologians and canon lawyers, who argued that the church was both a spiritual communion and ordered society, and that both elements belonged to its very nature, complementing each other in harmony. For good measure, the Catholics often invoked the "perfect society" theory to refute Sohm.

Undoubtedly, Sohm had been influenced by his own evangelical tradition which asserted that the church was a purely spiritual and invisible gathering of God's people. Nevertheless, his exaggerated views (which not even the German evangelicals accept in their original form any more) can serve as a healthy warning that charity should never be overshadowed by the law in a Christian community. Thus, in some way Sohm had a point: the church ought to be a community of love and not of law *as law is understood in the secular society*. But, and this is said in correction to Sohm, the church can have a legal system in an ecclesial sense; that is, a system which springs from, and remains under the control of, the theological virtue of charity.

Indeed, law in the church could be defined as *ordinatio caritatis*; it could be rightly called the "minimum of charity."[23] Unfortunately we do not have a proper name for ecclesiastical norms to distinguish them from civil law; canon "law" insinuates an analogy too close for comfort. The World Council of Churches prefers the expression "church order" in place of "law"; it certainly puts the emphasis on the ecclesial character of the norms.

A practical proposal

Presently we have a Code of Canon Law which contains not only norms concerning right and duty situations, but exhortations and encouragements which belong to the proper domain of moral theology.

---

23. For the expression "law is the minimum of charity," and even more for the doctrine that is behind it, I willingly give the credit to René Carpentier, once my professor of moral theology at the *Facultés St. Albert de Louvain* in Belgium. *See* also note 8 in this chapter.

Precisely because law in the Christian church is both a norm and act of charity, it must be open for exceptions and accommodations when so warranted. Thus the church received and developed the legal devices of *epieikeia*, equity, *oikonomia* and dispensation. The most theological among them is *oikonomia*, economy, honored in theory and practice in the Eastern church. For more information on these devices which can and must keep the law within the sphere of charity, *see* Ladislas Örsy, "General Norms, Notes," *The Code of Canon Law: a Text and Commentary*, James A. Coriden and others, eds. (New York: Paulist, 1985) 41–44.

It would help the community of the faithful if those two themes were physically separated from each other. There could be a "code" for strictly right and duty situations, such as legal relationships concerning contracts, properties, offices, etc.; and there could be a "Book of Christian Way of Life" exhorting the faithful to show their unity with the community by the devotional reception of the sacraments and by the observance of holy days and seasons.

If there is a resentment in the Christian community against canon law, it is not because the church makes laws for strictly right and duty situations, but because spiritual services have been put into the categories of a "juridical order" and imposed on people as such. They sense that something went wrong even if they cannot articulate it. In fact, what appears to be a "resentment" may well be the correct sentiment, dictated by nothing less than the *sensus fidelium* which does not arise without the assistance of the Spirit.

Conclusion

If it was not clear in the beginning it should be so by now that we are dealing with two sciences which are going through a period of ferment and change; it is all the more difficult to determine their relationship. Moral theology is in the process of shaking off much of its historical accretions, such as an excessive casuistry and a preoccupation with the negative aspects of morality. It is also surging to a new life, nourished from the authentic sources of Christian spirituality. Canon law is slowly abandoning a false autonomy and a dependence on secular legal philosophy nurtured mainly by the "perfect society" theory. It is also discovering itself as an ecclesial science in the service of faith, hope and love.[24]

Throughout our study we searched for the principles of a sound relationship between the two sciences, for a kind of universal equation that would do justice to both. Such an equation may not be precisely formulated as yet. But some elements of it have emerged with remarkable clarity and strength.

The most important among them is that every single piece of the law in the church must be in the service of values either defined or at least controlled by theological reflection.

---

24. On the impact of Vatican Council II on the development of canon law *see* Richard Potz, *Die Geltung kirchenrechlicher Normen* (Wien: Herder, 1978). For a study on the evolutionary nature of canon law *see* Helmuth Pree, *Die evolutive Interpretation der Rechtsnorm im Kanonischen Recht* (Wien: Springer, 1980).

Such a conclusion engages the legislator to approach his task with the conviction that every legal ordinance ought to be a manifestation of the redeeming action of the church. There cannot be any room for formality or legality: they have no saving value.

Further, whenever possible, the faithful must be guided to the point where they can see the values the law intends to uphold so that they can implement it with intelligence and freedom. Then obedience to the law will be a moral act in the best sense of the word because it will be an act of obedience to the luminous dictate of the conscience.

9

Models of Law and Their Impact on Interpretation

The purpose of the inquiry

The purpose of this chapter is twofold, theoretical and practical. In the theoretical order, it intends to give a brief survey of various a priori stances that can influence the understanding of the nature of canon law and the interpretation of its rules; and in the practical order it wishes to provide information that can help to discover, identify and evaluate hidden assumptions which can play a decisive role in its interpretation.[1]

An indubitable fact is that no inquirer ever approaches the law, even canon law for that matter, with a blank mind, a kind of mental tabula rasa. No interpreter ever constructs the meaning of the norms from the information gathered from the text and the context alone. All inquirers and interpreters, whether they are conscious of it or not, confront the law with certain fundamental assumptions in their minds: they search for its significance and construct its meaning with the help of previously accepted concepts and theories. If such assumptions are well grounded and correct, so will be the conclusions; if they lack proper balance or are downright defective, so will be the final interpretation.[2]

1. This chapter is concerned principally with approaches to presently valid law, but similar considerations apply also to approaches to law that has become history.

2. In every process of interpretation there are two dialectically opposed movements (balancing each other): one starting with the immediate meaning of the words and progressing into increasingly broader horizons, another starting from the extreme limits of the horizons and gradually reaching the crucial words.

This work focuses on the second movement, and its purpose is to assess criti-

To become aware in a general way of the existence of such a priori dispositions is to place oneself into a state of alertness concerning their influence. To know them specifically and to look at them critically is to protect oneself from pitfalls. Besides, such knowledge can be of great help in locating the reasons for seemingly insoluble conflicts in interpretation. When disputes flare up about the sense of a word or a clause, with no resolution in sight, the reason for disagreement often is not in the text or context but in the discordant approaches of the inquirers to the law itself. They may be using the same words but they mean different things; they may be quoting the same rules but they give different significance to them. Should such a situation occur, their disagreement cannot be resolved within the realm of the law; the debate should move back into the regions where their opinions first began to diverge, which could have been in the realm of philosophy, theology or other human sciences. Once the source of division is located, the disputants can retrace their steps to the precise point where their views parted and resume their discussion with a renewed hope of success.[3]

In my presentation I shall bring the approaches to canon law into focus gradually. First, I shall recall various approaches to law in general, applicable *mutatis mutandis* to civil law and canon law; then I shall center on others which are particular to canon law. Whenever possible, I shall put dialectically opposed trends side by side; the resulting contrast will show the distinct nature of each with greater clarity.[4]

Of course, the structure of reality is hardly ever so neat as the theoretical classifications describing it. While I present a few clear categories, I am aware that in the existential order they overlap and intermingle; yet, even so, a brief systematic exposition of them has a use-

---

cally some of the assumptions that may exist in the mind of the canonical interpreter. Not all of them have the same importance; yet, they deserve attention since they have the potential to influence the interpretation of the canonical texts.

3. Conflict situations often occur at conventions, especially when the participants come from different cultural milieus. It would be interesting to have a convention on the theme of "different approaches to canon law"; it could be instrumental if not for greater consensus at least for increased mutual understanding.

4. At this point it is useful to recall again the doctrine of horizon: the meaning of a word that is part of a text is determined not by its internal content alone (which is expressed in its definition) but also by its total environment in the text. For a theoretical exposition of this doctrine *see* Chapter Two in this book; for an interesting and creative practical application of it *see* John M. Huels, "Interpreting Canon Law in Diverse Cultures," *JUR* 47 (1987) 249-293.

ful purpose. The categories should be regarded as types, models or patterns of approaches; they offer workable clues toward identifying some main trends and they provide help for articulating hidden assumptions. Although I shall regularly refer to authors and schools, the nature of this essay remains in substance a survey of models, or a study in typology, and not an extended inquiry into the doctrines of individual authors or particular schools.[5]

APPROACHES TO LAW IN GENERAL

1. Univocal conception versus multivalent descriptions

The concept of law can be understood either as having one single meaning, with no variations, referring to the same phenomenon; or as multivalent and analogous, used to cover different meanings, referring to different types of norms.

• *The univocal conception* operates with one single definition that must be verified in any and every norm that claims to be law; outside of it there may be rules and regulations but there cannot be law. The consequences for the general understanding of the nature of canon law and for the classification of its inner content are far-reaching.

In general, there will be an overall tendency to handle canon law and civil law in the same manner. A typical question often raised (and answered) by those who use this approach is: Is canon law truly law? They mean: Does canon law fit into the one and exclusive category of law? Canon lawyers who consciously or unconsciously accept the same assumption are likely to respond defensively by proving that their science is indeed covered by the unique definition of law, hence that it is truly law. Once they take that position, logically enough, they will handle the norms of the holy church much in the same way as the norms of a secular empire: they all belong to the same species. They will make no allowance for the "metajuridical" fact that the laws of the state exist for the sake of justice, and the laws of the Christian community are there to help the believers to accept the gift of gratuitous redemption.

5. I use the term "model" in the title because I think it directly conveys to the reader something of the nature of this section—given the rather extensive use of the word "model" in the theological literature. At the same time I find the term unsatisfactory: here and now we are not dealing with preexisting patterns to which persons approaching canon law conform but with internal mental dispositions which a person has assimilated or developed previously.

The potential for such an approach is the greatest in secular universities, especially in the European continent, where canon law is part of the curriculum of civil law studies; the two systems are often handled in the same way.

Further, canon lawyers who accept this approach will regard all norms found in canonical documents as law in the one and exclusive sense of the word. For instance, commenting on the canons of the Code, they will allow no differentiation on the basis of literary forms; they will insist that all canons must be understood and implemented in the same way. They will not distinguish strict right and duty situations from broad spiritual exhortations: they will not differentiate between doctrinal statements and norms of action.[6]

- *The multivalent perception* regards the term law as analogous; that is, as referring to norms which are partly identical, partly different, with varying proportions of identity and difference.

It differentiates sharply between norms suitable for a necessary and compulsory secular society (intent on procuring the temporal welfare of the citizens), and norms fitting for a free and voluntary religious community (intent on accepting the gift of redemption).

In this perception, even if both types of norms (civil and religious, secular and sacred) are called law, they cannot be law in the same sense: one system is there to impose justice, if necessary with force; another to bring order into the acceptance of the gift of salvation. Clearly, for such different purposes norms of differing nature are necessary.

Accordingly, a number of Catholic "theoreticians of canon law" have taken the position that canon law is not law in the same sense as civil law; Mörsdorf, Corecco, Sobański would be the better known ones. The World Council of Churches avoids the term "law" in reference to norms in Christian communities; it prefers to speak of "church order."[7]

---

6. This approach may have caused some canonists in the past to search for sanctions in the case of norms concerning devotional exercises (Easter duty, Mass attendance, fasting, abstinence, recitation of the office, etc.). Not finding them in the ecclesiastical law, they had to invoke otherworldly sanctions, such as punishment in purgatory or even eternal damnation (an eternal sanction: it had to be eternal damnation). For them no law could exist without sanctions.

This same motive can be found in the reasoning of Sohm as well, but it led him to a very different conclusion: since there is no law without enforcement and sanctions, there cannot be any law in the church of divine charity. He, too, worked with a univocal concept of law.

7. The univocal perception of the concept of law must be due to a lack of

2. Static laws versus developing norms

The idea of law can be conceived either as a static norm that never changes, or a dynamic reality that is subject to change.

• *The static perception* originates in the classical world view that sees the structure of the universe through immutable essences which are not subject to developments. Its ideal is pragmatically expressed in the maxim *mutatio legis odiosa,* which can be literally rendered into English as "the change of the law is odious"; hence, it is to be avoided.[8]

---

epistemological alertness: a simplified concept is projected into a complex reality.

Historically, there is an interesting parallel to the univocal conception of law: the univocal conception of perfect society. There was one fascinating definition: a society that had all the means to reach its goal, and both the state and the church appeared to fall under it. Once this parallelism was established, it was easy to transfer many institutions and policies from the state to the church, among them the conception of the law. (E.g., the divisions of the Institutes of Justinian were used for the first Code of Canon law.) A community voluntarily gathered to receive supernatural gifts cannot be the same as a society held together by the sword of justice.

The uncritical (and mostly unconscious) transference of the elements of a secular "perfect society" to the church has caused harm to the community of believers. Vatican II discarded the expression.

8. Peter Green, the well known classical scholar (from the University of Texas at Austin) writes:
> The great paradox of the Graeco-Roman world for us today is the way in which its unparalleled intellectual and artistic fecundity of invention in the arts and sciences was dedicated throughout (with brief exceptions only) to the maintenance of a privileged *status quo*. . . . Stoic cosmology envisioned a changeless uniformity of order, in heaven as on earth, a 'natural law' that justified the prescriptive rule of imperial Rome or Byzantium, and was eagerly borrowed by medieval thinkers (who revamped it as the Ladder of Being) . . . Shakespeare gives vivid expression to this concept in *Troilus and Cressida* (?1603):
>> The heavens themselves, the planets and this centre
>> Observe degree, priority and place . . .
>> Take but degree away, untune that string,
>> And hark, what discord follows!
>
> It is no accident that the Greek and Roman verbs (*neoterizein, res novare*) habitually translated as 'to rebel' or 'to make a revolution' in fact simply mean 'to produce change (or novelty)': all change was, by definition, disruptive of the social order. The number of classics professors who are ferocious reactionaries should not really surprise us. *C'est leur métier*: conservation is, on every count, their proper business.

See Peter Green, *Classical Bearings: Interpreting Ancient History and Culture* (New York: Thames and Hudson, 1989) 17.

Logically, such a view can allow only an interpretation that is hardly more than the paraphrasing of the text with no creative element in it, no matter how much the circumstances have changed since the promulgation of the law and what new needs have emerged. The development of customs is similarly excluded. For such an approach, when put into practice, the price to be paid is high: the law loses touch with life, and an enmity develops between the rigid norms and the people.

This static approach is the result of a classical (but today regarded as simplistic) epistemology which leads to an imperfect understanding of the nature of the universe, of which law is a part. It is deficient because it misrepresents a continuously changing creation. Besides, it leads to an attitude that refuses to provide for the emerging needs of the people.

• *The dynamic perception* is ultimately nothing else than critical realism. It accepts the community and its laws as they are: subject to the universal law of life, which means change, the lack of which would spell stagnation and death.

Accordingly, all interpretations from a dynamic point of view will take into account the developing life of the community—there cannot be correct interpretation outside of that. Importance will be given not only to the promulgation but also to the reception of the laws. Also, customs will have an honored place in the system.

Historically it is not difficult to find examples for this developmental approach: it has played a prominent role in the creation and formation of canon law well into the Middle Ages and beyond. Nor can it ever stop.

An analogy may be helpful: we know that there is in the church an ongoing development in the intelligence of the revelation, or the word of God. It would be strange indeed if a parallel development were not taking place in the practical life of the same church.[9]

9. On the role of evolution in the interpretation of the law see the original and well balanced work by Helmuth Pree, *Die evolutive Interpretation der Rechtsnorm im Kanonischen Recht* (Wien: Springer, 1980). He sees the need to recognize explicitly the evolutionary character of canon law, and finds that this could be best accomplished by taking advantage of both the method of codification and that of case law. The two jointly could give to canon law the flexibility that it needs.

In the historical part of his book he effectively demonstrates how our canonical (and theological) tradition always accepted the developmental character of the law, and how various types of interpretations promoted it, even if no formal theory of it has been worked by our *jurisprudentes*. In the systematic part he pays much attention to the relationship of laws to values, and shows how the church is a mediator of values for canon law. He stresses the need for any legal system to be in touch with reality, which is historical and evolving.

3. Self sufficiency versus organic unity

The world of law can be conceived either as cut off from all other worlds; that is, totally autonomous; or as organically united with other worlds such as philosophy, religion, history, sociology, anthropology, etc.; that is, as part of a larger universe.

• *If the world of law is conceived as totally self sufficient,* the meaning of legal concepts cannot be modified or influenced from any other source than what is already contained in the law. The result is legal positivism and strict constructionism in interpretation.

Among the secular legal theories, Kelsen's "pure theory of law" would be the most striking example of this approach. In the field of canon law the influence of similar thinking is noticeable in manuals which give an absolute value to the legal norms without ever subjecting them to a critical examination from the point of view of values. Law becomes a value in itself, and is not in the service of values any more.

• *If the world of law is conceived as organically dependent on other worlds,* the meaning of every concept and principle can be influenced and modified by another world on which law is dependent. This should not be understood as other sciences taking over the place of the law; we are talking about an influence that is governed and moderated by an ontological connection.

In the field of secular jurisprudence, this organic approach to law has given place to various legal theories, such as historic, sociological, economic, and so forth.[10]

In the field of the post-Tridentine canon law there was a recognition of an ontological bond between the world of law and philosophy—of a sort, that is. By and large canonists paid little attention to developments in cognitional theories and epistemological inquiries. The "philosophy of law" taught in the schools prior to Vatican Council II was often a poor version of scholasticism that disguised its lack of depth by a superficial "clarity" in exposition.

Today significant effort is expended to show the dependence of canon law on theology; more of this in the second part of this chapter, and in Chapter Ten.

---

10. For a survey of various schools *see* the concise but substantial book by Carl Joachim Friedrich, *The Philosophy of Law in Historical Perspective,* second ed. rev. and enlarged (Chicago: Chicago University, 1963). Also, J. Walter Jones, *Historical Introduction to the Theory of Law,* reprint (New York: Augustus M. Kelly, 1969; originally Oxford: Clarendon, 1940).

4. Literary text versus norm of action

Legal texts can be approached either as literary productions with a myriad of meanings, or as norms which intend to determine specific actions.

This difference in approach is rarely attended to; in fact I know of no publication where it is discussed. Yet, it has an enormous significance for the style and more importantly for the content of interpretations offered.

The issue here is whether or not a legal text has a specific character that no other literary text has. I submit, it does. To understand it, however, we must return to the process that creates laws.

At the origin of that process there is an overriding intention: to impose a specific course of action. That is, the aim of the law maker (be it a constitutional legislator or the people through customs) is not to communicate knowledge through an elaborate text, but to convey a decision in view of an action. This intention then must become a primary hermeneutical factor in interpretation.[11]

- *When law is approached as if it were a piece of theoretical exposition,* the interpreter will search for knowledge. He or she will list every conceivable construction that the text can bear. This is to confuse the task and method of general literary analysis with the purpose and method of finding an intended action. The result may be commentaries with many fine distinctions and explanations responding to the demands of literary criticism but forgetting what the law is about. Such an approach can even be mistaken for an eminently learned one; in reality it is *magnus passus extra viam,* a great step in the wrong direction. Learning consists as much (or more) in the determination of the correct approach to the problem as in the accumulation of information.[12]

- *When the law is approached as conveying a decision,* the ultimate element that gives meaning to the law is the intended action; the inter-

---

11. A similar problem is much debated today in the field of biblical sciences. One scholar may offer an extended historical and philological explanation for every word in a passage but miss the message that gave birth to the passage; another may catch the message even without the fullness of the same scientific apparatus. This is not to deny the importance of history or philology but to stress the point that no research can be successful unless the literary form of a text is established and the hermeneutical factors for its explanation are determined.

12. Sometimes those who come to study canon law after having been trained to handle theological texts may find the transition confusing. In theology they had to search for knowledge in the documents; in canon law they are expected to detect the unique action that the text is prescribing.

preter, therefore, will discard all unnecessary diversions and distractions and will in a single-minded way search for that action. Thus, the resulting commentary will be clear, direct and concise, somewhat reminiscent of the classical lucidity and simplicity that we find in the works of the great jurists of Rome.[13]

5. Voluntarism versus rationality

Law can be conceived either as the projection of the sovereign will of the legislator, ordinatio voluntatis; *or a pattern set by reason to bring order into the life of the community,* ordinatio rationis.

• When the will of the law maker is named as the autonomous source for the existence of the law, the scope for its rational explanation and evaluation is reduced. After all, not much investigation is possible into a source that is not rational per se. There is an absurdity in this theory, because ordinarily we approach every single phenomenon in this universe with the assumption that there is an intelligent pattern in it, that it is a creature of reason; we are also convinced that once we find that pattern, we can understand and explain it better. Law (alone?), as this theory claims, would make an exception. Law reform in this conception is exceedingly difficult (at times even dangerous) because it means the reform of the will of the legislator.

Another shortcoming of this approach is that it does not treat the subjects as intelligent beings: their duty is not to inquire and understand but to accept and obey. No wonder that totalitarian regimes always tend to favor such an approach; a variation on the theme: *l'état, c'est moi!*

Among Catholic philosophers Suarez is the best known exponent of the theory that law is *ordinatio voluntatis*; that is, the reason for the law must be found in the will of the legislator. This is a weak point in his otherwise outstanding contribution to the development of Christian legal philosophy.

---

13. In the interpretation of law there are two kinds of simplicity, one by way of imperfection, another by way of perfection (in this I take my inspiration from Aquinas). Simplicity by way of imperfection does not notice the complexity of the issue and achieves conciseness and clarity by omitting substantial elements in the resolution of the case, or in the interpretation of the text; simplicity by way of perfection achieves brevity and lucidity by having found the essential elements through a maze of complexities. The great Roman jurists have displayed such a perfection, and set an ideal that would be hard to emulate.

Should the study of Roman law among canonists ever decline, simplicity by way of perfection in their laws, interpretations and decisions would also decline.

- *When reason is named as the principal agent* in the creation of laws, we are in a different landscape. The law makers appear as subjects, as being under a rule of law; that is, the law of reason. If they disobey and produce an unreasonable law, there is really no law. In saying this, we are right at the heart of Aquinas' theory. Like anything else in this creation, law must have an intelligible pattern, otherwise it cannot be law. The wisdom that produced it is entirely accessible to reason; it is likely to appeal to persons of good disposition. Further, law reform is conceivable because human beings can always come to better insights.

Thomas' theory expresses beautifully that all legislators are under the eternal law of God and must adjust to it whatever they may demand from their subjects. Nor does his theory take away anything of the authority of the legislator; quite the contrary, a clear intelligent pattern in the law enhances his authority, while at the same time it pays respect to the intelligence of the subjects.[14]

The approaches described to this point concern law in general, including canon law. There are other approaches which concern canon law alone.

APPROACHES TO CANON LAW IN PARTICULAR

6. No dependence on theology versus dependence on theology

Canon law can be approached either with no notice taken of its dependence on theology—theology in a broad sense, including beliefs, doctrines, and systematic expositions; or with an integrated vision in which theology and law are organically bound to each other.

These contrasting approaches are really variations on the ones described above under 3: *Self sufficiency versus organic unity.*

---

14. J. M. Häussling writes:
    . . . the philosophy of law of Thomas establishes that the "ratio" [reason] is the rule and measure of all human actions, against all voluntaristic foundation of the law; this reason must be aligned [adjusted] to the eternal law as it exists in the intelligence and wisdom of God . . .
See "Rechtsphilosophie," LTK 8:1051.
    It is difficult to see how a voluntaristic philosophy of law could have ever penetrated into Catholic thinking, otherwise so dedicated to the upholding of reason. To undermine the role of reason in the foundations of our legal system is bound to weaken the value and credibility of our theological inquiries.

Canon law, in fact, can be read at different levels, and bear a meaning on each. It can be read as a collection of purely legal texts, abstracting from their religious character; or it can be read as a particular expression of religious beliefs and attitudes.

• *No dependence on theology.* A "scientific" explanation may be proposed on the basis of the text, but since it cannot account for the religious dimension of the law, it may not serve the religious needs of the community. In particular, it may not appreciate adequately the values which have given existence and meaning to the law and to every part of it. It is bound to lead to a substantially deficient interpretation.

A person who does not share the faith of the community is likely to take this approach, but a believer may do so also on the basis of some philosophical assumption, such as "no metajuridical element should interfere with the purity of scientific interpretation."[15]

• *Dependence on theology.* In this approach Catholic beliefs and theological positions become important hermeneutical factors in the understanding of the nature of the law and in its interpretation. While it is not impossible for an unbeliever to take this route, a believer should be disposed to do so on the strength of his or her own faith.

This dependence can be seen in different ways.

7. External dependence versus internal integration

Even when it is admitted that canon law is substantially dependent on the authority of religion, that authority can be conceived either as being extrinsic to law, or as being fully integrated with the law.

• *External dependence* means that canon law is autonomous within its scientific sphere, but otherwise it is subject to the authority of the

15. This type of approach can be found within "the school" of the Italian lay canonists. Richard Puza (Professor of Canon Law at the University of Tübingen) writes:
> As good experts in modern legal science and methodology, the Italian lay canonists sought to bring about a reform of the science of canon law, but without any regard to its foundational problems. For them, it was not the task of a canonist to work out the theological foundations of canon law. Provided it could be empirically established, as a matter of fact, that the legal system of the Catholic church possessed all the characteristics of an *ordinamento primario e originario* [it contained primary and original norms], for these canonists, the conditions were there to work scientifically on the development of the science of the positive law of the church.

See Richard Puza, *Katholisches Kirchenrecht* (Heidelberg: Müller, 1986) 43.

(The present writer's query: is there an affinity between this doctrine and Kelsen's "pure theory of law"?)

magisterium which can make it, undo it or modify its texts. It follows that when it comes to interpretation, the ordinary rules (the same as in civil law) should apply, unless and until the proper authorities have given other directions. In the practical order, when an interpreter holding this approach comes to a difficulty, he or she is likely to request the magisterial authority to resolve it. Superiors thinking in the same way will regard the interpretation of the law as one of their essential tasks. In this approach the role of religion is extrinsic.[16]

• *Internal integration.* When canon law is perceived as integrated with theology, it will never be handled as any other law. Should difficulties in its interpretation arise, the subject, or the superior for that matter, will first and foremost seek a solution from theological sources and resources. This approach integrates law into the life of the church so that beliefs and norms of action are never separated.

The internal integration, too, can be explained in various ways.

8. Identity versus distinction in organic unity

Canon law can be conceived either as a part of theology, or as distinct from theology but organically united with it.

• Representative examples of this *doctrine of identification* can be found in the theories of Klaus Mörsdorf (d. 1989, longtime Professor at the University of Munich), Eugenio Corecco (formerly Professor at the University of Fribourg, Switzerland, now bishop of Lugano) and Remigiusz Sobański (Professor at the Catholic Academy in Warsaw).

Mörsdorf affirms that canon law is a theological discipline but one using a juridical method. In other terms, the world of theology includes canon law, but that particular part of theology must be handled on the pattern of the method used by secular jurists. This position, firmly held and many times repeated by its author, is difficult to understand. His notion of method is not clear, nor is it evident how a juridical

---

16. In connection with this approach the school of Navarra in Spain can be mentioned. Antonio Rouco Valera (formerly Professor at the Pontifical University of Salamanca, now Archbishop of Santiago de Compostela) writes:
> The ecclesial sense of faith that is a strong characteristic of this school moves its scholars to postulate . . . a pre-scientific subordination of the canonical science to the magisterium of the church. They designate the science of canon law as 'sciencia sagrada.' Nonetheless they explain canon law as being ontologically and logically a 'species generis iuris' . . .

See "Die katholische Rechtstheologie heute: Versuch eines analytischen Überblickes," *Archiv für katholisches Kirchenrecht* 145 (1976) 18.

method can be applicable to theology. Critics have pointed out that each science determines its method; it does not borrow it from somewhere else.[17]

Corecco affirms that canon law is *ordinatio fidei*, and not *ordinatio rationis*. The expression is ambivalent; it probably means both that the canons are somehow part of our Catholic faith, and that they originate in the faith of the community which senses the need for *ordinatio* and consequently brings a legal system into existence. Unfortunately Corecco's language is far from being precise, and he shuns exact definitions; thus we might be dealing with an intuition that needs further elaboration.[18]

Sobański sums up his own theory in this way:

> The law of the church cannot be separated from the church; it belongs to the church's reality. For this reason, the science of canon law has its genuine place within the science of the church [ecclesiology], also within the scientific discipline which is in the service of the intelligence of the faith, that is, theology. In the concept [nature] of the science of canon law there is a theological character in the same way as there is one in the concept [nature] of ecclesiology. It follows that it is really superfluous [idle] to speak of a theology of canon law because every canonical statement made in the light of faith has already a theological character.[19]

All three authors agree that canon law belongs to the field of theology although they explain this identity in different ways. Their theories, however, suffer from a common flaw: they do not distinguish sufficiently (or at all) between an inquiry into the meaning of a mystery (the object of theology), and an inquiry into the meaning of a norm of action (the object of a legal commentary). An inquiry into a mystery continuously expands and knows no end; an inquiry into a norm of action steadily narrows the scope of the field in order to determine with precision the action to be taken. The objects of the two are so different that they cannot form the same science.

---

17. Klaus Mörsdorf, *Schriften zum kanonischen Recht*, ed. Winfried Aymans, Karl-Theodor Geringer, Heribert Schmitz (Paderborn: Schöningh, 1989). This is a collection of Mörsdorf's major articles.

18. Eugenio Corecco, *Theologie des Kirchenrechts: Methodologische Ansätze* (Trier: Paulinus, 1980), esp. pp. 96–107 where he gives a summary of his theory and p. 113 with further references to his own writings.

19. Remigiusz Sobański, *Grundlagenproblematik des katholischen Kirchenrechts* (Wien: Böhlau, 1987) 141.

• *Distinction in organic unity.* Thus, the correct approach to canon law is to handle its norms as decisions for the appropriation of values needed for the welfare of the community. This is the approach that appears the best grounded since it is the only one that does justice to the theological roots of canonical norms, and at the same time it respects their practical and action oriented nature. The Christian values they pursue cannot become known in any other way than by theological inquiry; the action they propose cannot be determined in any other manner than by using the special hermeneutics applicable to action oriented speech.[20]

Summing up

At this point we are in position to summarize the assumptions that will lead to the correct understanding of the nature of canon law and to its critically well grounded interpretation. It consists in recognizing that

—the term "law" is not univocal but can be used for norms of different nature;

—law is not a static measuring rod but a dynamic instrument which regulates the activities of a living community;

—the world of the law is not an isolated autonomous reality but organically integrated with the fields of other human activities;

—the primary purpose of legal texts is not to convey knowledge but to impose a decision;

—law is more than an act of the will, it must contain an intelligible pattern composed by reason;

—the full meaning of canon law cannot be found without taking into account its religious origin;

—the bond of canon law with the realm of faith is not only in being subject to the magisterium but in its integration with the doctrine of faith;

—canon law is not identical with theology but organically united with it while remaining a science in its own right.[21]

---

20. This approach is rooted in a cognitional theory that looks at judgment and decision as really distinct parts of an organically united process.

21. An unrealistic proposal: it would be most enlightening for students of canon law if commentators would introduce their work by giving an account of the fundamental assumptions that govern their approach to canon law.

Since the proposal is unrealistic, it might well be extended from the theoretical to the practical order: it would be most profitable for every unit administering the

The body of civil law ought to respond to the question: How to organize a community on the basis of justice? The body of canon law ought to respond to the question: How to organize a community to receive the gift of redemption? Those two goals are so different that the rules they inspire and generate cannot be of the same nature even if they appear similar under many aspects.

The principal hermeneutical factor in interpreting canon law remains unique. It confronts the whole system as well as every part of it with the question: What is the redemptive value in this regulation?[22]

APPENDIX

In this Appendix I wish to present still another approach to law, so different from the others that I could not insert it well into the survey just concluded. In fact, it stands in contrast to all of them.

A studious person who desires to explain the meaning of the law ordinarily will focus on the external phenomenon of law in human society. Such a researcher will collect all the information (doctrinal and empirical) that can contribute to the understanding of this phenome-

---

law of the church (curias, tribunals, chanceries, etc.) to raise the question: What is our fundamental approach to the law?

A more realistic proposal of the pedagogical order: since the best way of leading students to increase their knowledge is to assess exactly where they are in the beginning, and then to build on that foundation, should not all introduction to canon law start by helping the students to discover their own assumptions concerning the law? If such discovery does not take place right in the beginning, there is a danger that the students will interpret all instructions in function of their own categories and of their own horizons. Besides, such exercise can sow the seeds of critical thinking, so essential for the legal profession.

22. Precisely because the primary purpose of canon law is to facilitate the acceptance of a gift, the church never regarded it as a rigidly closed system admitting no exceptions to the rules. From the beginning those in authority developed or admitted devices and practices which loosened the rules and let persons in need receive favors to which they were not entitled according to the law. The primary example of this magnanimity is the *oikonomia*, the healing of a wound that no law could cure, preserved in the tradition of the Eastern church. In the Western church there has been a tradition to recognize the legitimacy of *epieikeia* and equity, and a widespread use of kindred devices such as dispensation, sanation, privilege.

Canon law should obviously serve the cause of justice, but unlike civil law, it should not stop there: it should rise to the service of the theological virtues, faith, hope and charity. Admittedly, it will never be easy to maintain a legal system that must at the same time promote justice and imitate the generosity of God.

non, will examine various hypotheses to explain it (e.g., *ordinatio rationis*, social contract, sovereign command, tool of the ruling class, etc.) and will try to establish critically a valid one. The conclusion then can serve as a guide for creating the right type of law in the future—so that the people can live in harmony for ever afterwards.

The fact is that studious persons have produced such a great variety (some would say cacophony) of theories that many have despaired (with an academic despair, of course) and given up hope that a meaningful explanation of law can ever be found.

To find a way out of this impasse, David Granfield comes forth with a radical proposal: let us turn away from the observation of the external phenomenon of law and forget the innumerable theories which are trying to explain it. Instead, let us focus on the inner experience of the subject who is involved in the event of discovering, accepting and observing the law. This experience more than anything else will reveal the meaning of the law. Since this experience is available to anyone who has the capacity to reflect on his or her own inner world, and since the human spirit operates in every person in a similar manner, we may well come to the same discoveries, and find a meaning in the law that is common to us all. The justification for this meaning will not be in any conceptual theory but in the authenticity of the personal experience that can be verified by anyone who is willing to do the necessary introspection and is detached enough to report on it objectively. There is a path that bypasses the chaos of theories and can lead to a consensus.[23]

In proposing this alternative approach, Granfield takes his inspiration from Bernard Lonergan, the Canadian philosopher and theologian, whose major achievement was in the field of cognitional theory and epistemology. As Lonergan invited his readers to explore the inner process of the operations of the human spirit in order to discover the complex path to critically grounded knowledge, so Granfield invites us to explore our own participation in the "legal event" that takes place in our consciousness in order to find the ultimate meaning of the law.[24]

---

23. See David Granfield, *The Inner Experience of Law: A Jurisprudence of Subjectivity* (Washington, D.C.: Catholic University, 1988).

24. Granfield is not alone in undertaking a journey into human consciousness to find philosophical enlightenment. What he does has an affinity with the works of Maréchal, Rahner, Lotz, Coreth, Lonergan and others who are often described as belonging to the school of "transcendental Thomism"—an expression that covers a variety of approaches between rather wide parameters. See Otto Muck, *The Tran-*

Models of Law and Their Impact on Interpretation   155

He calls *nomosphere* that part of the inner world where we encounter the law, and recognizes four sections in it. He invites us to enter them one by one, and pause for reflection in each. He intimates what to expect.

As we stand alone in quiet reflection in the *monosphere*, we are bound to become aware of an internal drive towards meaning and value. As we let this drive have its scope and we pursue knowledge and good things, we soon learn that our moves have consequences, rewarding or punishing. This dialectic teaches us that we cannot be ourselves except by surrendering to certain norms; that is, as soon as our spirit moves, we find ourselves under the law. A condition we cannot escape.

Our next station in this introspective process is the *isosphere* where we take consciousness of what happens when we begin to interact with another person. We know that our partner too is experiencing a drive for meaning and value and wishes to reach out for them. Thus the imperative to divide what is available emerges, and with it the need for an objective measure to regulate the competition. This measure we call justice. The measure is then expressed in rules to be obeyed by both; otherwise the relationship is bound to turn destructive. In other terms, we discover that no two persons can live together in peace without surrendering to the rule of law.

Moving further in this internal journey, we come to the *koinosphere* where we reflect on our experience of being a member of a large community. We know that to give full scope to our internal drive for meaning and value, we need stable structures around us, a fair participation in the wealth of the community, and a peaceful climate that favors personal growth. The same need exists for all the others. We know again, with the deepest intuitive certainty, that such conditions cannot be achieved unless the whole community is willing to abide by certain norms.

The human spirit, however, remains restless until it finds an ultimate explanation for this universal need to surrender to a law. This explanation we can find in the *theosphere* where we become aware that the drive for meaning and value is a drive for the infinite truth and beauty, God. There we discover that the ultimate meaning of surren-

---

scendental Method, translated from the German (New York: Herder and Herder, 1968).

The movement, however, toward the philosophical exploration of consciousness is broader than any kind of Thomism; *see* e.g., the book by Eugene Webb, *Philosophers of Consciousness: Polanyi, Lonergan, Voegelin, Ricoeur, Girard, Kierkegaard* (Seattle: University of Washington, 1988).

dering to the law is in surrendering to God who is the source of all laws. Thus the process is completed: the inner experience of law leads to the inner experience of the divine.

From all this a unified vision of law emerges: all legal operations, in theory and in practice, have a meaning because we experience them as ultimately grounded in the divine, from where flow not only justice but also love, compassion and mercy.

The objective or theoretical question *What is law?* can then be answered out of this internal experience; and Granfield construes his answer with great care, historical erudition and good critical sense. Even from this brief summary one can see that the experience of the *theosphere* points toward the existence of a natural law and leads to the exclusion of legal theories that do not have an anchor in the Absolute. The need for law as discovered in the *koinosphere* can have worldwide applications: for the peaceful cooperation of the nations, for the equitable sharing of the earth's resources, for ordered processes in the states, and so forth; it excludes totalitarian excesses as well as belligerent conquests. The realization of the needs and rights of our neighbor in the *isosphere* lays the foundation for commutative justice and excludes the exploitation of human persons. In all these experiences (which in real life overlap and intermingle) we keep returning to the *monosphere* where the incessant drive for meaning and value reaffirms our human dignity that must be expressed also in an objective legal theory.

Thus out of the inner experience of law an objective theory of the nature of law can be construed. It rests on the experience of an unrestricted desire to reach out for values (which desire points towards the existence of an Absolute Being), and on the awareness that there are many other persons in this universe with similar desires. The desire of anyone for the Absolute, of course, need not be restricted; but when it comes to finite values, there is a luminous evidence in our consciousness that a pattern of order is necessary to assure a balance between desire and restraint so that all may prosper.

Granfield's approach to the discovery of the meaning of law is applicable perhaps even more to the discovery of basic ethical principles. But could it be used for building a theory of canon law?

The answer (or rather hint) is: yes and no. Yes, because the experiences of the diverse spheres in the *nomosphere* are as accessible to Christians as to other persons. Much, or perhaps all, that is discovered there *is* applicable to those who gather in the Lord's name. No, because in Christianity there is more than what we can perceive in our consciousness: there is the self revelation of God in time and space, a historical event. We live by his Word and by what his Word has been creating ever since it was first spoken, the sacraments—the principal one among them being the assembly of God's people, the *ecclesia*. The internal experience of the law in this *ecclesia* will always be coupled with the external and historical experience of the word of God.

10

Theology and Canon Law: An Inquiry into Their Relationship

Why this inquiry?

This inquiry is prompted by both historical events and contemporary reflections; that is, by facts and theories.

In recent history we have seen in fairly quick sequence first the emergence of a renewed doctrinal vision for the church through the work of Vatican Council II, and then the promulgation of the revised Code of Canon Law by the authority of Pope John Paul II. A refreshed understanding of our doctrinal tradition has led to the reform of our norms of action; the two were clearly organically connected. To search for a definition of this connection between theology and law makes good sense on several counts: it can enlighten us about our past history; it can help us to understand our present situation; and it can provide us with guidance for the planning of future developments.

Contemporary reflections on the mutual relationship of the two disciplines are gradually emerging and expanding. Although the inquirers are relatively few, their theories already display a variety of opinions: some see the relationship between theology and canon law as close, even to the point of virtual identification; some others view it as distant, even to the point of radical separation; others advocate a kinship of varying degrees between the two. As it is, such different approaches are not merging into any consensus, but they offer at least an opportunity: they stimulate exchanges, which in turn can bring progress. And progress we must, not only out of some intellectual curiosity but also for a pragmatic reason: it is likely that within a few decades there will be a new revision of the legal system (of the Code); and if so, guiding principles will be needed to proceed harmoniously from a renewed vision to fresh legislation, from doctrinal insights to practical norms.[1]

Yet, the multiplicity of different approaches constitutes also a warning: they conflict in so many ways that all of them clearly cannot be correct, even if we make an allowance for healthy pluralism. They must, therefore, be examined and critically evaluated in both their methodology and their substantive claims. Some of this work I intend to do. Fairness postulates, however, that before I raise questions about other approaches, I should give an account of my own way of proceeding.

The heuristic issue: what am I searching for? what do I intend to discover?

The answer is: I am searching for a well grounded understanding of the relationship between theology and canon law. In other terms: I want to discover the nature of the two disciplines *as they relate to each other*.

To move toward this goal, and eventually to achieve it, a heuristic structure is needed; that is, an orderly process that brings together the information needed to facilitate the discovery. From where could such information come?

I see two sources. One is in observing the dynamic pattern of the genesis of theology and canon law: how each of the two disciplines comes into existence; surely a relational pattern is bound to reveal it-

---

1. The first Code of Canon Law lasted from 1917 to the time of Vatican Council II when under the impact of the teaching of the council many of its norms, and even more its overall spirit and direction, had become obsolete. The prediction that the second Code will be subject to a thorough revision is based on the fact that it was composed fairly soon after the council when the new ideas had already made an impact on the church but the community by and large had not achieved "one mind and one heart" in their interpretation. A clearer and more uniform understanding of the council will undoubtedly emerge, and the developing theological insights will postulate new legislation. For a supporting (and clarifying) background to this reasoning see the essay by Walter Kasper, "The Continuing Challenge of the Second Vatican Council: The Hermeneutics of the Conciliar Statements" *Theology and Church* (New York: Crossroad, 1989) 166–176.

A significant change has occurred already with the promulgation in 1990 of the *Codex canonum ecclesiarum orientalium*: its first chapter concerns the *christifideles*, an order inspired no doubt by *Lumen gentium* which focuses in its beginning on the people of God. The general norms *De lege, de consuetudine et de actibus administrativis* are placed at the very end of that Code. The change may look small, yet it shows that a better understanding of Vatican Council II is gaining ground.

self in that process. Another is to look at them in their mature existence, a static picture, and compare their contents; such comparison will bring out similarities and differences.

Whatever my own search may yield could be then contrasted with some currently proposed theories; such an encounter would throw some more light on the matter. At the end of it, however, there will be still unresolved questions; I shall be adverting to a few of them.

Accordingly, this essay falls into four parts:

first, I shall look at the genesis of the two disciplines, theology and canon law (this means looking at a dynamic process);

second, I shall compare the nature of the two disciplines (this means to look at their images as captured statically);

third, I shall present a variety of opinions concerning the relationship of the two disciplines;

fourth, I shall add some more questions and comments.

Before all this, however, I wish to locate my own point of departure by giving an account of my understanding of some basic concepts.

Clarification of some basic concepts: what is meant by "theology," "canon law," and "relationship"?

While clarifying my use of some relevant concepts, I do not wish to imply that they could not be used in other senses; they could. I simply state the senses in which I am using them. My aim is to prevent misunderstanding.

I use "theology" in the sense of accumulated knowledge about God and his mighty deeds—creation, redemption, salvation, all included. The word translated literally means "God speech." This knowledge is composed of two elements, intimately blended together. One is the gift of God, his self revelation; we accept it with an act of surrender. The other is the result of our efforts to understand his gift: a quest undertaken with the help of human categories, which are the product of a culture. In theology divine and human elements intermingle.

By "canon law" I mean primarily a system of norms representing decisions on the part of the law maker and imposed with authority on the subjects (both statutory and customary laws are included here), secondarily the art and science of making and interpreting laws.

Some additional precisions must be added:

By canon law I do not mean simply the "canons" found in the Code since not all the canons are laws in the proper sense of that word, nor are all the church's laws incorporated as canons into the Code.

Further, by using the expression "canon law" I do not wish to prejudge the issue of whether the church should have "laws" in the same sense as a secular state has them, or should have not laws but guiding norms of a different nature.

"Relationship" is an abstraction: in reality no such entity exists by itself. There are only persons or things related to each other. Hence, the correct way of formulating our questions is: "How does theology relate to canon law?" and "How does canon law relate to theology?" Or, "What is in the nature of theology that makes it relate to canon law?" and "What is in the nature of canon law that refers it to theology?" To discover the relationship between the two disciplines, the inquiry must focus on the nature of each; the clue for discovering the relationship is built into their very nature.

Methodologically this means that the nature of the two disciplines must be determined before there can be any talk about their relationship. The nature reveals itself first historically, in its genesis, and then through an analysis of its structure. This is the path I am going to follow.

My inquiry, therefore, will not be an investigation into the impact of contemporary doctrinal perceptions on current legislation. My aim is to discover and describe the deep lying bond embedded in the nature of the two disciplines, so that we can have a norm for ordering them to each other correctly. Once we have this "meta-physical" (beyond empirical) knowledge, the present situations with their myriads of details can be objectively assessed—confirmed or corrected.

The preliminaries over, let us begin the process of discovery.

PART ONE
THEOLOGY AND CANON LAW IN THEIR GENESIS

In this part, my inquiry will move from the observation of the most empirical phenomenon (*language*) to what is still external in its exercise but spiritual in its source (*authority*) to what is plainly internal (*intentionality*).

An empirical beginning:
what is the testimony of the language?

To ask what is the testimony of the language of theology and of canon law appears to be a humble beginning, but in fact it is of importance because the first signs we encounter in searching for the meaning of a communication are precisely in the grammatical structure of the language. There, and nowhere else, are the initial clues for the discovery of deeper meanings.

The two disciplines are couched in two different types of language: theological discourse is in the indicative mood; canonical norms are in the imperative mood.

Theology is composed of affirmative judgments; it speaks of what *is*. It conveys knowledge acquired either through revelation or reflection on the revealed data. It speaks of God's mighty deeds in history and of our own human response to them. When the discourse is concluded, no order is issued. This is not to say that theology does not speak of God's commands: it does. It reports on them, it conveys the knowledge of them. The authority to command, however, remains with God.[2]

Canonical enactments are in the imperative mood; they speak of what *ought to be*. They convey a specific command, coming from an ecclesiastical (that is, human) authority and demanding action. This is true even when *seemingly* they are plain affirmations of rights and duties: in the context the only purpose of the indication of those rights and duties is to impose on all a behavior that will respect them.[3]

The reasons for such difference in the language must lie deeper than the conventions of human speech; the different moods point to different types of communication.

On a deeper level: what authority governs the world of theology? what authority rules the world of canon law?

The authority that governs the world of theology is that of faith and reason. Theology at its highest level mediates God's self revelation received through faith; at a lower level it consists of the fruits of human reflection on the same divine revelation—all that faith has found in seeking understanding. Theology is concerned with the assertion of truth,

---

2. A typical expression of this indicative theological mood is the Creed: it consists of a series of affirmations.

3. Both the "ought" of a legal obligation and the "ought" of a moral obligation are commands perceived by an informed conscience. In the case of a moral obligation the source of knowledge for the conscience is the revealed doctrine or the discovery of natural law; in the case of legal obligation the act of promulgation as well is a source of information for the conscience. Note, however, that all legal obligation must pass through the conscience: the final decision belongs there.

supported either by the testimony of the Spirit in the heart of the believers, or by the strength of reason enlightened by faith.

The authority that rules the world of canon law is that of ecclesiastical power, divine in its origin but human in its exercise. Canon law commands actions to be performed. It mediates decisions made by an ecclesiastical superior who has the power to bind the subjects. Remotely, all such decisions must hinge on the knowledge of the values necessary or useful for the community, a knowledge acquired through the cultivation of theology and by a good dose of human wisdom as well. The decisions become law through a specific process: the formulating and promulgating of laws, a series of authoritative acts. The authority behind them is an identifiable societal authority to bring order into the life of the community.

Another way to show the contrast is to say that theology narrates how the church has received God's self revelation; canon law reveals how the church uses its own authority to organize the community. Disagreement with the former results in disbelief or argument. Disagreement with the latter results in refusing to perform an action.

Thus, two distinct types of communication arise from the consciousness of the church, theology and canon law. The next step in our inquiry then is to turn to that consciousness to see how the two are conceived and given birth there.

In the consciousness of the church: how do theology and canon law emerge?

There must be a reason for the different modes of speaking. There must be a reason for the different types of authorities. Those reasons are ultimately found in the different intentionalities in the consciousness of the church.

We must begin by recalling that the church is a living body. As such, it must undergo continuous development and growth. This process is assured by an internal drive that compels the community to seek more knowledge and to reach out for values that are both life sustaining for the community and life giving for the human family. The origin of this drive is in the Spirit present in the body. There is a rhythm in the resulting activity of the church: a movement from knowledge to decision.

When the church is doing theology, it intends to know. When the church promulgates a law, it intends to impose a decision that leads to action.

All such activities are parts of the same process: the church as a collective person moves from the knowledge of the Christian way of life to a decision to impose on the members of the community the appropriation of certain values.

Theology and canon law are the specifically distinct fruits of the rhythm of the internal life of the church: at one stage faith is seeking understanding, at another stage the ecclesiastical authority is imposing a decision in view of action.

As the two stages in the process are distinct, so are their fruits.

This is the time to pause for a moment. Thus far the inquiry has revealed both the organic unity of theology and canon law and their specific diversity.

They are organically united to the point of inseparability. They are produced by the same subject: the church.[4]

They are fruits of the same process: of the dynamism that drives the church to knowledge, and from knowledge to action. To separate the two would be to dismember one continuous and integrated activity, a never ending drive to sustain and increase life in the body.

But they are distinct entities. Theology emerges from the consciousness of the whole church *as the fruit of faith seeking understanding.* Canon law emerges from the consciousness of legitimate authority *as the fruit of faith seeking decisions and actions,* leading to a set of commands to the community, or to some members of it, directing them to appropriate values which are important for the entire social body.

Perhaps the strength of these positive statements can be best illustrated by the absurdity of their opposites:

If theology and canon law were the same discipline, there would be really no difference in the human psyche (personal or collective) between knowledge and decision. We all know that they are not the same; one can even exist without the other—which is often the prelude to tragedy. We can know the right and do nothing about it; we can also act against our own best judgment.

Conversely, if theology and canon law could be separated so that one had nothing to do with the other, there would be no continuity in the internal drive of the church from knowledge to action—the sign of an erratic and senseless existence.

---

4. Although the subject that brings forth theology and canon law is the same (that is, the church) the way of producing them is not the same. The faithful at large can have a much broader participation in the generation of theological insights than in the drafting of new laws. The church is an organic body; its operations must show an organic division of labor.

Add to these that if ecclesiastical authority played the same role in theology as it does in canon law, theology would become a set of rules to obey. Similarly, if ecclesiastical authority played the same role in canon law as it does in theology, the canons would become theses for profession and reflection.

The only relationship that can be reasonably sustained is that of distinct specificity in an organic unity.

PART TWO
THE CONTENT OF THE TWO DISCIPLINES COMPARED

The following reflections should be read as a report on a thought experiment, and unfinished at that, since in no way will they exhaust the topic.

Mentally, I shall place theology and canon law side by side, and then observe and describe their relationship, trying to answer the twin questions: in what are they different? in what are they similar?

But the matter is not that simple. Neither of the two is an unchangeable, static object; both of them have a dynamic existence. Hence, to represent them in a "frozen state" may be misleading unless we continuously keep in mind that a vital dimension is missing. Besides, even if they can be so represented, theology and canon law are not like two material constructions which can be physically measured and meticulously compared. They have all the subtlety of a product of the mind.

They are also impervious to any simple comparison. Whatever I say, therefore, is exposed to the classical objection that I am trying to compare apples and oranges.

Yet, even apples and oranges can stand some comparison since there is a lot in common between those two delicious fruits, their differences notwithstanding. It should, therefore, be possible to describe their relationship, even if the results cannot be neatly tabulated.

To return to theology and canon law: there are some sharp differences.

Body of knowledge versus system of commands

The first and striking difference between theology and canon law is the one that I have already described: the former contains a body of organized knowledge obtained through revelation and reflection on what was revealed; the latter consists of a system of norms of action issued by an ecclesiastical authority. As we have seen, the acts of generating and receiving each are radically different. There is little doubt that the Christian community always sensed that difference. From very early times it has differentiated between heresy and schism: one was regarded as a crime against doctrine, the other as a breach with legitimate authority.

Further, the institution of separate schools of canon law and theology, a separation that took place in the Middle Ages and has been kept up ever since, speaks of a certain common sense perception of a radical difference between the two—even if today we should judge that the divorce has gone too far.

Aquinas himself defined law as a species of *ordinatio*, clearly distinct from *doctrina*. He understood *ordinatio* as an authoritative act intent on bringing order into a situation where otherwise disorder would reign.[5]

An unlimited horizon versus a well defined field

Another radical difference comes into sight when one looks at the area that each discipline covers: theology knows no limiting horizon, while the field of canon law is circumscribed with precision.

Theology is interested in knowing the uncreated and created universe, God and all his mysteries revealed to, or discovered by, human beings, from the beginning of time to our present days, and beyond, as far as human intelligence can ever advance in reaching them. Its world knows no limits; nothing in this God-related universe is beyond its interest.

Canon law covers a well defined field: it contains the *ordinationes*, ordering norms, issued by an ecclesiastical authority. Each of them is recognizable as such: no rule can be part of the system unless it has been marked by the same authority; that is, unless it has been publicly promulgated or otherwise approved as a norm binding on the community: a field with precise boundaries.

The two disciplines cover two distinct worlds.

5. The difference between theology and canon law could be expressed also by using the scholastic categories of material and formal object. The material object consists of all that constitutes the material for an inquiry, the formal object is the particular aspect under which it is investigated. Thus, the material object of theology is the mysteries; the formal object is the same mysteries as "true," hence "knowable." The material object of canon law is the values; the formal object is the same values as "good," hence desirable. (Remember Aristotle's "transcendentals" of being: one, true, and good?)

Hermeneutics for expansion versus hermeneutics for restriction

Another sign of difference between the two disciplines is that they require diametrically opposed hermeneutics to find in them the correct meanings.

In the world of theology, with no limiting horizon, hermeneutics will direct the inquirer to search for all the meanings that can be found, since the purpose of discovery is to learn as much as possible about the mysteries—a never ending, always expanding, task. We can never know all of them, and cannot know any of them fully. The purpose of the search is knowledge, with no end.

In the world of canon law, in a well defined field, hermeneutics will direct the interpreter to find the actions that the law maker has intended—an extremely limited scope.[6]

The two approaches cannot be mixed: if the hermeneutics suitable for theology were applied in the field of canon law, the practical life of the church would be beset with endless uncertainties and hesitations as to what should be done, and confusion would reign supreme. If the hermeneutics of canon law were applied in the world of theology, the discipline would be strangled with simplistic and one-sided answers, and the intellectual life of the church would be strangled too.

The internal dynamics of theology prompt a person toward seeking deeper insights and discovering more meanings; the internal dynamics of canon law direct a person to narrow the search steadily until the intended actions are determined.

---

6. If this hermeneutical rule were respected, it would soon put an end to diffuse commentaries and would give us canon law books marked by concise lucidity. The process of discovery in commenting on a legal text should focus on the unique intended action, and not on every conceivable construction that the words can bear.

To find that unique action and to express it with classical brevity and clarity is hardly ever easy: to reach the required certainty a great deal of historical and doctrinal background study is needed.

This "action-oriented hermeneutics" should not be interpreted as denying the fact that some legal texts or cases can pose very complex problems. It simply means that no matter how complex a problem is, the aim is to find (in a maze, maybe) the action warranted in the circumstances; the aim is not to accumulate probabilities on the basis of abstract conceptual analyses. To do the latter would be to ignore the intention in which all legal norms are grounded.

Secular philosophy versus secular jurisprudence as matrices for the two disciplines

In each discipline the Christian content is received in a rich secular matrix, but those matrices are different. Let me explain. Theology in many ways mediates between revelation and contemporary culture. Theologians, therefore, have kept reaching out for philosophical categories through which the mysteries can be made more accessible. Augustine did it, Aquinas did it, Rahner did it, and John Paul II, the former professor of philosophy, is doing it.

The organizational norms of the church, too, needed a cultural matrix to facilitate the operations of the community, such as the spreading of the word of God and the reception of the sacraments. The medieval canonists found the juridical system of the Romans eminently adaptable for such purposes: they called on its principles and institutions and filled them with a new content.

There again is a difference between the two disciplines: a good part of each consists of a cultural matrix, for the one mostly philosophical, for the other mostly juridical. Such *matrices* are not purely accidental; they belong to the integral existence of each.

Beyond the sharp differences there are also similarities, but they hardly ever amount to identities.

Similar concepts in different horizons

Undoubtedly, there are identical sounding concepts in both disciplines, and they are numerous: church, *communio*, faithful, primacy, episcopacy, magisterium, sacraments—to mention just a few. On a closer examination, however, most of these concepts take on a special shade of meaning in the field of canon law. Thus, dissertations are not rare about the canonical meaning of *communio*, *consortium*, intention, and so forth—with a subtle hint or explicit claim that side by side with their theological meaning there is also a canonical meaning. The hint or claim may well be true, since in canon law all the theological concepts appear in a specific horizon in which everything is ordered to action; a situation that certainly impacts on their meaning.[7]

---

7. If all the above is correct (as it is), the question is how far theology has a right and duty to critically evaluate canonical conceptions and, whenever necessary, to point out the need for correction of the legal use of theological terms.
    Theologians could certainly argue that if an ecclesiastical institution is of a theological nature, no law can change it, and consequently the law ought to be steadily

Transcendence through knowledge versus transcendence through action

Another similarity is that both theology and canon law are signs of life and growth in the church. In more philosophical language, they show that the church is able to transcend itself (its present state) continuously by arriving at new insights and making new decisions.

Through theology (faith seeking understanding) the community comes to a better knowledge of the mysteries; through canon law (faith seeking action) the community is prompted to appropriate values for a greater abundance of life. The former is primarily a process of growing internally because the acquisition of knowledge is an internal process. The latter is principally a process aimed at bringing about changes, either within the community or in the world surrounding it. The same internal drive in the church to perfect itself operates in two distinct directions.

evaluated from a theological point of view. Some canonists would, no doubt, resist any such effort on the basis that the autonomy of their discipline must not be violated. They should remember, however, that their science was not autonomous enough to create the theological realities that are the objects of canonical legislation.

The problem with the "canonical meaning" of theological realities is that law cannot create realities but can only adjust to them. When this adjustment is not correct, the law creates a fiction and operates on the basis of such fiction. Such deviation, when it occurs, carries its own built in penalty: the subjects soon perceive the shadows of formalism or legalism, and a contempt for law follows. Reality (including theological reality) has its own way of taking revenge.

This does not mean that research into the "canonical meaning" of (say) *communio* is not legitimate; on the contrary, it is of supreme importance to discover how far canon law has adjusted to the theological reality of *communio*. The researcher, however, should be aware that the study is not completed until it is shown how far the canonical concept corresponds to, or deviates from, the only existing reality, which is theological.

Like so many other sciences, canon law too has suffered from a methodology that used an "atomistic" approach to reality instead of a "holistic" one. The "atomistic" approach focuses on the part, and pays no attention to the whole. Thus in medicine, a cardiologist could concentrate on the aching heart and remain uninterested in the rest of the humanity of his patient—often missing thereby the source of the trouble. Yet, we know that there is no other correct medicine than the "holistic" one.

Similarly, there is no other correct approach to theological realities than a holistic one. An approach to them through canon law alone is not holistic.

One process, two products

The organic connection between the two disciplines is an ontological fact: each is a product of the same internal and vital drive of the "spirit" of the church. The unity due to their common origin cannot be taken away. There is an unbreakable bond between them.

Their common origin, however, creates a relationship of intrinsic dependence between them: the possession of knowledge is the mother of action. It follows that for canon law to be authentic, it must be dependent on theology, not only in some external way (e.g., whenever the teaching authority intervenes), but in its innermost being—and meanings.

This imperative, because an imperative it is, is best understood through the analogy between the operations of the church, a collective person, and the operations of a human being, an individual person. A human being achieves integrity when there is a flawless harmony between his or her vision and actions. If someone thinks in one way and acts in another way, there is a breakdown in his or her personality. The same principle stands for a collective person, in our case, the church. If the understanding of revelation does not govern and control the decisions of the church as reflected in its own laws, there is a breakdown, with potentially disastrous consequences. The credibility of the proclamation is bound to be affected, and the faithful may be hurt.

Differences and similarities in Aristotelian categories

Before we conclude this part on differences and similarities, the question can be raised if the differences and similarities could be expressed through the Aristotelian categories of four causes: efficient, material, formal and final.

The answer is that those categories were really not constructed to explain the relationship between the various activities of the Christian church, and yet, an attempt can be made to use those "causes" analogously to illustrate such a relationship. What follows, therefore, should not be taken as a metaphysical statement, but rather as an attempt to clarify further what has been explained above.

Let us take theology first.

Efficient cause. The first task is then to identify the agent who brings into existence and sustains the dynamics of theological knowledge. It is clearly the church itself, and in the church all those who participate in the process of reflecting over the deposit of revelation. There is a group of persons who dedicate their life to such reflection; they are known as the professional theologians.

Material cause. By material cause we should understand the material component that theologians reflect over. It clearly includes the data of revelation, but it includes also the philosophical categories developed to handle all beings—revealed ones included. On such material the one who reflects will work, seeking all the time a better understanding of the mysteries, their relationships to each other, and so forth. It is an exercise in *intel-legere*, with the help of insights. But as long as the insights are tentatively floated, there is no conclusion—there is no form added to the material.

Formal cause. The formal element is added to the material component by critically tested judgments which affirm the truth concerning the mysteries, as far as it can be established. When this happens, we may have a well reasoned treatise on Christology, or sacramental theology, or any other kind of theology.

Final cause. The final cause is described by the Aristotelian as the first in intention and the last in execution. In ordinary English, the issue is the purpose of the thing under consideration: what is it for? The main purpose of theology is to let the church advance in the understanding of the mysteries, which brings with it a better and more effective way of communicating them.

This description of theology should be contrasted now with an explanation of canon law through its own causes.

Efficient cause. The agent that brings into existence canon law is the law maker, who could be a collective person (members and head acting together, as their status allows, e.g., an ecumenical council), or a specifically designated individual legislator (e.g., the pope, a bishop). In the church the pope or an ecumenical council is the author of universal laws, and bishops, alone or in council, are the makers of particular laws.

Material cause. The material over which the law maker works appears to be composed of two elements: a description of values necessary or convenient for the community, and a description of the capacity of the community to appropriate those values. In themselves a shapeless mass again, over which judicious selections must be made.

Formal cause. The formal cause really consists of decisions: they single out certain values and determine actions that are to be performed. In other words, the formal cause consists of a system of commands.

Final cause. In the classical tradition one should say that the purpose of those commands is to bring order into the life of the community, order in view of peace, but that is not all. The actions commanded aim to promote orderly growth in the community and the service of the whole human family.[8]

After all these expositions the next heading should bring no surprise:

Theology judges canon law

Theology has the capacity out of its own resources to form a judgment over the fittingness of canonical norms for theological institutions. It has the means to determine if the rules are well proportioned for the purpose of upholding the values in question: if they go as far as necessary but do not go beyond what is needed. By way of concrete examples: in recent times theological criticism has brought about significant changes in the laws concerning the eucharist (cf. the rules of fasting), the sacrament of the sick (cf. the broader conception of illness), or marriage (cf. the understanding of the ends).[9]

Canon law has no capacity at all to judge theology because legal *ordinationes* are not meant to be judgments. Besides, it would have no criteria; in its genesis it depends on theological affirmations concerning values. Admittedly, there are canons which seem to be exercising jurisdiction over theology, such as the ones which prescribe *obsequium*

---

8. The classical approach is often to say that the purpose of law is to bring peace into the life of the community, and then peace is defined as *tranquillitas in ordine*, tranquillity that springs from an ordered state. This approach does not take into account that any growth, including that of God's kingdom, takes place through the play of vital forces that often oppose each other before coming to a harmonious balance.

If a legislator (civil or ecclesiastical) understands the law's primary purpose as an instrument to bring order into the community, such a legislator will always lean towards a legal fundamentalism and be slow to monitor the developing needs of the community and to provide for the people accordingly.

9. There are other sciences besides theology that can judge canon law under some partial aspects: e.g., medicine, psychiatry and psychology can judge the fittingness of certain rules concerning the sacrament of marriage; philosophy can judge the way canon law employs certain metaphysical concepts, such as "mind," "will," "intention," etc.

to the ordinary teaching of the magisterium. Their purpose, however, is to impose an attitude on the subjects and not to impose a specific point of doctrine.[10]

A summing up in a somewhat schematic way:
Theology and canon law are really distinct disciplines because
—the one affirms the mysteries, the other organizes the community;
—the one contemplates God and his created universe with no limits, the other operates on a well defined field;
—each yields its meanings through the use of its own specific hermeneutical rules only;
—each has its own specific cultural matrix, the one philosophy, the other jurisprudence.

Yet, theology and canon law are organically united because
—both of them are concerned with Christian mysteries, and in speaking of them they use the same words and expressions;
—both are the product of the internal drive of the church toward a deeper understanding of the mysteries and toward an enrichment by the appropriation of values;
—the decisions represented by canon law flow from a vision of values that is presented by theology;
—theology retains the power to judge canon law.

---

10. There have been theologians and canonists who held that the power to teach was part of the jurisdictional power of the church, the other part being the power to legislate and issue precepts.

Such a theory not only displays a defective epistemology, since it confuses the nature of communicating knowledge with the nature of issuing a command, but more seriously it shows a lack of understanding of how God himself communicates with us. He does not simply issue commands as to what to believe, but he speaks the truth and then sends his Spirit to testify in our hearts to the truth of his Word.

Although few today would defend explicitly the theory that the power to teach is an aspect of the power of jurisdiction, in the practical order ecclesiastical superiors may still be tempted to act on it. When someone who has the power to govern attempts to impose a point of teaching by a sheer act of jurisdiction, without referring it to the deposit of revelation, without showing how it is linked to the tradition of the apostles, he is unconsciously inspired by the discredited theory that there is no difference between the communication of truth and the issuing of a disciplinary order.

See Ladislas Örsy, "Teaching Authority," *The Church: Learning and Teaching* (Wilmington, Del.: Glazier, 1987) 45-78.

PART THREE
VARIOUS THEORIES

The theories range from affirming a rather loose connection between theology and canon law to advocating the virtual identity of the two. My intention is not to give an exhaustive account of all of them, or of any of them, but to draw the attention of the reader to some of the better known ones. Unless otherwise noted, the authors named are of the Roman Catholic tradition.

Whenever I group the authors into various "schools," the reader should keep in mind that I am proposing a tentative classification meant to facilitate the understanding of several complex positions; I do not wish to imply that there are no further differences within a school, or that the boundaries among the schools are as clear in reality as they appear in theory.

Also, although some of the authors mentioned have worked out far reaching theories concerning particular ecclesiastical institutions (e.g., episcopacy, laity, etc.), using both theology and canon law as their sources, I shall not enter into those discussions. I shall confine myself to the issue as stated in the beginning of this inquiry: what is the relationship between theology and canon law?

For each author, or school, I shall give a summary of their theory, and I shall point to what appears to be their positive contribution toward the resolution of our question, but I shall indicate also what seems to be unsatisfactory in their approach either from a methodological or a substantive point of view.

As the reader will no doubt discover, there is a fundamental difference between the pattern of discovery I have followed in searching for the answer to our initial question and the approach by the various authors to be presented. In my pattern the operations of the *subject*, in this case the church knowing, deciding and acting play a decisive role in establishing both the unity and diversity between canon law and theology. In their approach the identity or difference is found on the basis of the *objective content* of the two disciplines. My submission is that while it is correct and necessary to take into consideration the content, that is not enough to resolve the issue correctly because a vital part of relevant information is left out.

The answer I propose is intimately connected with a cognitional theory, which admittedly is complex but whose principal elements are verifiable by anyone. It affirms that values are known through judgments, and decisions ought to flow from value judgments. Laws cannot be anything else than decisions put before the community. They reverberate in the conscience of each one of the subjects, so that each has the opportunity and the duty to make his or her own decisions. Then, actions can follow. In this theory (if a theory it is; it could be considered a report on direct experience) full justice is done: the power of the legislator is recognized, and the rights of the personal conscience are upheld.

Authors who tend to identify the two disciplines
Klaus Mörsdorf[11]

Mörsdorf's insight is usually summed up with the statement that canon law is a theological discipline but one with a juridical method. So, there is one discipline that divides into two on the basis of two distinct methods, theological and juridical.[12]

Mörsdorf translates this principle into practice, and he makes ample use of theology and canon law as virtually one discipline for his "theologizing"; in particular he uses canonical texts as sources or "loci" to buttress theological assertions; e.g., concerning membership in the church, episcopal power, etc. This is a highly questionable method since as a rule the legislator's intention is not to determine a point of doctrine when he communicates a decision.

The positive aspect of this approach is that it recognizes the organic unity between theology and canon law. In an oblique way it recognizes also the importance of method: it provides the criterion for the distinction of the two disciplines.

It has, however, an overall negative aspect: it goes too far in affirming the unity of the two disciplines, even to the point of making them virtually identical, by denying all real distinction between them, except in method. The objection to this position is that a specific method is always formulated in function of a specific discipline; nature determines the method and never vice-versa.

---

11. Klaus Mörsdorf (1909–1989), of German nationality, was the founder and director of the Institute of Canon Law at the University of Munich. For an introduction to his thoughts *see* the representative collection of his writings: Klaus Mörsdorf, *Schriften zum kanonischen Recht*, ed. Winfried Aymans, Karl-Theodor Geringer, Heribert Schmitz (Paderborn: Schöningh, 1989).

12. On the theories of Mörsdorf and Corecco *see* Myriam Wijlens, *Theology and Canon Law: The Theories of Klaus Mörsdorf and Eugenio Corecco* (Lanham, Md.: University Press of America, 1992). In her Bibliography she lists the publications of both authors with additional references to relevant literature.

In particular, Mörsdorf takes no notice of the internal process of cognition and decision: he displays little awareness, if any, of the radical difference between theology and canon law in their respective origins. Further, he fails to account with precision for his concepts; throughout his writings there remains some ambivalence about what he means by theological discipline (doctrine of revelation? reflection on revelation? legislative enactments?—all of them?) and by canon law (a discipline with no specific content? a mere method?).

He seems to base his identification of the two disciplines on the fact that both of them are concerned with divine mysteries; but he fails to see that the formal objects of the two are different: one aims to understand the mysteries, the other aims to bring about actions to support the mysteries.

Mörsdorf should be considered a pioneer in the search for understanding the correct relationship between theology and canon law. He is raising many good questions, but by and large his answers tend to be all too simple for resolving the complex issues, especially the epistemological ones.

Eugenio Corecco[13]

Corecco's fundamental insight is that canon law should be defined not as *ordinatio rationis*, but as *ordinatio fidei*. Reason is competent to bring order into a secular society, but faith alone can regulate a believing community.

In the church, therefore, we have a legal system born of faith; a system essentially different from the one that reason can produce. Our norms, therefore, can be "laws" in an analogous sense only; to do justice to them, we had better abandon the expression "canon law" and speak of "church order," or use a similar expression.

Corecco certainly sees a unity between faith, doctrine and canon law. However, he adverts little, if at all, to the distinctions among them.

The initial problem with his position is that he does not critically clarify, still less justify, his own terminology. Much of what he is saying is the articulation of a basic intuition explained in rather general terms. His cardinal assertion that canon law is *ordinatio fidei* introduces an ambivalence right from the beginning. Does he mean that the faith

---

13. Eugenio Corecco (1931–) was ordinary professor of canon law at the University in Fribourg in Switzerland until he was appointed bishop of Lugano in 1986. He sums up his own theory in his book, *Theologie des Kirchenrechts: Methodologische Ansätze* (Trier: Paulinus, 1980) 96–107.

of the community brings order into its own life, or that the doctrine of faith is expressed in the canonical norms? He substitutes *fides* for *ratio* in the classical definition of Aquinas, but there is no parity there. *Ratio* for Aquinas is a "faculty" of the soul, and the practical *ratio* is an ordering agent; but *fides* for him is a theological virtue, *habitus*, that has for its primary object God himself, not the making of legal rules! Undoubtedly, Thomas would object to a general definition of law in function of the virtue of prudence, as *ordinatio prudentiae*; logically, then, he should object also to *ordinatio fidei*.

Corecco speaks repeatedly of epistemology, especially epistemology of faith, but again, it is far from clear if he refers to a cognitional theory (if so, we do not have its elements), or to the science of epistemology that explains the *why* of any such theory. At any rate, his principal interest is much more in that content of canon law which has a close link with theology.

Perhaps the strongest objection that can be raised against Corecco's position is that he over-exalts canon law and seems to give it the same standing that is due to revealed doctrine. After all, if the law is *ordinatio fidei*, the response of the faithful should be *oboedientia fidei*; a response to be given to the word of God alone.

Further, any reform of law in this vision is difficult to advocate: how could anyone call a norm enacted by faith "misguided," or "outdated"? Yet, Corecco himself is highly critical of certain provisions of the new Code—a puzzling feature.[14]

Overall, Corecco's theory does not take sufficient account of the humanity of the church. Surely, we have *ordinationes fidei* in the Ten Commandments, or in the precepts of the Sermon on the Mount, but to extend that dignity to all the norms, big and small, that the church has ever imposed on the faithful, is certainly going too far.

Remigiusz Sobański[15]

Sobański is probably the one who goes the furthest in identifying theology and canon law. For him, canon law is part of the event of

14. See "Aspects of the Reception of Vatican II in the Code of Canon Law," *The Reception of Vatican II*, ed. Giuseppe Alberigo and others (Washington, D.C.: Catholic University, 1987) 249–296; and "Theological Justifications of the Codification of the Latin Canon Law," *The New Code of Canon Law*, Proceedings of the 5th International Congress of Canon Law (Ottawa: St. Paul University, 1986) 69–96.

15. Remigiusz Sobański is ordinary professor at the Canon Law Faculty of the Catholic Academy in Warsaw. A synthesis of his theories can be found in *Grundlagenproblematik des katholischen Kirchenrechts* (Wien: Böhlau, 1987), a series of lectures given at the University of Mainz in Germany.

salvation, because it is part of the church, the primary salvific event. To stress this point, he rejects even the expression "theology of canon law," because canon law cannot exist as a distinct and specific object of theology; it is subsumed in the church that teaches the Word and dispenses the sacraments.

He is innocent of the cognitional issues; the difference between knowledge (as theology is) and imposing a decision (as canon law does) is virtually unknown to him. Consequently, he does not perceive the specific origin of canon law as an authoritative act of the ecclesiastical superior; the result is that in his system there seems to be no difference between the norms of morality imposed by the word of God and the norms of action imposed by a human legislator.

Hans Dombois[16]

Dombois, of evangelical (Lutheran) tradition, has construed a very complex system that is virtually impossible to sum up in a few paragraphs. His fundamental intention, however, can be stated succinctly: the data of revelation and our understanding of them could be and should be presented anew in juridical categories. Thus, for instance, the title of one of his major treatises is *Das Recht der Gnade,* "Law of Grace": he offers it in place of a customary "Theology of Grace." If one looked for a similar effort in Catholic tradition, the treatise of St. Anselm of Canterbury *Cur Deus homo*? comes into mind: the archbishop made use of legal concepts in explaining the work of our redemption. Dombois, however, is far more thorough and far reaching in representing all theological institutions in a legal framework. The result is a unification of theology and law, but at a price.

Much of the richness of traditional theology is lost: the juridical categories are insufficient to handle all the details and nuances that Christians developed in their search for a better understanding of the mysteries. There is also the problem of unresolved cognitional issues in Dombois' approach: he does not sufficiently advert to the difference that exists between an affirmative judgment and an authoritative command.

16. Hans Dombois (1907–), of German nationality, is a civil lawyer; he held the positions of state attorney and judge. Throughout his life he was much involved in canon law work for the Lutheran church in Germany. His major work is *Das Recht der Gnade,* cf. Bibliography.

I take this opportunity to pay tribute to the memory of Herman van Golde, a talented, and for the science of canon law promising, young Jesuit from the Netherlands who worked for several years on a major study on Dombois. He intended to present it as a doctoral dissertation at The Catholic University in Washington, and was well advanced in his research and reflection when his untimely death in 1991 cut short his life and labors; a great loss.

A philosophical approach
Wilhelm Bertrams[17]

Bertrams' main interest is not in the relationship of the two disciplines but in explaining the nature of ecclesiastical institutions. He sees them as composed of internal and external structures. The internal structures are constituted by theological or philosophical realities, the external ones by juridical dispositions. The two are organically united, and at the same time distinct, even separable. He applies this theory consistently to all institutions that he studies. A good example to show its application is the office of the bishop. The internal structure is brought into existence by the episcopal ordination that confers all the power necessary for the office; the external one is provided by the insertion of the ordained person into the visible organization of the church. This insertion brings with it the right to exercise the power already granted. Another example could be the formation of Christian marriage. The internal structure is provided by the consent of the parties, the external one by the observance of the canonical form. A similar pattern, Bertrams asserts, can be found in all institutions that operate within the legal framework of the church.

This theory may work well for some institutions, but not for all of them. Many structures in the church are pragmatic constructs on the basis of accumulated experience.[18]

Bertrams should be given credit for drawing attention to and explaining the relationship between the theological/philosophical and the juridical components of our institutions. His studies can be of help to-

---

17. Wilhelm Bertrams (1907–), of German nationality, is professor *emeritus* of the Gregorian University, Rome.

18. Concerning the episcopal and papal office *see* Wilhelm Bertrams, *De relatione inter episcopatum et primatum. Principia philosophica et theologica quibus relatio iuridica fundatur inter officium episcopale et primitiale* (Rome: Università Gregoriana, 1963). This book is significant because Bertrams participated in the drafting of the famous *Nota praevia* added as an instrument of interpretation to *Lumen gentium*, and some ideas expressed in the book are present in the *Nota* as well.

Concerning the sacrament of marriage *see* Wilhelm Bertrams and others, *De matrimonio coniectanea* (Rome: Università Gregoriana, 1970). Two essays in particular can give a good idea of his method and the content of his philosophy: "De effectu consensus matrimonialis naturaliter validi," 1–23; and "Notae aliquae quoad instructuram metaphysicam amoris coniugalis," 75–82.

For a list of Bertrams' writings *see* Antonio Arza and others [authors, no editor], *Investigationes theologico-canonicae* (*Festschrift* honoring Bertrams) (Rome: Università Gregoriana, 1978).

ward clarifying the relationship between theology and canon law, but he himself has not focused specifically on that issue, certainly not from a cognitional point of view. His theory is of classical "essentialist" inspiration, somewhat reminiscent of the scholastics' "matter and form" hypothesis. It shares the limitations of that school of thought: a tendency to force complex and multiform realities into a rigid metaphysical framework and a lack of sensitivity for historical changes.

Norms as expressing sacramental relationships
Peter Huizing[19]

Huizing proposes to change the focus of all the norms in the church on historical and theological grounds. He explains that originally, in the early church, rights and duties in the community related to the celebration of the eucharist. With the development of the primacy, the center shifted, and rights and duties were defined in relation to the papacy. Since the government by the pope appeared similar to secular monarchies, their law served as a model for building a canonical system—a shift from the sacramental to the hierarchical. Huizing proposes that we should return to defining rights and duties in relationship to the eucharist, and thus have a "sacramental" system of norms which could not be properly called "canon law" but should be known as "church order."

There is nothing in Huizing's theory that would not fit harmoniously into our understanding of the relationship between theology and canon law. He shows how doctrinal understanding should guide and direct the development of the legal system, and how theology can bring correction into the course of evolution that the law has taken.

He himself has not specifically worked on the epistemological foundations of the relationship between theology and canon law; he is rather intuitively applying certain doctrinal principles which are capable of preserving both the organic unity and the specific autonomy of both disciplines.

---

19. Peter Huizing (1911-) is of Dutch nationality. He taught at the Gregorian University in Rome, and at the Catholic University of Nijmegen in the Netherlands. For an exposition of his doctrine and for a list of his publications see the dissertation by Karl-Christoph Kuhn, *Kirchenordnung als rechtstheologisches Begründungmodell* (Frankfurt am Main: Peter Lang, 1990).

Schools that stress the autonomy of canon law
The School of Navarra[20]

This school does not really speak of a relationship between theology and canon law but of the relationship between the ecclesiastical authority and the science of canon law. Its aim is to strike a fine balance between the seemingly conflicting demands of scientific autonomy and ecclesiastical dependence. It preserves autonomy by asserting that canon law is no less and no more law than any other legal system, and hence all the acquisitions of modern juridical science are fully applicable to it. It upholds dependence by affirming that canon law in its existence and in its interpretation remains always subject to ecclesiastical authority. In other terms, the ecclesiastical authority can create a system, or can modify the existing one, but once its work is terminated it must leave its analytical and systematic explanation to the *jurisprudentes* who will do their work according to the rules of modern jurisprudence. Thus the science of canon law takes its place as fully equal to the science of any other law; yet canon law itself retains its dependence on the religious authority that makes it and sustains it.

In this view canon law is not integrated with theology; it has rather an external relationship to church authority. This approach to canon law generates also a vast *sui generis* literature which elaborates on the "canonical" meaning of theological terms. For example, since the school is prevented by its own principles from explaining *communio* from theological sources, it is compelled to compose a concept of *communio* from purely canonical resources. The result cannot but be a deficient concept since *communio* is a theological reality, too rich to be adequately represented by any canon. The danger is that such a partial expression can be taken for the full expression of reality, and that opens the way to legalism in both speech and action.[21]

---

20. Names of canonists usually associated with this school: Amadeo de Fuenmayor, Javier Hervada, Pedro Lombardia, Pedro Juan Viladrich and others mostly professors at the University of Navarra in Spain.

21. It is, of course, perfectly legitimate to research into the representation of any theological reality in canonical sources as long as the author and the readers are clear of the limited scope of the research: the result is not meant to be the full representation of a reality.

Ideally, when a canonical investigation into a theological institution is completed, the results should be referred to the theological understanding of the same institution, and the shortcomings of the legal concept should be identified and demonstrated. The existence of shortcomings in no way is a blemish on the law: no juridical

182 *Theology and Canon Law: An Inquiry into Their Relationship*

The Italian School[22]

The position to be explained here is by and large attributed to the so called "Italian school" which consists mostly of Italian canon lawyers teaching "ecclesiastical law" in "faculties" of civil law at state universities. It is, however, reasonable to assume that a similar approach is common in secular universities well beyond the boundaries of Italy, hence the title is likely to be a misnomer.

The position consists in fully accepting canon law as a proper object of juridical science but disregarding entirely its connection with theology. Anything that is not contained in the legal system is seen as meta-juridical, and hence beyond the proper field of the legal scholar. Although the connection between theology and canon law is not denied, it is seen as irrelevant for the understanding of the law.

This approach has, undoubtedly, something akin to the pure theory of law proposed by Kelsen; it is interested in the scientific examination of the edifice of the law, nothing else. The dependence of the law on a body of doctrine or on ecclesiastical authority is neither affirmed nor denied: meta-juridical facts are beyond the competence of the pure science of (in this case) canon law.

Rejection of canon law
Rudolph Sohm[23]

Sohm, of the evangelical (Lutheran) tradition, sees "church" and "law" as mutually exclusive. The church is an assembly bound together by love, law by its very nature requires coercion which is a type of

---

concepts (human constructs, to be sure) can ever emulate the riches of "faith seeking understanding."

If the referral to such riches is excluded from the interpretation of the law, the community will be the poorer for it.

22. As representatives of this school (perhaps trend would be a better term) the following could be named: Pio Ciprotti, Pietro d'Avack, Pio Fedele, Pietro Gismondi, and numerous others.

23. Rudolph Sohm (1841-1917), of German nationality, was a professor of civil law and legal history with a keen interest in the development and theoretical foundations of church law, on which his main work is *Kirchenrecht*, Vol. 1: *Die Geschichtliche Grundlagen*, Vol. 2: *Katholisches Kirchenrecht*, reprint (München: 1923). For an assessment of the relevance of his ideas for our own times *see* Yves Congar, "Rudolf Sohm nous interroge encore," *Droit ancien et structures ecclésiales* (London: Variorum, 1982), iv/263-294.

violence. They cannot exist together in the same community. He knows well that historically the church produced laws, lived by them and enforced them, but he considers all such developments as deviations from the primitive Christian ideal.

It is logical to deduce from his ideas that for him there could not be any talk about the relationship between theology and canon law, except historically, in a demonstration of how the Christians abandoned their genuine tradition.

Sohm works with a concept of law that stresses both its reliance on physical coercion and its vindictive character in case of its violation. He has a point: there is indeed a certain type of law, relying on coercion and disrespectful of consciences, which is unsuitable for the disciples of the teacher of the Beatitudes and contradicts the very nature of the church.

Sohm, however, seems to miss the point that there cannot be a community without some norms that can create a common mind in practical matters and bring about a common pattern in its actions. Even if a common mind can be created by the evangelical teaching, to follow a common pattern in actions requires some normative directions. Yet, Sohm's position, as it is, can be taken as a warning: even if the church has a legal system, it cannot be in the same sense that a secular state has it.

One could speculate and ask what Sohm would have thought if he had been able to come to a more nuanced and analogous understanding of the concept of law. Be that as it may, we can go some way with his insight and affirm that law as he understands it is incompatible with the Christian ideal of love. We may even admit that deviations have indeed taken place in history, and that they should not be repeated. But we cannot go so far as to exclude all kinds of norms of action in the church, because without some commonly followed directions no unity in practical matters is possible in any community of human beings. In truth, the very notion of community includes the existence of accepted norms of action. Paul did not hesitate to give directions to the Corinthians, and he did so quite forcefully.

Summing up

A fundamental criticism: none of the authors or schools pays sufficient attention to the cognitional and decisional process through which theology and canon law emerge in the consciousness of the church, nor do they explain why such an omission is justified. They leave themselves open to the question: If they do not give a critically well grounded account of the geneses of the two disciplines, how can they speak with certainty about the nature of those two disciplines and their mutual relationship?

Moreover, Mörsdorf, Corecco, and Sobański fail, in too many cases, to give precise descriptions or definitions of the concepts, categories and expressions they are using. All three advocate a close unity between theology and canon law but in different ways. Mörsdorf makes canon law into a theological discipline distinguishable only by its juridical method; Corecco retains the distinctiveness of canon law by keeping it in the category of *ordinatio* but then places it *en bloc* into that of faith; Sobański makes canon law part of the salvific action of God through the Word and the sacraments and leaves no specific existence for it.

Dombois reaches out for theological realities, transposes them into the horizons of the law, and presents them in legal categories. Thus, he effectively reduces the two sciences into one which seeks to understand the mysteries with the help of juridical traditions and positions.

Bertrams' interest is in the "metaphysical" structure of divine and ecclesiastical institutions, and he writes mainly about the interplay between them. In his system the theological and legal structures are organically united, without losing their specific identity; thus far his thought can serve as an inspiration to find a similar pattern for the explanation of the relationship between theology and canon law.

Huizing asserts that in the early centuries the rights and duties of the faithful were defined in relationship to the eucharist; in later times the center shifted and the rights and duties were defined in relationship to the papacy. He wishes to restore a legal system where the juridical relations reflect the relationship of the faithful to the central sacrament of the church.

The school of Navarra and the Italian school are above all anxious to defend the scientific character of canonical work and research, and they do so by asserting the autonomy of their science. The scholars from Navarra, however, balance this autonomy with another legal fact: the whole canonical system is legally subject to the acts and interventions of the ecclesiastical authority, in particular the magisterium. The Italian school regards any such consideration beyond the concern of the *jurisprudentes*.

For Sohm there is no conceivable relation between the church and a system of laws; theology can only point out the incompatibility of the two.

PART FOUR
ADDITIONAL QUESTIONS AND COMMENTS

• *What is the relationship between the doctrine of faith and canon law?*

This chapter handles the issue of the relationship between theology and canon law, theology being defined as containing both the revealed doctrine and reflections on it. The question, however, could be raised: what is the relationship between doctrine in the strict sense and canon law? It is not an idle query, since some authors come close to an identification of the two.

Doctrine here means the deposit of revelation as it both is preserved and keeps unfolding in history; it means formulations of belief which we accept with an act of faith.

There is a direct relationship between the two when canon law gives effect to divine law. This must not be confused with the often encountered situation when canon law repeats a divine law: the divine law still has its authority from God. I am speaking of a far more delicate situation. Let me explain it by examples. All sacraments exist by divine law but in the case of some sacraments the church has the power to determine the structure of the symbol that constitutes the sacrament.[24] When this happens, it is of divine law that a structure should exist, but it is of human law what the structure ought to be. The case is delicate because in such circumstances it is easy to transfer the divine character of the basic exigency to the contingent response chosen by the church.[25]

---

24. This principle is eloquently stated by Pius XII in his Apostolic Constitution, *Sacramentum ordinis*, November 30, 1947:
> If it [*the traditio instrumentorum*] was at one time necessary even for validity [*of the ordination*] by the will and command of the Church, every one knows that the Church has the power to change and abrogate what she herself has established.

Cf. CLD 3: 396–399.

25. Today we are able to witness the search for human laws to express adequately the demands of episcopal collegiality, which is of divine institution. It is a slow process.

History shows also that once a contingent structure is introduced in response to a divine demand, the church is slow to allow further changes. This can be demonstrated through the study of the sacraments of penance, anointing of the sick, order, and marriage; also through the study of the history of divinely instituted offices, such as primacy and episcopacy, which must operate through human laws.

Ecclesiastical laws that exist in order to fulfill a divine law should be distinguished from those which are of completely human creation. Greater care is required to

Also, the primacy, episcopacy and episcopal collegiality exist by divine law, but the norms which regulate the exercise of the power vested in them are largely of human creation. Thus, there is a direct connection between the doctrines of primacy, episcopacy and collegiality, and canon law: by divine law the fundamental structures are given, by human law their exercise is regulated.[26]

The relationship, however, is never that of identity. Ecclesiastical law must not be identified, ever, with the deposit of revelation—not even with its unfolding reality; this is equivalent to saying that canon law must never be elevated to the dignity of the word of God. The revelation is protected by the Holy Spirit to the point that the church can never lose it, or falsify it; this is the ultimate meaning of infallibility. Canon law is a manifestation of the humanity of the church. This is, of course, not to deny the assistance of the Spirit to the church in building structures; such assistance, however, never amounts to a guarantee of finding, with inerrancy, the most prudent laws conceivable.

Some caution must be exercised also when canon law is presented as part of the sacramental structure of the church. True, for the church to be visible, some visible structures are necessary. But while the need to have some norms is as permanent as the church is, whenever those norms are not of divine origin those norms remain changeable.

- *Can there be a theology of canon law?*

The meaning of this question is: in what sense can the system of legal *ordinationes* constitute the object of theological reflection? In other terms: can the church *knowing* reflect with the help of theological principle and method on its own system of laws?

The answer must be obviously, yes. There is no reason to exclude such reflections. It will have to be done, however, within fairly well defined limits.

Theologians can surely reflect on the church's own being as structured from the beginning (e.g., all the baptized, the twelve, the deacons, the presbyters, and other ministers); all such structures were upheld by some kind of norms of action (which did not merely describe them) and signifying an *ought*. Those norms can be the proper object of theological investigation.

---

formulate the former ones, and once they are in place, they should enjoy great stability—but never so much as divine laws proper.

26. Understandably, the church has been always cautious and slow in changing the sacramental symbols.

Also, theologians can reflect on developments in the church by examining the evolution of its institutions and norms of actions—much of it canon law, of course.

Further, theologians can reflect on the present system of laws and examine them critically to assess how far they support the divine and human values by which, and for which, the church lives.

All such reflections can be called "theology of canon law" although a more correct terminology for it would be "theology of the church" that is a structured community and operates through norms of action.

- *How far should the church make use of secular legal science?*

Starting with the "enactment" of the Twelve Tables in Rome (450 B.C.), the West developed a highly sophisticated system of laws, based first on experience, or common sense wisdom, and later perfected through general principles obtained by reflection and abstraction.

In all legal systems there is one common purpose: to bring balance into the life and operations of a human community. Now the church is a human community; therefore, to use the wisdom accumulated in legal tradition is obviously fitting for the church, although its use must be always selective and have due respect for the specific nature of a religious community.

Secular legal science should be regarded by the church as a store where much practical wisdom can be found, some of it helpful, some of it not suitable for the believing community.

- *Does history bear out the contention that theology has priority over canon law?*

At this point an insightful objection can be raised: it can be shown historically that the church has reached out for values through legislation without first defining them theologically. It follows that the principle that theology has priority over canon law cannot be sustained.

The objection states a historical fact correctly: normative directions from the church (whether in the form of laws or otherwise) often preceded theological articulations. It happened especially before the development of critical and systematic theology in the Middle Ages. Ample illustrations could be found, for instance, in the history of ecumenical councils and that of the sacraments.

It would be hasty to conclude, however, that in such developments praxis preceded theory, or that legislation was the mother of theology. Natural processes cannot be reversed, not even in the case of the church.

The clue to the correct assessment of this apparent reversal is in the understanding that there are several ways of knowing an object. Aquinas points out that a Christian may know evangelical morality in two ways: by the use of reason enlightened by faith, or "by affinity": that is, perceiving intuitively what is the way to the kingdom. Such intuitive perception, however, is an act of knowing even if it is not articulated conceptually. What is true of an individual Christian is true also of the church: the Spirit-filled community can intuitively perceive a value and decide to appropriate it even before that value is conceptually defined.

It follows that there is no reversal in the natural process: a theological intuition always precedes a decision. Yet, because the knowledge is intuitive and not articulated, it appears as if praxis had preceded theory.

In this context Newman's explanation of dogmatic development can be recalled: the church is in possession of an "idea" that somehow contains all that is in the tradition but not in the form of propositions. As history progresses, the church, guided by the Spirit, lets the "idea" unfold and its content be revealed in articulated formulations. Before this unfolding happens, however, the "idea" may already inspire practical norms, but this is really nothing else than an intuitive vision leading to a decision. Knowledge, even though implicit, remains the mother of action.

INSTEAD OF A CONCLUSION

At the end of this inquiry, the temptation may arise to regard it all as a subtle conceptual play; important perhaps for scholars but of little significance for anybody else.

The truth is that the conception of the relationship between theological realities and the laws of the church has consequences that mark the life of the community and touch the lives of individuals far and wide. There is a logical and psychological link between the theory one holds (consciously or otherwise) and the practical attitude that one takes toward legal norms.

Those who hold that canon law is part of theology are often inclined to transfer the qualities of theological realities to legal institutions and norms of action. Since the word of God is permanent, so should be the practical rules supporting it. Or, since the sacraments are timeless gifts, the laws protecting them should not be subject to change. There is a lack of attention in this approach to the difference between two essential needs: to preserve the Word and the sacraments on the one side, and to make constant accommodation to necessary developments in a human society on the other. When these two needs are not sufficiently distinguished, misguided practical attitudes will follow. Most of the time this means a trend to resist sensible changes in the law, and to demand a devotion to it that is due only to the word of God and to his sacraments.

Those who hold that canon law, once enacted, is emancipated from theology, will tend to cut it off from its roots, the theological reality. Since the purpose of any legal norm in the church is to uphold and promote values that can be known through theology only, to seek the meaning of a law while remaining indifferent to the value that it serves is to make its interpretation into a conceptual exercise that is not controlled by reality. The predictable consequence is that the law is presented as a value that needs no other justification than the fact that it was correctly enacted; an approach that is bound to lead to legalism.

There is the challenge on both theoretical and practical levels.

There should be a constant effort in the church to show how the legal system as a whole and all its parts are in the service of Christian and human values.

There should be a constant effort to lead the faithful to an intelligence of the laws, which means to lead them to the perception and appreciation of the values that the laws are meant to promote and serve. When they reach that understanding, and only then, they will be able to obey with that freedom that belongs to the children of God.

Acknowledgments

The chapters in this book are the revised versions of the following publications by the author:

Chapter 1: "*Novus habitus mentis*: New Attitude of Mind," *JUR* 45 (1985) 251-258.
    Developed from an address given at the meeting of the Canon Law Society of Australia and New Zealand, in Perth, 1984.

Chapter 2: "The Meaning of *novus habitus mentis*: The Search for New Horizons," *JUR* 48 (1988) 429-447.

Chapters 3 and 4: "The Interpreter and his Art," *JUR* 40 (1980) 27-56; "The Interpretation of Laws: New Variations on an Old Theme," *SC* 17 (1983) 44-79. The *Studia* article was partially reprinted in James A. Coriden and others, *The Art of Interpretation* (Washington, D.C.: Canon Law Society of America, 1982).
    Developed also from a paper presented at the Silver Jubilee Conference of the Canon Law Society of Great Britain and Ireland, in London, 1982.

Chapter 5: "Reception and Non-Reception of law: A Canonical and Theological Consideration," *Proceedings of the 46th Annual convention,* Washington, D.C.: Canon Law Society of America, 1984, 66-70.
    Paper presented at the convention.

Chapter 6: "The Relationship Between Values and Laws," *JUR* 47 (1987) 471-483.
    Revised text of a talk given at the Eastern Regional Conference of the Canon Law Society of America, Paterson, N.J., 1986.

Chapter 7: "Integrated Interpretation; or, The Role of Theology in the Interpretation of Canon Law," *SC* 22, 1988, 245-264.
    Developed from a talk given at the annual meeting of the Canadian Canon Law Society, in Montreal, 1987.

Chapter 8: "Moral theology and Canon Law: The Quest for a Sound Relationship," *TS* 50 (1989) 151–167.

Chapter 9: "Models of Approaches to Canon Law and Their Impact on Interpretation," *JUR* 50 (1990) 83–101.

Chapter 10: "Theology and Canon Law," *JUR* 50 (1990) 401–431.

The author is indebted to Professor John P. McIntyre, S.J. (Faculty of Canon Law, St. Paul University, Ottawa) for reading the material assembled for publication and for offering helpful suggestions.

References:
Interpretations by the Author

This book is an answer to the question: *What is interpretation?*—a theoretical approach. Interpretation, however, is a practical art as well. Hence, it is essential to show how the guidelines work when applied to the legal norms; that is, how the theory is able to animate practice. There is the crucial test for speculative insights. In the case of canon law this amounts to verification.

The scope of the present book did not permit many examples. It seems therefore advisable, as a service to my readers, to refer them to some of my publications where the transition from theory to practice is further described, and where the theory was put to work in practice. The studies listed show also a development toward a theologically better grounded and more value oriented understanding of the laws.

"Legal Judgment and Legal Eduction," *JUR* 38 (1978) 1-47.
> A proposal for an educational program that fosters creativity in the field of canon law.

The Evolving Church and the Sacrament of Penance. (Denville, N.J.: Dimension Books, 1978).
> This book is on theology and law. It attempts to create a method for legislation that is based on doctrine. It surveys the history of penance in order to find the permanent elements of the sacrament, and, thus, to determine the accretions that can be freely changed or abandoned. From such a critical study a much greater freedom for future legislation emerges than is generally assumed. The method followed could be applied to other institutions to achieve the correct balance between dogma and law.

"Lonergan's Cognitional Theory and Foundational Issues in Canon Law." *Studia Canonica* 13 (1979) 177-243.
> The art of making and interpreting the laws ought to be grounded in a sound cognitional theory.

"The Mandate to Teach Theological Disciplines: Glosses on Canon 812 of the New Code." *TS* 44 (1983) 476-488.

"Matrimonial Consent in the New Code: *Glossae* on Canons 1057, 1095-1103, 1107." *JUR* 43 (1983) 29-68.

"The Issue of Indissolubility: An Inquiry." *Thought* 59 (1984) 360-372.
In reference to canon 1056 on indissolubility.

"General Absolution: New Law, Old Traditions, Some Questions." *TS* 45 (1984) 676-689.
The same issue as in the book *Evolving Church* . . . but reflected on after the promulgation of the new Code.

"Book I: General Norms." In *The Code of Canon Law: A Text and Commentary*, ed. J. Coriden and others (New York: Paulist Press, 1985) 25-45.
It contains the explanation of the standard canonical rules of interpretation, not handled in this book.

From Vision to Legislation: From the Council to a Code of Laws. The Père Marquette Theology Lecture. (Milwaukee, Wis.: Marquette University Press, 1985).
On the passage from the new insights of the council to the new ordering of the practical life of the church.

"The Sacrament of Penance: Problem Areas and Disputed Questions." *Proceedings*, Canon Law Society of America 48 (1986) 29-45.
Canons 959-962, 978, 988, 989 and 914 are interpreted on the basis of the theological values which they are meant to serve.

Marriage in Canon Law. (Wilmington, Del.: Glazier, 1986).
Three principles of interpretation are constantly at play: the literary form of every canon must be respected, the values behind the norms must be made explicit, and the pastoral character of the legislation ought to be upheld.

The Church: Learning and Teaching. Magisterium, Assent, Dissent, Academic Freedom. Second revised edition. (Collegeville, Minn.: The Liturgical Press, 1992).
From the doctrine of teaching authority to the practical legislation for universities. An interpretation of the term *obsequium* in canon 752.

"Reflections on the Teaching Authority of the Episcopal Conferences." *Episcopal Conferences: Historical, Canonical and Theological Studies*, ed. Thomas J. Reese. (Washington, D.C.: Georgetown University, 1989) 233-252.
Background to the interpretation of canon 753.

The Profession of Faith and the Oath of Fidelity: A Theological and Canonical Analysis. (Wilmington, Del.: Glazier, 1990).
An explanation of the authority of the law and an interpretation of the prescribed formulas.

Bibliography

Titles listed here are significant for the overall topic of this book. Works which are relevant for a particular issue only are referred to in the appropriate footnotes. Throughout this book, several authors have been judged worthy of attention because they raise good questions, even if they fail to give well grounded answers.

AA. VV. [*Autori varii*: various authors]. *Teologia e diritto canonico.* Città del Vaticano: Editrice Vaticana, 1987.

Alberigo, Giuseppe, Jean-Pierre Jossua, and Joseph A. Komonchak, eds. *The Reception of Vatican II.* Washington, D.C.: Catholic University, 1987.
    A collection of reflective essays; the one by Eugenio Corecco on "Aspects of the Reception of Vatican II in the Code of Canon Law" (pp. 249-296) is excellent.

Bartocetti, Victorius. *De regulis iuris canonici.* Roma: Blardetti, 1955.
    The author takes the well-known eighty-eight rules from the sixth book of the Decretals of Boniface VIII, and relocates each one as far as possible into its original context. Then he describes the evolution of each and determines its place and role, if any, in the Code of Canon Law (1917). His appendices contain good tables of references to historical sources and to the Code of 1917.

Bastian, Hans-Dieter. *Theologie der Frage. Ideen zur Grundlegung einer theologischen Didaktik und zur Kommunikation der Kirche in der Gegenwart.* Munich: Kaiser, 1970.
    The author is of the Evangelical tradition. It is refreshing to read about the importance of the question in all communications among Christians: it prompts the mind and the heart to search for light. In our teaching, preaching, and discussions sectarian affirmations often dominate unduly and close the way to mutual understanding.

Beddard, Ralph. *Human Rights and Europe.* London: Sweet & Maxwell, 1980.
    In the forum of international law there are many declarations uphold-

ing human rights, but only the European Community has a machinery to protect them. A significant success story. In the new Code we have good definitions of the rights of the faithful but no efficient procedures to protect them; we need to look at different models not for imitation but for inspiration.

Berman, Harold J. *Law and Revolution. The Formation of the Western Legal Tradition.* Cambridge, Mass.: Harvard University Press, 1983.
Much in this book is on the immensely important role that canon law has played in the development of the two legal traditions of the West, the Continental and the English.

Bertolino, Rinaldo. *Il nuovo diritto ecclesiale tra coscienza dell'uomo e istituzione.* Torino: Giappichelli, 1989.
The main theme of the book is the relationship between the individual conscience and the institutional norms; the issue is handled in a broad theological framework.

Bertrams, Wilhelm. *Quaestiones fundamentales iuris canonici.* Roma: Università Gregoriana, 1969.
A collection of articles published in Latin and German. The main themes are: the nature of canon law; the structures of the Church (the essay on the *grades of communio* is important for ecumenism), primacy, episcopacy, and subsidiarity in the Church. The orientation of the author is more philosophical than theological: every ecclesiastical institution has an "internal metaphysical structure" to which corresponds an "external juridical structure."

Betti, Emilio. *Teoria generale della interpretazione.* 2 vols. Milano: Giuffrè, 1955.
Little known in English-speaking countries, Emilio Betti was a pioneer in applying modern hermeneutical principles to the understanding of laws. This work is a summa of the broadest scope. It begins with a discussion of broad epistemological issues. From there, he moves to a discussion of the process of interpretation and the question of hermeneutical methodology. He describes the different types of interpretation, philological, historical, technical—even dramatic and musical—before he comes to the examination of legal and theological types of interpretation. Canon lawyers can learn much from this author even if they cannot share all his opinions.

Betti, Emilio. *Interpretazione della legge e degli atti giuridici.* Ed. Giuliano Crifo. Milano: Giuffrè, 1971.
A systematic treatise on the interpretation of laws of mainly civil law countries, especially Germany. Throughout his scholarly life, Betti was in close intellectual contact with his German colleagues; he carried on a long dispute with Gadamer concerning "subjective" and "objective" interpretation.

196 *Bibliography*

Bleicher, Josef. *Contemporary Hermeneutics: Hermeneutics as Method, Philosophy and Critique.* London: Routledge & Kegan Paul, 1980.

Bodenheimer, Edgar. *The Philosophy and Method of Law.* 2nd edition. Cambridge, Mass.: Harvard University Press, 1974.
    An introductory work; concise, clear, and informative; its author is a philosopher of law. Part Three on "The Sources and Techniques of the Law," 269–386, has a great deal on interpretation, with significant insights about the evolutionary character of all legal systems.

Cardozo, Benjamin J. *The Nature of the Judicial Process.* Reprint. New Haven: Yale University Press, 1975.
    A small classic in modern common law; instructive reading for comparative purposes.

Chadwick, Owen. *From Bossuet to Newman.* 2nd Edition. Cambridge: Cambridge University Press, 1987.
    Newman's attempt to explain the development of doctrine could be a case study in horizon development. He struggled for a long time before he was able to enter into a new field of vision, and when he did, he was able to see the history of dogma in a refreshingly new way, and account for the changes. But many theologians and hierarchs recoiled. By the time of Vatican Council II, however, a slow conversion to his theory had taken place, and thus, he who once "was under a cloud" became a source of enlightenment for the Council. The book brings out well the contrast between the horizon of Bossuet and that of Newman.

Congar, Yves. *Vraie et fausse réforme dans l'Eglise.* 2nd revised and enlarged edition. Paris: Cerf, 1968.
    One could speak also of true and false reform of canon law; Congar shows the way.

Congar, Yves. *I Believe in the Holy Spirit.* Vol. 2. *Lord and Giver of Life.* Translated from the French. New York: Seabury, 1983.
    Part One, pp. 1–66, is on "The Spirit Animates the Church." Ecclesiology at its best. The purpose of canon law is to create a favorable environment for the presence and operations of the Spirit.

Congar, Yves. *Droit ancien et structures ecclésiales.* London: Variorum Reprints, 1982.
    Collected articles.

Corecco, Eugenio. *Theologie des Kirchenrechts. Methodologische Ansätze.* Translation from the Italian. Trier: Paulinus, 1980.
    Canon law is *ordinatio fidei*, not *rationis*: there is the difference from civil law. The author makes canon law more rooted in the divine than it is; leaves little room for the humanity (and the failures) of canon law.

Corecco, Eugenio. *Théologie et droit canon. Ecrit pour une nouvelle théorie générale du Droit canon*. Edited under the direction of Patrick Le Gal. Fribourg: Editions Universitaires, 1991.

Crowe, Frederick E. *Theology of the Christian Word: A Study in History*. New York: Paulist Press, 1978.
> The history of the development of our understanding of the word of God offers some clues for the understanding of the evolution of our laws as well.

D'Entrèves, A. P. *Natural Law*. 2nd revised edition. London: Hutchinson University Library, 1970.
> A historical and systematic introduction into the varied (sometimes discordant) theories of natural law.

Davitt, Thomas E. *The Basic Values in Law*. Revised edition. Milwaukee: Marquette University Press, 1978.
> The principal values discussed in their relation to law are: life, sex, knowledge, decision, property, association. Ample references to relevant literature and court decisions.

de Finance, Joseph. *L'affrontement de l'autre*. Rome: Università Gregoriana, 1973.
> The author describes the scope of his book as a study of the actions of human persons in the world and affecting the world. Actions prompted by law would certainly fall into this category. Of particular interest are Chapters Five *"L'alterité sociale"* and Chapter Six *"L'alterité des valeurs.*

De Vries, Wilhelm. *Orient et Occident: Les structures ecclésiales vues dans l'histoire des sept premiers conciles oecuméniques*. Paris: Cerf, 1974.
> There are few studies that can be more enlightening and broadening for a canon lawyer than the study of our ancient structures: history has a way of revealing how many of our modern legal institutions, categories, and principles are contingent and changeable.

De-Mauri, L. *Regulae iuris*. Milano: Hoepli, 1980.
> A collection of two thousand rules in their original Latin version and in Italian translation, grouped under alphabetically arranged systematic headings, e.g., *Libertas, Licitum, Lis*, etc. The source of each rule is given, but there are no cross-references or indices.

Del Vecchio, Giorgio. *Philosophy of Law*. Translated from the Italian 8th edition (1952). Washington, D.C.: Catholic University Press, 1953.
> A classic in Italian legal literature. The first part is historical. It is concise, clear, and erudite. The second part is systematic. It deals mainly in "the concept of law" with rather short reflections added on the origin, evolution, and rational foundation of law. Del Vecchio is often classified as a representative of Kantian idealism. But he may be closer to the natural law school than is generally assumed.

Devlin, Patrick. *The Enforcement of Morals*. Oxford: Oxford University Press, 1965.

On the eternal problem: how far should law go to enforce morals? Useful for comparative reflections.

Doe, Norman. *Fundamental Authority in Late Medieval English Law.* Cambridge: Cambridge University Press, 1991.
Questions about the foundations of law are not new: they were already raised in the Middle Ages. This book describes the disputes and tensions between two schools of thought: one saw the authority of law arising from morality, the other from the will of the legislator.

Dombois, Hans. *Das Recht der Gnade. Oekumenisches Kirchenrecht.* Vol. 1. Witten: Luther Verlag, 1961; Vol. 2. Bielefeld: Luther Verlag, 1974; Vol. 3. Bielefeld: Luther Verlag, 1983.

Dworkin, R. M., ed. *The Philosophy of Law.* Readings. Oxford: Oxford University Press, 1977.
A collection of readings for law school students; how do *others* think of the law?

Erickson, John H. *The Challenge of our Past: Studies in Orthodox Canon Law and Church History.* Crestwood, NY: St. Vladimir's Seminary Press, 1991.
Reliable information about the development and role of canon law in the Orthodox church.

Faivre, Alexandre. *Naissance d'une hierarchie. Les premières étapes du cursus clérical.* Paris: Beauchesne, 1977.
On the origins of the distinction between the clergy and the laity.

Fasso, Guido. *Storia della filosofia del diritto.* Vol. 1, *Antichità e Medioevo,* 3rd edition, 1974. Vol. 2, *L'età moderna,* 1968. Vol. 3, *Ottocento e Novecento,* 1970. Milano: Il Mulino.
One of the best in recent literature. The philosophy of law of a thinker is carefully set into the context of his philosophical system as a whole. Historical derivations and interdependence of the authors are noted and explained. Bibliographical references are abundant; primary sources are distinguished from subsequent critical studies.

Finnis, John. *Natural Law and Natural Rights.* Oxford: Clarendon Press, 1980.
A modern attempt to explain natural law; a theory based more on empirical facts than on metaphysical speculations.

Gadamer, Hans-Georg. *Truth and Method.* Translated from the 2nd Edition in German. New York: Seabury, 1975.
One of the pioneer works in hermeneutics and horizon studies.

Fransen, Piet F. *Hermeneutics of the Councils and Other Studies.* Ed. H. E. Mertens and F. de Graeve. Leuven: University Press, 1985.
Fransen's penetrating research concerning the meaning of the decrees and canons of the Council of Trent has already led to the revision of some previously held convictions: not all that is upheld under the penalty of

an *anathema* is necessarily part of the deposit of revelation. The discovery of the original intention of the council can have significant repercussions for the re-assessment of some traditional canonical norms, and even more so for the making of new laws.

Friedrich, Carl Joachim. *The Philosophy of Law in Historical Perspective*. 2nd edition, revised and enlarged. Chicago: University of Chicago Press, 1963.
A concise and clear introduction into the philosophy of law.

Gallagher, John A. *Time Past, Time Future: An Historical Study of Catholic Moral Theology*. New York: Paulist, 1990.
This study is not as far reaching in history as that of Mahoney, nor does it discuss as many factors as he does, but in some other ways it is complementary to his work. It focuses mainly on the manualist tradition of the last four hundred years, it describes the impact of the neo-Thomistic revival, and it gives an account of the development of the theory of proportionalism.

Geffré, Claude. *Le christianisme au risque de l'interprétation*. Paris: Cerf, 1983.
The author's point is that we must fear an interpretation that amounts to the betrayal of our faith, but we should not fear to take the risk of seeking a creative interpretation of our faith that brings it closer to our contemporaries. There is a great deal of inspiration in this book toward a creative approach to the revision of our laws.

Granfield, David. *The Inner Experience of Law: A Jurisprudence of Subjectivity*. Washington, D.C.: Catholic University, 1988.
See the "Appendix" at the end of Chapter Nine.

Groupe des Dombes. *Pour la conversion des Eglises*. Paris: Centurion, 1991.
Christian unity cannot be achieved unless all the churches and communions are open to the grace of conversion, which implies also a readiness to change the structures and laws not instituted by divine command.

Grundmann, Siegfried. *Abhandlungen zum Kirchenrecht*. Köln: Böhlau, 1969.
A collection of twenty-seven reflective articles and extracts from the books of the late Professor Grundmann, a Lutheran interested in theology and ecclesiastical law, edited by his students. His interest ranged far and wide: the legal problems of all the German Evangelical churches in a theological context; ecumenical questions; Church and State. He displays extraordinary learning and a capacity for synthesis, but he shows little acquaintance with pre-Protestant Christian traditions or with Catholic thought.

Hart, H. L. A. *The Concept of Law*. Oxford: Clarendon Press, 1961.
Hart is probably the best representative of the trend, in English-speaking countries, of applying the principles and methods of linguistic analysis to philosophy—philosophy of law. The influence of Austin, Kelsen and, of course, Wittgenstein, can easily be perceived in his writings. He admits

no metaphysical foundations for law; in fact, he is opposed to any metalegal consideration. These thinkers have, however, exacting standards in the use of the language; to pass through the crucible of their method, provided it is kept within due bounds, can be beneficial even to canon lawyers.

Hart, H. L. A. *Essays in Jurisprudence and Philosophy*. Oxford: Clarendon Press, 1988.

Hinder, Paul. *Grundrechte in der Kirche*. Freiburg, Switzerland: Universitätsverlag, 1977.

A well organized and closely reasoned study, written in clear concise style. The problem is well defined. There is a critical survey of present-day writings on the topic (quite abundant) and the position of the author. His theological reflections have depth, his proposals for legislation show good practical sense. *Utinam* his suggestions were accepted! A useful bibliography.

Hohfeld, W. N. *Fundamental Legal Conceptions as Applied in Judicial Reasoning*. London: Greenwood, 1978.

First published posthumously in 1923, this work had a far-reaching impact of the understanding of legal concepts in those countries where common law is the law of the land.

Hommes, Hendrik Jan van Eikema. *Major Trends in the History of Legal Philosophy*. Amsterdam: North-Holland, 1979.

Very good, clear, comprehensive.

Jacobs, Uwe Kai. *Die Regula Benedicti als Rechtsbuch. Eine rechtshistorische und rechtstheologische Untersuchung*. Köln: Böhlau, 1987.

The Rule of Benedict is a classical example of the harmony that must exist between the legal and the spiritual. In a Christian community all laws must be grounded in charity, and must be tempered by equity and discretion. (One could add that the Rule of Benedict is one of the masterpieces of legislation in the best classical Roman tradition.)

Jeanrond, Werner J. *Text and Interpretation as Categories of Theological Thinking*. New York: Crossroad, 1988.

The author reflects critically on the hermeneutical positions of Gadamer and Ricoeur; he elaborates his own theory. Pertinent insights hidden behind a cumbersome style.

Krahe, Maria Judith. *Der Herr ist der Geist: Studien zur Theologie Odo Casels, II: Das Mysterium vom Pneuma Christi*. St. Ottilien: EOS Verlag.

A study on the presence and operations of the Spirit in the church. The chapter on "Die unheilige Kirche" ("The Unholy Church") contains helpful insights for the understanding of the role of the law. *See* pp. 126–136.

Krämer, Paul. *Theologische Grundlegung des kirchlichen Rechts.* Trier: Paulinus, 1977.
   This study is mainly a critique of the positions of Hans Barion and Joseph Klein: two German scholars who addressed themselves to the problem of the theological foundation of law in Christian churches. It gives also a short introduction into the *Problematik* of theology of law, and provides a long chapter on how to lay the foundations for good law in the light of Vatican II. Extensive bibliography.

Kuhn, Karl-Christoph. *Kirchenordnung als rechtstheologisches Begründungsmodell. Konturen eines neuen Begriffs und Modells Katholischer Rechtstheologie unter besonderer Berücksichtigung von Peter J. M. J. Huizing.* Frankfurt/M: Peter Lang, 1990.

Kuttner, Stephan. *Harmony from Dissonance: An Interpretation of Medieval Canon Law.* Latrobe, Penn.: Archabbey Press, 1960.

Kuttner, Stephan. *The History of Ideas and Doctrines of Canon Law in the Middle Ages.* London: Variorum Reprints, 1980.

Kuttner, Stephan. *Gratian and the Schools of Law: 1140–1234.* London: Variorum Reprints, 1983.

Le Guillou, M. J. *Christ and Church: A Theology of the Mystery.* Translated from the French. New York: Desclée, 1966.
   Aquinas wrote no treatise on the theology of the church: the author collected his thoughts on it.

Liebs, Detlef. *Lateinische Rechtsregeln und Rechtssprichwörter.* München: Beck, 1982.
   This book is a treat for lovers of reflective jurisprudence. It contains some sixteen hundred rules in their Latin original and in German translation, many of them directly concerned with interpretation. With its references and cross-references and indices of Latin and German terms, the book is a small mine of legal wisdom as it has been distilled by *jurisprudentes* of past ages.

Lies, Lothar. *Sacramententheologie: eine personale Sicht.* Graz: Styria, 1990.
   The author proposes a new understanding of the sacraments, inspired by Trinitarian theology and a renewed understanding of communication among free persons. There is an interesting topic for study: if such a new perception ever prevailed in the church, should our laws change as well? and if so, how?

Lonergan, Bernard. *Method in Theology.* New York: Herder and Herder, 1972.
   The very nature of the theological enterprise depends on the horizon of the person who does it: the believer perceives the mysteries differently from the unbeliever. Also, the transition from one horizon into another requires genuine conversion: intellectual, moral or religious.

Lonergan, Bernard. *Insight: A Study of Human Understanding.* New York: Longmans, 1967.

Mahoney, John. *The Making of Moral Theology.* Oxford: Clarendon Press, 1987.
One of the best contributions to the understanding of moral theology as it developed into our times. Chapter Six on "The Language of the Law" should be of particular interest to canon lawyers interested in the hermeneutics of the law.

Marshall, Geoffrey. *Constitutional Theory.* Oxford: Clarendon Press, 1971.
A good and readable introduction into the basic ideas underlying the British and American system of constitutional government. Highly recommended for canon lawyers who are anxious to broaden their horizons.

McCool, Gerald A. *Catholic Theology in the Nineteenth Century.* New York: Seabury, 1977.
The history of neo-Thomism in the Catholic Church is traced from Leo XIII's *Aeterni patris*.

McEvenue, Sean E., and Ben F. Meyer, eds. *Lonergan's Hermeneutics. Its Development and Application.* Washington, D.C.: Catholic University Press, 1989.

McIntyre, John P. *Customary Law in the Corpus Iuris Canonici.* San Francisco: Mellen Research University Press, 1990.
A reflective historical study enlivened with much erudition. Originally a doctoral dissertation presented at The Catholic University of America.

Meyendorff, John. *Byzantine Theology: Historical Trends and Doctrinal Themes.* 2nd edition. New York: Fordham University Press, 1979.
The understanding of the Eastern church concerning the role of law and order in the Christian community has been historically different from the perception of Western church.

Monden, Louis. *Sin, Liberty and Law.* Translated from the Dutch. New York: Sheed and Ward, 1965.
The author's judicial remarks about the relationship between law and conscience have a permanent value.

Mühlen, Heribert. *Una Mystica Persona. Die Kirche als das Mysterium der heilsgeschichtlichen Identität des Heiligen Geistes in Christus und den Christen: Eine Person in vielen Personen.* 2nd enlarged edition. Munich: Schöningh, 1960.
One of the best of post-conciliar ecclesiologies, marked by spiritual depth, respect for the tradition, and well grounded new insights.

Mussner, Franz. *Geschichte der Hermeneutik von Schleiermacher bis zur Gegenwart. Handbuch der Dogmengeschichte,* Vol. 1, Fascicle 3c, Second part. 2nd enlarged edition. Freiburg im Breisgau: Herder, 1976.
Rich information presented in concise encyclopedic style.

Newman, John Henry. *An Essay on the Development of Christian Doctrine.* Re-

print. Notre Dame, Ind.: University of Notre Dame Press, 1980.
   There is an analogy between the development of doctrine and the evolution of structures and norms of action in the church.

Palmer, Richard E. *Hermeneutics. Interpretation Theory in Schleiermacher, Dilthey, Heidegger, and Gadamer.* Evanston, Ill.: Northwestern University Press, 1975.
   A widely used introduction into the science of hermeneutics.

Paul VI. *Allocutiones de iure canonico.* J. Beyer, ed., 2nd edition. Rome: Università Gregoriana, 1980.

Potz, Richard. *Die Geltung kirchenrechtlicher Normen: Prolegomena zu einer kritisch-hermeneutischen Theorie des Kirchenrechts.* Wien: Herder, 1978.
   The author is among the first to raise the hermeneutical issue in canon law. He turns to three sources to broaden our horizons and enrich our understanding: modern theories of law as they are found in German language literature, legal theories as they were developed by theologians and canonists from Gratian to Vatican II, and opinions on the meaning, authority or validity of ecclesiastical laws as proposed by writers after the council.

Pree, Helmuth. *Die evolutive Interpretation der Rechtsnorm im Kanonischen Recht.* Wien: Springer, 1980.
   The book falls into two parts, one historical and the other systematic. The historical part is quite ecumenical; side by side with the "Catholic" developments, the approach of the reformers to church law is explained, as well as the theories of some modern secular thinkers. The focus is on the evolving understanding of interpretation throughout. The systematic part displays an unusual depth and breadth; vast erudition goes hand in hand with balanced judgments. The bibliography lists some three hundred works published mainly on the continent of Europe; the work would have been enriched by more attention to the relevant literature in English-speaking countries.

Prodi, Paolo. *The Papal Prince. One body and two souls: the papal monarchy in early modern Europe.* Translated from the Italian. Cambridge: Cambridge University Press, 1987.
   Chapter Four is on the interplay of canon law and civil law in the papal states. The same sovereign had to operate with two legal systems. An interesting question: how far the civil system in the papal states influenced the development and understanding of canon law?

Ramallo, Valentin. *El derecho y el misterio de la iglesia.* Roma: Università Gregoriana, 1972.
   A reflective study. It embraces too much historically and systematically to be precise on any single issue, but it presents an overall view of the ideal role of law in the Church. It is to uphold the transcendental orientation of the community toward the Spirit.

204 Bibliography

Ramsey, Ian T. *Models and Mystery.* London: Oxford University Press, 1964.

Resweber, Jean-Paul. *Qu'est-ce qu'interpréter? Essai sur les fondements de l'herméneutique.* Paris: Cerf, 1988.

Ricoeur, Paul. *Le conflit des interprétations. Essais d'herméneutique.* Paris: Seuil, 1969.

Ricoeur, Paul. *Du text à l'action. Essais d'herméneutique, II.* Paris: Seuil, 1986.

Sawyer, Geoffrey. *Law in Society.* Oxford: Clarendon, 1973.
A sociology of law, written for lawyers.

Schlier, Heinrich. *Der Geist und die Kirche.* Freiburg im Breisgau: Herder, 1980.

Schlier, Heinrich. *Die Zeit der Kirche.* Freiburg im Breisgau: Herder, 1972.

Sharkey, Michael, ed. *International Theological commission. Texts and Documents 1969–1985.* San Francisco: Ignatius, 1989.

Sobański, Remigiusz. *Grundlagenproblematik des katholischen Kirchenrechts.* Wien: Böhlau, 1987.

Sohm, Rudolph. *Kirchenrecht.* Vol. 1: *Die Geschichtliche Grundlagen.* Vol. 2: *Katholisches Kirchenrecht.* Reprint. München: 1923.
See Chapters 8 and 10.

Stein, Peter and John Shand. *Legal Values in Western Society.* Edinburgh: Edinburgh University Press, 1974.
There is no chapter entitled "Interpretation" in this book, but much of the discussion on legal values really concerns the interpretation of legal norms. See especially Chapter Three on "Justice and Just Procedure" and Chapter Four on "Just Decisions" (pp. 59-113). The interest of the authors extends over the broad field of legal systems used in the Western world. An analogous volume could be written in canon law: "Legal Values in the Western Church."

Stiegler, Anton. *Der kirchliche Rechtsbegriff: Elemente und Phasen seiner Erkenntnisgeschichte.* München: Schnell und Steiner, 1958.
A historical survey, in six chapters, of the development of the concept of law from the earliest documents of the Old Testament to Suarez. The first chapter is a rapid survey of terminology in Hebrew, Greek, Latin, and modern tongues. The remaining five chapters go deeper to enlighten us on the concept of law in Biblical writings; in the Greek and Latin literature (including the Fathers); in Gratian and his commentators; in the scholastics' treatises, especially in St. Thomas; and finally in Suarez, after whom (the author says) no major development occurred. A useful summary, a guide to primary sources—betraying great industry, but no originality. Richer in documentation than in thought.

Tillard, J-M. R. *Eglise d'églises. L'ecclésiologie de communion.* Paris: Cerf, 1987.

All our canon law, as a whole and in parts, exists within the church of Christ, which embraces non-Roman Catholic churches and ecclesial communions as well. Does such an existence have any consequences for interpretation?

Tracy, David. *The Achievement of Bernard Lonergan*. New York: Herder and Herder, 1970.
    This study contains a good explanation of the doctrine of horizon, with references to the history of theology and philosophy.

Useros, Manuel Carretero. *"Statuta ecclesiae" y "sacramenta ecclesiae" en la Eclesiologia de St. Tomás*. Roma: Università Gregoriana, 1962.
    A historical study, done with competence and erudition. In the center of it is Aquinas' understanding of the Church as a "radical sacrament" or sacramental *communio*. In the concrete order, law is an indispensable instrument of its corporate life. There are many references to modern problems and authors.

Vago, Steven. *Law and Society*. Englewood Cliffs, N.J.: Prentice-Hall, 1981.
    More sociology than philosophy but interesting; it tells how law is in the service of social values.

Van Riet, Georges. *Problèmes d'épistémologie*. Louvain: Publications Universitaires, 1960.
    See the chapter "Le problème moral et son épistémologie particulière" on prudential judgment; that is, judgment concerning value.

Verdross, Alfred. *Abendländische Rechtsphilosophie: Ihre Grundlagen und Hauptprobleme in geschichtlicher Schau*. Wien: Springer, 1963.
    A most comprehensive survey of the history of Western legal philosophy (beginning with Homer), with increased emphasis on the modern writers, and, at the end of the book, with critical reflections.

Virt, Günter. *Epikie—verantwortlicher Umgang mit Normen. Eine historisch-systematische Untersuchung*. Mainz: Matthias-Grünewald, 1983.
    A study of *epieikeia* in the writings of Aristotle, Aquinas, and Suarez, and some reflections on the help that *epieikeia* can bring to solve the problems of our present age.

Voegelin, *In Search of Order*. Baton Rouge, La.: Louisiana State University Press, 1987.
    This is the fifth and last volume of Voegelin's *Order in History*, but it can stand on its own by reason of its specific subject. It is the elucidation of the experience of transcendence in the search for order in human society. Voegelin can teach us to raise pertinent questions: what kind of order has the Christian community, *as experiencing the transcendent*, been searching for in the course of its history, and what sort of order is it searching for today?

Wächter, Lothar. *Gesetz im kanonischen Recht. Eine rechtssprachliche und systematisch-normative Untersuchung zu Grundproblemen der Erfassung des Gesetzes im Katholischen Kirchenrecht.* St. Ottilien: EOS Verlag, 1989.

Walgrave, Jan. *Unfolding Revelation. The Nature of Doctrinal Development.* Philadelphia: Westminster, 1972.

> A historical and systematic treatise on the development of doctrine, much of it having relevance for the developments of structures and norms of action.

Wijlens, Myriam. *Theology and Canon Law: The Theories of Klaus Mörsdorf and Eugenio Corecco.* Lanham, MD: University Press of America, 1992.

> A systematic presentation of the theories of Mörsdorf and Corecco, followed by a well reasoned critical evaluation of their method and doctrine. Originally a doctoral dissertation presented at St. Paul University, Ottawa, Canada.

Wojtyła, Karol. Pope John Paul II. *The Acting Person.* Translated from the Polish. Dordrecht, Netherlands: Reidel, 1979.

> This book is relevant under two aspects: first, to make laws and to receive them is to be an "acting person"; further, its emphasis on participation (see especially Part Four) can serve as inspiration for the cooperation of the entire community for the formulation and implementation of the laws.

Analytical Index

Entries refer to the main text and its footnotes; entries in bold designate themes discussed more extensively; Bibliography is not included.

civil law 29, 32, 33, 39, 44, 46, 47, 49, 52, 58, 59, 60, 62, 70, 76, 109, 110, 133, 134, 135, 136, 140, 141, 142, 150, 153, 182
Code/1983 16, 17, 26, 30, 31, 32, 52, 54, 56–57, 58, 59, 70, 72, 76, 81, 83–86, 92, 94, 95, 98, 99, 102, 105, 107, 111, 117, 121, 130, 132, 133, 136, 137, 142, 158, 159, 160, 177, 193
Code/1917 25, 32, 39, 59, 60, 70, 102, 105, 107, 121, 143
culture 20, 49, 50, 68, 69, 70, 74, 76, 79, 108, 140, 143, 160, 168
custom 24, 38, 39, 42, 49, 60, 71, 79, 80, 85, 87, 92, 99, 116, 117, 121, 126, 144, 146, 160

devotional practices and legislation 29, 62, 71, 102, 103, 111, 137, 142

ecumenical issues 13, 15, 20, 26, 29, 59, 67, 74, 87, 93, 130
English law 44, 48, 61, 62, 70, 85
evolution of legal system 13, 35, 39, 50, 56, 63–65, 81, 92, 137, 144, 180, 187

Gospel and law 70–73

image of God 29–30, 77
implementation of the Code 83–88
    community, role of 83–88
    customs developing 87
    horizons, expanding 86
    inquiry, ongoing 86
    reception 85–87
    state of the question 83
interpretation 53–82
    authority 80–81
    communication 82
    cultural context 79
    dialectics 82
    economy, *oikonomia* 73–74
    epiky, *epieikeia* 42–44
    equity 60–63
    evangelical 70–73
    evolution 63–64, 81
    general principles 53–77
    hermeneutics 68–70
    historical 50–51, 78
    horizon, role of 65–68
    human dignity 80
    light to the nations 79
    literary forms 53–58, 78

208   *Analytical Index*

    rules 77–82
    theoretical background 78
    universality 79
    values 59–60, 80, 109
interpreters 46–52
    administrators 49
    courts 48–49
    doctors 49
    legislator 47–48
    people 49
    qualities 50–52

juridical order: *ordo iuridicus* 32, 105, 110, 128, 134, 135, 137

lack of law: *lacuna* 95
law and canon law 37–43, 92–96, 139–153, 160–173
    essential definition 37–38
    existential significance 38–39
    life span of 40–43
    reception of 45–46
    state of the question 37–39
literary forms in the Code 52–58
    dogmatic statement 53–54, 56
    empirical/scientific 56, 57
    exhortation 55, 57
    moral doctrine 55, 56
    philosophical theory 55, 57
    right and duty 56, 57
    theological opinion 54, 56

models of law and of canon law 138–157
    canon law in particular 148–152
    dynamic 143–144
    integrated 145
    law in general 141–148
    literary text 146–147
    multivalent 141–142
    norm of action 146–147
    rational 147–148
    self sufficient 145
    state of the question 138–141
    static 143–144
    univocal 141–142
    voluntaristic 147–148

moral theology and canon law 119–138
    alienation 119–120
    assistance of the Spirit 132
    continuity 124–125
    creation of legal system 123–124
    diversity 125–127
    emergence of moral rules 122–123
    priority 128–129, 187–188
    prudence 132
    science of canon law 133–136
    state of the question 119–122

new attitude of mind: ongoing inquiry 9–17
    communion: *communio* 12, 15
    dynamism 13, 15
    ecumenism 13
    expansive presence 13, 15
    higher viewpoint 14
    misconceptions 10–11
    state of the question 9–10
    Vatican II 11–16
new attitude of mind: new horizons 18–34
    church redeeming 29
    commentaries 31–32
    conversion 21–24
    dialogues 33
    discovery 21–24
    ecumenism 20
    education 31
    empirical sciences 31
    history of canon law 24–27
    horizons expanding 18–34
    image of God 29
    law reform 18
    service 30
    state of the question 19–20

Orthodox church 73–75

perfect society 25, 66, 105, 136, 137, 143

post-Tridentine period 25, 26, 28, 30, 96–99, 101, 119, 120, 133, 145

reception of laws 39, 40, 41, 43, 45–46, 60–61, 77, 109, 124, 133, 144, 177, 190
revision of laws 16, 18, 26, 78, 79, 98, 99, 105, 115, 117, 158, 159
Roman law 12, 24, 35, 44, 60, 62, 74, 78, 79, 85, 104, 127, 133, 143, 147, 168

sensus fidei 86, 87, 88
sensus fidelium 61, 71, 81, 137
simplicity 127, 147

theology and canon law 158–189
authority 162–163
canon law, meaning of 160–161
causality 170–172
consciousness of the church 163–165
command 165–166
content 165–173
genesis 161–165
hermeneutics 167
horizons 166, 168
knowledge 165–166
language 161–162
matrices 168
priority 172, 187–188
relationship, meaning of 161
state of the question 158–160
teaching power 173
theology, meaning of 160
transcendence 169
theological (integrated) interpretation 102–118
confession (canon 960) 113
faithful, role of 115–117
hermeneutics 110–112
historical references 102–103
legal positivism 104
marriage contract (canon 1055) 113

obsequium (canon 752) 112
principle of integration 103
state of the question 105–106
temporal goods (canon 1254) 114
theological horizon 110
theology, role of 109
values 106–108
theories (modern) of canon law
Bertrams 179–180
Corecco 150–152, 176–177
Dombois 178
Huizing 180
Italian school 149, 182
Mörsdorf 150–152, 175–176
Navarra, school of 181
Örsy 159–173
Sobanski 150–152, 177–178
Sohm 135–136, 182–183
tribunals 48–49, 68

values and laws 89–101
beauty of laws 101
distortion of values 94–96
integrated community 94–96
nominalism, legal 96–99
revision of laws 99–100
state of the question 88–89
Trent 96–99
values described/defined 90–93
Vatican II 99–100
Vatican Council II
inquiring spirit 9–17
higher viewpoints 18–34
implementation 83–88
revision of laws 99–100

Index of Persons

*See also **Bibliography**.*

Alberigo 133, 177
Aquinas 20, 21, 38, 42, 45, 64, 65, 84, 90, 92, 97, 129, 131, 147, 148, 166, 168, 177, 188
Aristotle 19, 20, 21, 45, 46, 65, 68, 74, 84, 166, 170
Arza 179
Aymans 175

Baudot 144
Bertrams 179–180, 184
Beyer 9
Boniface VIII 77

Carpentier 124, 136
Ciprotti 182
Congar 86, 182
Corecco 133, 142, 151, 176–177, 184
Coreth 154
Coriden 136
Crowe 106

d'Avack 182
Dante 69
de Fuenmayor 181
de Finance 126
Dombois 178, 184

Fedele 182
Felici 98
Fransen 96
Friedrich 145

Gadamer 20
Gaius 127
Gallagher 119
Gismondi 182
Granfield 153–157
Gratian 24, 26, 97
Green 143

Häussling 148
Hervada 181
Hinder 130
Huels 70, 140
Huizing 180, 184

Isaiah 111

John XXIII 12, 69
John Paul II 9, 16, 26, 168
John, Ev. 77
Jones 145
Justinian 143

Kasper 159

Index of Persons 211

Kelsen 145, 149
Kuhn 180

Lefèvbre 34
Lombardía 181
Lonergan 8, 106, 126, 154
Lotz 154

Mahoney 104, 119
Maréchal 154
Matthew, Ev. 36
McIntyre 191
Morrisey 56
Mörsdorf 142, 151, 175-176, 184
Muck 154

Newman 117, 188

Örsy 16, 57, 100, 107, 113, 136, 173, 192-193

Paul VI 9, 10, 11, 33, 105, 110
Paul, Ap. 36, 95, 111
Peter, Ap. 84
Pius XII 184
Pius IV 98
Plato 84

Potz 136
Pree 144
Puza 149

Rahner 154, 168
Roberts, 67

Sequeira 113
Shan 121
Sharkey 114
Sobański 177-178, 184
Socrates 35, 120, 142, 151
Sohm 135, 136, 142, 182, 184
Stein 121
Suarez 97, 98, 147

Tracy 19

Useros 129

Vago 37
Valera 150
van der Golde 178
Viladrich 181

Webb 155
Wijlens 175